FINITUDE AND TRANSCENDENCE IN THE PLATONIC DIALOGUES

☙☙

SUNY SERIES IN ANCIENT GREEK PHILOSOPHY

ANTHONY PREUS, EDITOR

Finitude and Transcendence in the Platonic Dialogues

❧❧ ❧❧ ❧❧

Drew A. Hyland

State University of New York Press

Published by
State University of New York Press, Albany

For information, address State University of New York Press,
State University Plaza, Albany, N.Y. 12246

Production by M.R. Mulholland
Marketing by Theresa A. Swierzowski

Library of Congress Cataloging-in-Publication Data

Hyland, Drew A.
    Finitude and transcendence in the Platonic dialogues / Drew A.
Hyland.
        p.   cm. — (SUNY series in ancient Greek philosophy)
    Includes bibliographical references and index.
    ISBN 0-7914-2509-6 (HC : alk. paper). — ISBN 0-7914-2510-X (PB :
alk. paper)
    1. Plato.   2. Transcendence (Philosophy)   I. Title.   II. Series.
B398.T7H95   1994
184—dc20   94-29564
                                                                    CIP

10 9 8 7 6 5 4 3 2 1

FOR CHARLES GRISWOLD, BOB PIPPIN, AND DAVID ROOCHNIK:
ONCE BEST OF STUDENTS, NOW BEST OF FRIENDS.

ᛒᚷ

CONTENTS

PREFACE

If Plato teaches us nothing else, he teaches us that philosophy is inseparable from dialogue with others. This book has been deeply informed and improved by dialogues, sometimes continuing over the years, with philosophic friends. Helen Lang and Daryl Tress, two colleagues at Trinity College, have discussed these issues in its halls as well as in study groups and private conversations. Charles Griswold, Bob Pippin, and David Roochnik, to whom the book is dedicated, have read all or parts of it and been immeasureably helpful, though this is but a small part of the blessing that their sustained philosophic friendship has been over the years. Jacob Howland and Mitchell Miller, from whose works as well as conversations I have learned so much, made their names known to me as readers of my manuscript for SUNY Press, and their comments have greatly added to the worth of this book, if worthwhile it be. I wish also to thank the other, unnamed readers of the manuscript for comments that were most constructive and constituted a genuine engagement with my work. I should add that the positive and deep influence of my teacher, Stanley Rosen, will be obvious throughout the book.

Finally, as always, I am most grateful of all to my wife, Anne, for her support, her direct philosophic help—especially in matters of the "long-standing war between art and philosophy"—and her sustaining good company.

INTRODUCTION

This book was originally conceived as a work on irony in Plato, an issue which has become the subject of one of its chapters. It became a single chapter because as I developed it I began to see that the presence and role of irony in the Platonic dialogues was really one of many instantiations of a broader theme that was the one genuinely guiding my thinking on irony, the theme adumbrated in the title of the book as "finitude and transcendence." Each chapter will develop that theme in a specifically different way in which it is found in the dialogues. In this introduction, I want briefly to develop the theme in a more general or abstract way, an abstraction, I hasten to add, that is nowhere found in the dialogues themselves. One might thus consider the introduction a statement of the thesis that the various chapters will attempt to instantiate in specific ways, ways more true to the way the theme is presented in the dialogues. Long before Kierkegaard, Plato had established himself as a master of "indirect communication," and the guiding theme of this book is one that is at once pervasive in the dialogues, yet always, so far as I can tell, presented "indirectly." The chapters will therefore appear to be on widely diverse topics, but I hope I can show that they center on a common theme.

In recent years much convincing work has been done on the so-called dramatic aspect of the Platonic dialogues. Perhaps the most general thesis of this body of work is that the dialogue form in which Plato presents his thinking has not merely literary but philosophical importance as well. Its significance must therefore be considered in any adequate discussion of the "arguments" contained therein, and certainly in any claim to gain access to "Plato's philosophy."[1] I accept this general hermeneutical

---

1. The list of authors and works that have adopted this standpoint is now, happily, so large as to make short summary impossible. For my own efforts in this direction, see especially "Why Plato Wrote

standpoint, and in the pages that follow I shall attempt both to set out its principles and to embody some of its results. Before turning to that task, however, I must contrast the hermeneutical standpoint I accept with its most pervasive alternative, an alternative which, for the time, may still be called the "orthodox" method of interpretation, at least in English-language scholarship.

That orthodox view, to put it most simply, assumes that the dramatic context of the dialogues, including the personnae, the locus, and the various "existential" aspects of the situation portrayed, contribute nothing substantial to the philosophical content of the dialogue itself. To the contrary, the position continues, the philosophic content, usually in the form of a set of "arguments" for a universalizable "theory" or "doctrine," can be lifted without distortion from its (presumably merely literary) context and stated as "Plato's theory" of this or that. The reason that task is relatively easy is that these scholars assume that "Plato's theory" is essentially articulated by one individual in each dialogue who is thus "Plato's mouthpiece" in that work. The rest of the dialogue, by implication, is more or less literary dross. In most dialogues that mouthpiece is Socrates, but if Socrates happens to be silent or absent in a given dialogue, there is no need to worry: Plato has simply switched mouthpieces for some reason of his own, to Timaeus, or to the Eleatic Stranger, or to the Athenian Stranger.

Probably the most famous exponent of this orthodox view is Gregory Vlastos, who achieved early renown as a Plato scholar with his 1954 article, "The Third Man Argument in the *Parmenides*," in which he leaps into that discussion and analyzes its logic with no reference to its dramatic context.[2] In his most

---

Dialogues," in *Philosophy and Rhetoric* 1, no. 1 (1968): 38–50; and *The Virtue of Philosophy: An Interpretation of Plato's Charmides* (Athens: Ohio University Press, 1981). For an instructive study of the history of Platonic interpretation, see E. N. Tigerstedt, *Interpreting Plato* (Uppsala: Almquist & Wicksell, 1977), and the helpful critical evaluation of it by Alan Bowen, "On Interpreting Plato," in *Platonic Writings, Platonic Readings*, ed. Charles Griswold (New York: Routledge, 1988), 49–65.

2. Gregory Vlastos, "The Third Man Argument in the *Parmenides*," *Philosophical Review* 63 (1954): 319–49.

recent work, *Socrates, Ironist and Moral Philosopher*, Vlastos nicely articulates his principle of interpretation that Socrates (or, presumably, some other main interlocutor) is Plato's mouthpiece: "In any given dialogue, Plato allows the persona of Socrates only what he (Plato), at the time, considers true," and in a footnote he helpfully labels this the "grand methodological hypothesis on which my whole interpretation of Socrates in Plato is predicated."[3] One can infer, therefore, that if that hypothesis proves defective, so is his "whole interpretation." Beginning with chapter 1, I shall attempt to demonstrate in detail the utter inadequacy of this orthodox hypothesis.

There is, however, something very tempting about it; it enables us to resolve with apparent ease what is otherwise an enormously complex and vexing question about the dialogues. One need only read any two dialogues to recognize that Plato has Socrates (or the main interlocutor) say different things in different dialogues, things that are often incompatible. If differences in dramatic context are by hypothesis to be ignored, how are we to explain the different positions put into the mouth of Socrates from dialogue to dialogue? The answer for the friends of the orthodox position is easy: the "developmental hypothesis!" Since Socrates is simply Plato's mouthpiece, the differences from dialogue to dialogue record Plato's own intellectual development, his changes of mind, and occasionally his vacillation on important issues. Often, part of this supposed "development" is Plato's gradual liberation from the teaching of his master, the historical Socrates. Hence, the "early" dialogues (as opposed to the "transitional," "middle," or "late" ones) present not just "the young Plato's" view, but, more or less, that of the historical Socrates.[4]

Crucial to this entire method of interpretation, therefore, is the ability to date the dialogues. Without the ability to tell "early" from "middle" or "late" dialogues, we would be unable to determine in anything but a haphazard fashion the course of Plato's

---

3. Gregory Vlastos, *Socrates, Ironist and Moral Philosopher*, (Ithaca, N.Y.: Cornell University Press, 1991), 117 and note 50.

4. This is a central contention of Vlastos's *Socrates, Ironist and Moral Philosopher*, see esp. chapter 2, "Socrates *contra* Socrates in Plato."

"development." Students of Plato who, contrary to this view, argue that the dialogical contexts are important and even determinative, have long objected to the circularity of the major attempts to date the dialogues chronologically. Recently, however, the procedure of dating the dialogues has been decisively refuted by Jacob Howland in a landmark article.[5]

In any case, my central contention, that the exigencies of the dialogue form cannot be ignored in the determination of the philosophic import of the dialogues but are crucial to Plato's teaching, will best be exhibited positively in the pages that follow. Indeed, if the "orthodox" view were correct, the guiding theme of this book, to which I shall now present a skeletal introduction, could not even arise, since it is not explicitly articulated or rendered thematic by *any* major speaker in *any* dialogue. Nevertheless, I shall argue that it is pervasively present as a philosophic issue, but present precisely in those so-called dramatic aspects of the dialogues, without attention to which, therefore, the full philosophic richness of the dialogues cannot be appreciated. To be sure, many of the "arguments" in the dialogues will bear on my guiding theme, and I shall have occasion to examine some of those arguments with what I hope will be exemplary care. But the guiding theme itself is never made the explicit subject of the argument. Let me turn to an introductory statement of that theme.

In dialogue after dialogue, and in a number of different ways, Plato emphasizes by what happens therein that the occasion of philosophy, and perhaps the human occasion altogether, is almost always one in which we are forced to confront a situationally specific form of finitude, limitation, or negation. Hegel notwithstanding, there are next to no "absolute," "infinite," or totalizing possibilities presented to human being, and certainly not regarding the occasion for and possibility of philosophy, or so the dialogues intimate.

---

5. Jacob Howland, "Re-Reading Plato: The Problem of Platonic Chronology," *Phoenix* 45, no. 3 (1991): 189–214. This article should become required reading for all Ph.D. candidates contemplating writing dissertations on Plato. For a different attack that focuses more specifically on Vlastos's developmentalism, see Debra Nails, "Problems with Vlastos' Platonic Developmentalism," *Ancient Philosophy* 13, no. 2 (1993): 273–92.

One of the important consequences of Plato's employment of the dramatic form of dialogue is that every one of his philosophic "works" begins by placing the chief interlocutor, usually but not always Socrates, in a specific situation, one initial consequence of which is to present the interlocutor with limitation, with finitude. Every dialogue does this. That limitation often has to do in part with the participants in the dialogue, and it is instructive, as others have observed, that Plato never presents a dialogue between two mature philosophers, much less between two "wise" people. More generally, the situation itself in which the dialogue occurs—the place, the occasion, the temporal exigency—all have the effect of presenting the interlocutor with an initial limitation, an occasion of finitude, that he or she must confront.[6]

One might counter that a moment's reflection makes clear that of course every human situation is one of finitude, that every specified place or specified time, not to mention the specific people one encounters, self-evidently is one of finitude or limitation. True enough. But how many philosophers make that initiating fact, however obvious, explicitly present as a factor of interpretation in their writing? What we must recognize and take account of is that Plato does; he takes this "obvious" fact of situational finitude and begins every one of his philosophic works by making specific its presence and inviting us to reflect, in conjunction with the announced "question" of the dialogue ("What is justice?," "What is piety?," "What is knowledge?") on its significance.[7]

Every Platonic dialogue thus begins with at least two themes, the one explicitly formulated as the matter for discussion and the other the limiting conditions under which that discussion is to take place. It is hardly an exaggeration to say that, notwithstanding its "self-evident" character, the second theme has, until

---

6. The feminine pronoun is not simply politically correct. Consider Diotima in the *Symposium* or Aspasia in the *Menexenus*.

7. In keeping with the diverse manifestations of such finitude or limitation in the dialogues (not to mention in life), I shall intentionally use the terms in as broad a sense as possible, not trying to limit their range with an arbitrarily precise "definition." Hopefully, something of their range of meanings will become evident in what follows.

recently, largely been ignored by Platonic scholarship. I intend this book to illustrate that the very omnipresence of this theme testifies rather to its importance and provocativeness for Plato than to its obviousness as a fact that can quickly be passed over.

When we encounter finitude, there are a number of ways in which we can respond. One, an aggressive but often tempting strategy, is to try to demolish the limiting condition, to conquer or overwhelm it, to remove its limitation from our lives. From the Greek sophists to the modern attempts to master or conquer nature, this strategy is one with enduring appeal to human being. As I shall show in the next chapter, Plato usually shows such an aggressive strategy toward finitude to be inadequate.

A second strategy, no less appealing on occasion, is simply to submit to the finitude, to capitulate to it and be dominated by it. What we might call this "counsel of resignation" has been a recommendation only slightly less appealing in Western culture than the stance of dominance or mastery. But again, we shall see that Plato presents such a strategy as usually unsatisfactory.

The "dialectic" between these two apparently opposite standpoints through the history of the West would make a worthy and instructive study. It can be seen in the biblical injunction to "have dominion over the earth," as well as in the exhortation to accept this life as a "veil of tears," in the seventeenth-century call to "master nature," and in the twentieth-century advice to "submit" to the "happening" of historically manifested Being. It has surely pervaded the history of our ethical thought, our political philosophy, our understanding of the place of human being in the world, even the possibility and pursuit of knowledge itself.

There is a third strategy, however, which on the one hand does not pretend that our finitude can be comprehensively overcome, yet does not on the other hand passively capitulate to it. This is to acknowledge and understand the finitude as what it is, to recognize it in its depth and complexity, but to respond to that limiting condition by transforming it into possibility, to engage in what we may call "finite transcendence." It is this third strategy, I shall argue, that the Platonic dialogues set out in numerous ways, and at least implicitly recommend as the more adequate stance, indeed, as the stance of philosophy. As the dialogues show, this third stance is a delicate and precarious one, always in danger of falling off into one of its poles, either a passive acceptance of "the way things are," or, perhaps more often, a claim to demolish or conquer the limitations that confront us.

The human situation, then, is such that we are faced again and again with some fundamental manifestation of finitude, and faced with the choice of an attempt at domination, submission, or an acknowledgment of the finitude that transforms it into possibility. The presentation of this theme, together with the implication that the more adequate response is the third, is so prevalent in the Platonic dialogues that it is hard to resist the conclusion that it is an informing theme of Platonic philosophy itself. In the chapters that follow, I shall argue that tragedy, comedy, irony, the founding of a city, and—decisively— philosophy and the pursuit of truth itself are just some of the topics whose presence in the dialogues reflects Plato's meditation on this issue.

The book will not, however, develop this theme "systematically" because it is not developed systematically in the dialogues. I take this to be no accident, nor an indication that the very idea of "systematic" thought had not yet occurred to Plato. Yet another consequence of the pervasive emphasis in the dialogues on context, on the literally de-fining character of situation, is that it makes anything like "systematization" of Plato's thought immensely more problematic than has been recognized by many scholars. Plato never has Socrates, or any other character, speak of his "moral theory," nor of his "theory of forms," his "theory of knowledge," or his "metaphysics." Only Platonic scholars speak of such things, and one reason they so easily do so is that they ignore the pervasive presence of context, of situational finitude, that informs every specific discussion of ethical issues, of forms, of knowledge, or of Being, in the dialogues.

I hope to avoid this error by paying heed to the power of the limiting conditions that inform every philosophic speech presented by Plato, although I shall certainly, with all due caution, attempt to make appropriate generalizations. No character in the dialogues ever suggests that we are completely limited to, or radically determined by, the specific situation in which we find ourselves, nor does Plato imply it. But the dialogues suggest that we must always begin with that situation, and transcend it only with great caution and thoughtfulness, and always with the recognition of the finitude or partiality of all human transcendence.

Accordingly, the chapters of the book will attempt to illustrate some of the many different ways in which the theme of finitude and transcendence is developed in the dialogues. Rather than the image of a "system," I suggest that the dialogues, and the themes developed within them, be thought of more after the image of a spoked wheel, where each spoke begins on the perimeter, at a different specific place, but, via its own path, eventually converges on a common center.[8] My chapters will, as it were, trace a few of the many spokes.

Nevertheless, I have tried to give the book a certain dramatic or organic unity by writing it with constant reference to the *Republic*. Many of my examples and many of the issues explicitly discussed are taken from that dialogue. Given the broad nature of my topic, however, it would have been misleading to choose my examples only from one dialogue. My point, after all, is that the theme of finitude and transcendence is a pervasive theme throughout Plato's writing. I have tried to use a sufficient number of examples from other dialogues to make that thesis plausible, while giving the book a certain dramatic or literary unity by choosing the preponderance of my examples from the *Republic*.

In chapter 1, then, I set the stage for the other chapters by developing a certain "hermeneutic" of the dialogue form. I emphasize the significance of the situation, the *topos* in that broad sense, of each dialogue, and set the stage for the recognition that one lesson of the Platonic dialogues is that the situation out of which every philosophic discussion arises functions at once as a

---

8. If this metaphor is an apt one for the dialogues, then obviously the date of composition of any particular "spoke" is of little importance. Much more important is the aptness of the context for a certain type of soul.

limitation and a possibility, that we must always begin with a self-conscious recognition of that situation and its constraints, while at the same time recognizing the challenge to transcend the merely idiosyncratic elements in that situation. The "place" of each dialogue, then, sets the stage for the theme of finite transcendence.

Chapter 2, on book 2 of the *Republic*, takes the founding of a city as a core example of this originating situation of finitude and possibility, and shows how the rest of that great dialogue is determined in fundamental ways by the alternatives that are presented. In particular, Glaucon and Socrates, in their very different accounts of the origin of justice and the city, both present us with variations on the limiting character of the political situation and how we might respond to it. Their different perspectives remain fundamental throughout the dialogue.

Chapter 3, on the famous "three waves" of the *Republic*, books 5–7, shows how tempting and problematic at once is the urge to respond to the limitations of the political situation by creating a "utopia," a "solution" to the political problem. Plato demonstrates the complexity of this urge by treating each of the three "waves" in different ways that suggest different attitudes toward their possibility and desirability in each case, as I attempt to demonstrate.

In chapter 4, still concentrating on the *Republic* but beginning to move beyond its boundaries, I develop an interpretation of Socratic and Platonic irony that claims that irony itself is a core and pervasive instance in the dialogues of the recognition of finitude (in this case a form of "negativity") and the effort to transform that finitude into possibility. Plato accomplishes this by making irony "dialectical," taking what begins as something negative and transforming it into something positive.

Chapter 5 treats comedy and tragedy as intimately connected versions of the same movement. They both in different ways recognize the human situation as one of limitation or finitude, yet suggest that such limitation can be transformed into possibility. The focus of this chapter, as it is in the dialogues, is on how philosophy itself is a decisive instance of what Socrates once calls "the whole tragedy and comedy of life."

If chapter 5 begins to focus more explicitly on philosophy itself as an instance of this finite transcendence, chapter 6, on the Greek notion of truth (*aletheia*) and its pursuit, makes this theme central. I focus on this issue through a critical examination of that twentieth-century philosopher who has made the most thorough and sustained reflection on the Greek notion of *aletheia*, Martin Heidegger. I argue that in the case of Plato, Heidegger decisively misunderstands the significance of *aletheia* and so of philosophy, and does so precisely by ignoring what he of all people should have appreciated, the way in which *aletheia* functions dramatically in the dialogues rather than being presented as some "theory of truth." Correctly appreciated in the dialogues, *aletheia*, even as Heidegger himself suggests, is itself perhaps the most fundamental instance in human life of finite transcendence.

The final chapter confronts what on the surface would seem to be a substantial obstacle in the dialogues to my interpretation, the so-called theory of forms. By a careful examination of the ways that the "forms" or "ideas" are discussed in the dialogues, I argue that in fact their presence and the ways that they are discussed and employed supports rather than confutes my reading, that the ideas, as ultimate objects of knowledge, are part of a human "world" in which a kind of epistemological transcendence (which we call "knowledge") is indeed possible, but always and only in a finite way.

This book, then, attempts not to be comprehensive but illustrative. I make no claim herein to exhaust any of the topics I address; most especially, I in no sense intend this book as a comprehensive interpretation of the *Republic*. The theme of the book, as the title announces, is finitude and transcendence. I intend to develop some of the striking ways in which that theme is manifested. If I am successful, my book will no doubt lead readers to think of other cases; I could not hope for more.

Given that intention, I have tried to keep reference to secondary scholarship to a reasonable minimum. For the most part, I shall cite scholars whose work expands on points I am making or supports them in different ways. Sometimes, I shall cite striking contrasts to my own interpretations. Only rarely, when I think the matter decisive, shall I take issue explicitly with opposing scholarship. My book, after all, is not fundamentally about my differences with other scholars. It is intended to be about the dialogues themselves.

The book that follows, then, seeks not closure, but opening, and in that sense seeks to imitate the Platonic dialogues it addresses.

1

THE PLACE OF PHILOSOPHY

In this first chapter, I wish to discuss what is at once perhaps the most pervasive locus for the presence of the theme of finitude and transcendence in the dialogues, and at the same time the condition for all the other manifestations thereof.[9] I refer to a crucial aspect of the dramatic element in the dialogue form, the "place" of each dialogue. I take the notion of place, as the dialogues themselves do, in a double sense. In a narrow sense, it can refer to the spatial location of the dialogue, such as a private home, a jail, or the agora. Or, the sense of place can be sufficiently broad to include the "situation" in which we find ourselves, the occasion for our being there, and the people with whom we interact. This broad sense is implicit in English usage, as when we say "a woman's place is in the house...and senate."

In this chapter, I shall touch on the narrower sense of place as spatial location but shall focus on the significance of "place" in the broader sense of "situation" alluded to above, namely, the way in which the *Umwelt*, the "environment" that occasions each dialogue, is used by Plato to open up the themes of finitude and transcendence. One must note the irony that notwithstanding the pervasive presence of "place" in the Platonic dialogues, when scholars turn to a thematic treatment of this issue, they too often ignore its manifest presence in the dramatic context of every dialogue and turn instead to the more abstract and often explicitly mythical speeches about "space," such as the famous discussion

---

9. An earlier version of this chapter was presented at the Metaphysical Society of America conference held in March 1991 at Pennsylvania State University. A later version appears as "Potentiality and Presence: The Significance of Place in the Platonic Dialogues," *Journal of Speculative Philosophy* 8, no. 1 (1994): 28–43.

in the *Timaeus*. In doing so, they do justice neither to place nor to Plato.[10]

Perhaps the single most distinguishing feature of the Platonic dialogue compared to other formats of philosophic writing is that the dialogue always begins in a specific place, a specific situation, within which the limitations as well as the possibilities of each dialogue arise. In this the Platonic dialogue is realistic in a way matched by no other philosophic writing, quite especially the dominant one, the philosophic essay or treatise. All of our own philosophic discussions take place (note the phrase) in a specific place, on a specific occasion, and what is said in the conversation is always tinged by that situation; both its potentialities and its limitations are literally de-fined by the place of its presence. Most contemporary philosophic treatises and essays, of course, are usually presented as if the place of their saying were irrelevant, as if they were said, literally, in no place; but a moment's reflection reveals that this is pretense. Although it is rarely treated as an issue in its own right, we do speak, for example, of "American philosophy," "German philosophy," or "British empiricism," thus identifying, however superficially, certain philosophical positions by the place of their origin.[11] Perhaps more important is the striking and increasing dominance of the university as the place of so much of contemporary philosophy, and derivative from that, the near hegemony of the article or the book as the locus of written philosophical discourse, even when most of those writings remain silent or, more often, unself-conscious about such influences.[12]

Surely Plato could claim to be the realist on this issue, teaching by example that there is truly no such thing as abstract

---

10. For an interesting discussion of this issue, see Paul Friedlander, *Plato: An Introduction*, vol. 1 (New York: Pantheon Books, 1958), esp. chaps. 14, "Plato as Physicist," and 15, "Plato as Geographer."

11. So-called continental philosophy is a good example of the superficiality of these labels, since most of it seems now to be done in the United States. I am indebted to Bob Pippin for this example.

12. A separate and disturbing work could be written on the negative effects of the conventions of the academy on philosophy in the last few centuries.

philosophy, philosophy that occurs in no place, philosophy the *topos* of which has no significance for the content of the thought. One might profitably begin the process of understanding the role of place in the dialogues by developing a topology of the places in which dialogues occur. Here is a brief list:[13]

Apology: lawcourt of Athens

Crito: prison

Phaedo: prison

Charmides: Palaestra of Taureas

Laches: apparently a public place, unspecified

Lysis: Palaestra of Miccus (between the Academy and the Lyceum!)

Euthyphro: on the steps of the Stoa Basilike (near the agora)

Menexenus: on the streets near the agora

Hippias Minor: apparently in a private home

Ion: apparently a public place, but unspecified

Gorgias: agora

Protagoras: frame: agora; contents: home of Callias

Meno: unspecified, but possibly a palaestra

Euthydemus: frame: possibly at Crito's house; contents: Lyceum

---

13. I use the dialogues translated in Edith Hamilton and Huntington Cairns, *The Collected Dialogues of Plato*, in their order, and with thanks to an unnamed reviewer for suggesting that I present the list. For an insightful discussion of the "universe" of the Platonic dialogues, see Diskin Clay, "Gaps in the 'Universe' of the Platonic Dialogues," and the largely supportive commentary by Mitchell Miller, "Commentary on Clay," in *Proceedings of the Boston Area Colloquium in Ancient Philosophy*, vol. 3, ed. John J. Cleary (New York: University Press of America, 1988), 131–64.

Cratylus: unspecified

Phaedrus: outside of town, on the banks of the Ilissus

Symposium: first frame: unspecified; second frame: between Phalerum and downtown Athens; contents: Agathon's house

Republic: first frame: unspecified; second frame: Piraeus; contents: house of Cephalos

Theaetetus: frame: Euclides's house; contents: a palaestra

Parmenides: frame: agora, then Antiphon's house; contents: house of Pythodorus

Sophist: apparently same palaestra as *Theaetetus*

Statesman: apparently same palaestra

Philebus: unspecified, probably indoors

Timaeus: unspecified, presumably a private home

Critias: same as *Timaeus*

Laws: walking outdoors, in Crete (from Knossos to the Cave of Zeus)

Epinomis: unspecified, presumably in Crete

Hippias Major: indefinite location in Athens

The place of a discussion can have an effect on its content in a number of ways. At the most concrete level, for example, whether it is an extraordinary place, laden with drama, or a more everyday place can have a direct effect both on the subject of a conversation and on what is said about it. A dialogue that takes place at a trial, or on the day of one's death, will have an altogether different nuance and impact from one that takes place, say, at a private party or while walking in the country. What are the chances that a discussion we might have together would have the same topic, or that we would say the same things in the same way, if it took place at a party where one of us was celebrating the winning of a MacArthur Award, as opposed to its taking place in a jail, where one of us was imprisoned for civil disobedience? Plato's writing exhibits the conviction that the place of a dialogue is nothing incidental to the content or character of the discussion that ensues therein. Once we recognize this truth, we can see that even those occasions when the context of a discussion seems ordinary and everyday, such that it does not seem so dramatically to affect the discussion, even that becomes significant in contrast to the more striking alternatives. Sometimes, and we see this reflected in several Platonic dialogues, we are vouchsafed a "free space" for discussion, where the place of our talk determines and so confines what is said less than it sometimes does.[14]

A crucial dimension of place in the broader sense surely must be the "time" of the dialogue. It goes without saying that anything that happens in a place also happens at a given time. Strictly speaking, therefore, I should say that in the dialogues place in the narrower sense is co-primordial with time. The dramatic date of various dialogues (as opposed to the speculation as to the date of their composition by Plato) should be significant in our interpretations. The relative age of Socrates (for example, that he is a precocious adolescent when his juvenile "theory of forms" is refuted in the *Parmenides*), is, or should be, an important element in our understanding of that dialogue. Or consider the usually ignored fact that Plato has Socrates engage in at least eight dialogues (counting "The Philosopher") during the last fortnight or so of his life.[15] Surely the sense of urgency that would mark those last days should be a factor in our understanding of those dialogues, as it would be in a similar event in our own lives; but how many commentators on those dialogues take account of

---

14. Though we must always wonder whether such "everydayness" is not more insidious than innocent. Consider again the undramatic but altogether powerful and not always beneficial effect of the university and its conventions on contemporary philosophic discourse, written and oral.

15. The dialogues are *Theaetetus, Euthyphro, Sophist, Statesman,* "*Philosopher,*" *Apology, Crito,* and *Phaedo.* It is to be noted that those dialogues range throughout the conventional chronology of their supposed composition by Plato, from "early" ones such as the *Crito* or *Euthyphro* to "late" ones such as the *Sophist* or *Statesman.*

those existentially powerful factors? Clearly, then, the dramatic time of the dialogues is an important aspect of its "place" in the broader sense.

The place of a dialogue can also take on symbolic significance, especially as it is employed in the literary artifact which is the Platonic dialogue. Dialogues that take place in gymnasia invite reflection on the dominance of the body in our lives and on our speech, on the possibilities and the limitations conferred by embodiment.[16] Or they could invoke the theme of play. The playful eroticism of the opening scene in Plato's *Charmides* and the appropriateness therefore of the particular discussion of the nature of *sophrosyne* that ensues, could hardly be imagined, say, at a funeral, or at a trial for one's life. Dialogues in prisons invoke the theme of constraint, coercion, or the urgency conferred by impending death, even when nothing is explicitly mentioned concerning those topics. Dialogues in the agora remind us that philosophy must confront the public, even if that confrontation is fraught with tension and danger.

As a somewhat extended example of the significance of place in the Platonic dialogues, let us briefly consider the opening scene of the *Republic*.[17] The dialogue begins, "I went down yesterday to the Piraeus...." When we couple this statement with what soon happens, that after the festival Socrates wishes to go back up to Athens but is constrained by his companions, however playfully, to remain down in the Piraeus and discuss the nature of justice, we recognize that Plato has set the dialogue up so as directly to reflect the situation that he later suggests will confront the philosopher in the cave analogy, who, once escaped from the cave, must be coerced to go back down into it in order to lead the people in the direction of a just city. The element of constraint is of special significance here. Just as the philosopher-king of the

---

16. Not to mention the significance of the fact that this "place of nakedness," a place for bodily exercise, should become a center of social life for Athenian males.

17. The gist of what I note here has already been discussed by writers such as Leo Strauss and Allan Bloom in their work on the *Republic*, but I repeat it here with special emphasis on the significance of place for what ensues.

cave analogy will participate in politics only under constraint, so Socrates conducts the very dialogue that presents that teaching under conditions of constraint himself. We would be mistaken to take this symmetry merely as literary flare on Plato's part. Would Socrates have said the same things about justice without the same coercive conditions? Would Plato have written the same things about the tension between philosophy and politics if Socrates had not in his own life fallen prey precisely to those tensions? If we decide that in our own place, for whatever reasons, such tensions between philosophy and politics no longer exist or not in the same way, how should that affect our reading of the *Republic*?

Socrates goes down to the Piraeus with a purpose, to see a religious festival, where he is no less impressed by the foreign, Thracian procession than by the native one. Socrates, we note, has no natural commitment to orthodox piety. Yet he and his companions soon go to the house of Cephalos, who before long leaves the discussion of justice engendered by Socrates, and leaves precisely in the name of orthodox piety: he goes out to perform religious rites. In the discussion soon to take place, Socrates will institute radical reforms, or at least, radical changes, into Athenian religion. In the opening scene, we see that he is no pious respecter of traditional religion, and that those who are so pious, such as Cephalos, simply will not listen to him. We are also invited to remember that Socrates was brought to trial for impiety. As with the tension cited earlier between politics and philosophy, so here, we ask, is the tension between Socrates and conventional religious piety a peculiarity of Socrates and Athenian religion, or is it indicative of a more general and fundamental tension between philosophy and orthodox piety altogether?

Already present in the preceding remarks is an element of place often more decisive than the literal locus of the discussion. In our own philosophic discussions, by and large, what is most fundamentally determinative of the content and character of what is said is less the literal location of the discussion than the people with whom we are speaking. In our own experience, the people who are present are often virtually determinative of what we talk about and the manner in which we discuss it. We talk about some things, in certain ways, when in the company of professional philosophers; we talk about other things, in other ways, in different company. These differences, I hasten to add, are not manifestations of hypocrisy. They are rather an indication of a moderate sensitivity to the nuances of human situations and the differences they entail.

Why do we ignore this simple recognition when we turn to the Platonic dialogues, especially since Plato always reminds us of its significance by placing every dialogue in a specific context with specific people who are participating in the discussion? When we read a book of more orthodox philosophic format, such as the *Critique of Pure Reason*, the almost complete absence of reference to context invites us to suppose that Kant is speaking as a "pure mind," that he is speaking universally, that he would say much the same thing to anyone, at any time.[18] We are justified in making no such assumption when we read Platonic dialogues, where the leading interlocutor, and Socrates in particular, always says what he says to *specific* people, to *particular* character types.

Let me again begin by citing some general types of interlocutors, before I reflect on the significance of some particular examples. Consider first dialogues such as the *Gorgias, Protagoras,* and the first book of the *Republic*, where Socrates' primary interlocutor is a professional Sophist, but where impressionable youths are also present. In those situations, Socrates is at his rhetorically most fierce. Not only does he question his interlocutor and call into question his views; he demolishes his opponent, embarrasses and humiliates him, sometimes to the point where we are almost lead to a certain sympathy with the refuted Sophist who suffers Socrates' rhetorical cruelty.

Is Socrates' conduct in these situations simply a function of his polemical character, or is the presence of impressionable youths as important a factor as that of the Sophists? Is Socrates here refuting Sophists in part as therapy for youths? We get a clue when we compare his behavior in other dialogues, where his chief, or at least initial, interlocutors are youths: Lysis and Menexenus in the *Lysis*, Charmides in the *Charmides*, or

---

18. Or, no less striking, that a specific audience, that of academic philosophy, is silently assumed.

Theaetetus in the dialogue named after him. In these situations, Socrates becomes, in his own famous metaphor, a midwife; his choice of topic as well as his more gentle, maieutic manner is determined by the character of the youths with whom he speaks. With Lysis and Menexenus, two young boys who consider themselves friends, he conducts a dialogue on friendship, gently leading them to the recognition that they don't know what friendship is. With the handsome Charmides, who suffers, strangely, from headaches in the morning (presumably a function of his behavior the night before!), and who will eventually become one of the thirty tyrants, he engages in a dialogue on *sophrosyne*. With the not-so-handsome but intellectually gifted Theaetetus, he discusses the nature of knowledge. In these encounters there is none of the humiliating repetition of questions unanswerable, forcing the interlocutor to publically admit defeat, that we see in Socrates' dialogues with Sophists.

To take a different example, consider Socrates' conduct in the short dialogue, the *Crito*. Socrates is in jail awaiting his death. His friend Crito enters, and the dialogue that ensues takes place between Crito and Socrates alone. That dialogue is decisively determined, I suggest, by the person of Crito and by the project he brings to Socrates' attention. Crito, we note, is an old friend of Socrates, a wealthy businessman who has often been his financial patron. He is no philosopher. Of particular importance is the fact that he has attained early admission to the jail by bribing the guards, and he comes with the news that he has obtained the necessary bribes to assure Socrates' escape, if only Socrates will cooperate. With what kind of man is Socrates here confronted? Crito seems to be following the principle that if he cannot obtain justice (justice as he sees it) by legal means, he shall obtain it by any means at all, and money is the means by which Crito is usually able to obtain what he wants. Socrates then conducts a dialogue with Crito on the injustice of his escaping, the immediate effect of which is that Socrates refuses to escape, but the longer term effect, perhaps, is to restore Crito to his status as an obedient citizen.

As most undergraduates can see, there are a number of curiosities in Socrates' arguments with Crito. There are, in particular, several obvious lacunae in the arguments which Crito, not being a philosopher or perhaps because of his emotional state at the time, does not observe. For example, at 53b ff, Socrates, speaking in behalf of the laws of Athens, begins his concluding argument as to why he will not leave. Where would he go? He allows two possibilities: he could go to a nearby, civilized city, such as Thebes or Megara, but there his reputation would follow him, and in any case, he would soon be in the same difficulties he suffered at Athens. Or, he could go to a distant, uncivilized city, such as Thessaly, but who would want to live in a city devoid of philosophy? In allowing a nearby, civilized city, or a distant, uncivilized city, Socrates leaves out an obvious alternative, which Crito fails to supply: a distant, civilized city—an alternative for which Socrates would have to develop new arguments.[19] And just in case one needed a geographical reminder, on the previous page, at 53a, Socrates had mentioned just such a city: Crete. Obviously, Socrates is not considering all the arguments for leaving.

He makes this virtually explicit in his closing remarks of the dialogue.

> "Be sure, my dear friend Crito, that this is what I seem to hear, as the worshippers of Cybele seem, in their passion, to hear the music of flutes; and the sound of these arguments rings so loudly in my ears *that I cannot hear any other arguments.* And I feel sure that if you try to change my mind you will speak in vain. Nevertheless, if you think that you will succeed, speak." (54d; my emphasis)

Crito declines and the dialogue ends. But Socrates' remark is a clear provocation to the reader: what other arguments is Socrates not hearing? Would they, under other circumstances, convince Socrates to escape? We do not know, but we are invited to speculate. Earlier, Socrates had indicated that another reason why it would be unjust for him to escape now is that he has always

---

19. Richard Kraut, in his often thorough and helpful reading of the *Crito*, passes over this problem; see *Socrates and the State* (Princeton, N.J.: Princeton University Press, 1984), 179, 222–23.

been free to try to persuade the laws to change if he so wished (that is, to engage in legislative persuasion), and he has also always been free to leave Athens for another city, but has never done so (*Crito*, 51d, ff). Socrates does not say what his position would be if he lived in a city that did not give him the opportunity to participate in the determination of the laws, or if he lived behind an iron curtain. What would Socrates' response have been if he lived in a nondemocratic regime? Would his arguments be the same? Socrates' arguments for not leaving, that is, quietly *assume* the political structure of a democracy. Perhaps in his life Socrates was a less harsh critic of democracy than he sometimes seems in his speeches.

This much is clear from these closing lines. Socrates, and surely Plato, know well that these arguments presented in the *Crito* are neither abstractly universal nor conclusive. They are not comprehensive, context-neutral arguments against anyone escaping from jail, and they certainly do not present "Plato's position on civil disobedience." But they do succeed in their existential intention; they convince Crito of what, as most students realize, Socrates has himself become convinced long before this discussion with Crito: that it is better for him to remain in Athens and to die.[20]

One way to put the general point I am making is to say that what the dialogues capture, and what most philosophical essays ignore, is that most of our philosophic discussions are, in a nonpejorative sense of the terms, ad hominem and ad locum. They take place in given contexts and with given people, and these factors are often determinative both of the content and the manner of our discussion.

It seems clear that Plato was sufficiently impressed by this "existential" aspect of philosophic discourse that he chose to bring it home vividly in all his formal works. But it has rather powerful

---

20. For a discussion of the *Crito* compatible with my own, see Clifford Orwin's discussion of Richard Kraut's *Socrates and the State*, entitled "Liberalizing the *Crito*: Richard Kraut on Socrates and the State," in *Platonic Writings, Platonic Readings*, ed. Charles Griswold (New York: Routledge, 1988), 171–76.

and often ignored consequences for our reading of Plato. If the content and the manner of presentation of the speeches in the dialogues are functions in part of the place and the participants, then we should be far, far more cautious than we usually are about making comprehensive pronouncements about "Plato's philosophy," about, for example, "Plato's criticism of art," "Plato's earlier metaphysics," or "Plato's moral theory." If Plato had such abstract or totalizing philosophic "theories," and wanted to make them available to all readers, he surely could have done it best, as he himself reminds us in the Seventh Letter.[21] But he does not; he chooses instead to bring home another, perhaps deeper, lesson about philosophic discourse: its irreducibly existential character, that its place and its participants cannot be ignored in reflecting on what is said.

There is an obvious objection that might be raised at this point, one that students of the dramatic aspects of Plato's writing have come to know as "the Aristotle question." If Plato had wanted to be read in the way I suggest, surely Aristotle, his outstanding student of many years, would have understood that. But Aristotle, as we know, has no hesitation about attributing all sorts of abstract pronouncements to Plato—usually promptly to criticize them! If Aristotle read Plato with little or no attention to the dramatic significance of the dialogues, aren't we thereby justified in doing so too?

First, it should be noted that Aristotle more often attacks "the Platonists," presumably of the Academy, than Plato himself or the dialogues in particular. But in any case, second, Aristotle's specific criticisms of Plato would be more of a problem if there were evidence that the Stagirite was trying to be objectively fair to his predecessors, acting as a good historian of philosophy; but there is no such evidence. He is not "fair" in this sense to the pre-Socratics, so why should we expect him to be fair to Plato? Aristotle, in a proto-Hegelian strategy, is interested in his predecessors primarily insofar as they lead partially up to him (Thales and the other Milesians saw the presence of "material cause,"

---

21. Plato, Seventh Letter, 341d: "Besides, this at any rate I know, that if there were to be a treatise or a lecture on this subject, I could do it best."

Empedocles added "efficient cause," and so on.).[22] To read one's predecessors primarily insofar as they prepare the way for your own thought is hardly the basis of an objectively fair reading.

Our own problems in this regard are increased by the historical fact that, over the course of centuries and particularly with the advent of modern philosophy, the essay or treatise form gradually attained dominance as the standard form of philosophic writing. It is important to recognize that such simply was not the case for Plato. He had before him a rich pallette of philosophic styles from which to choose. There surely was no standard or conventional format. He had, to be sure, the "Concerning Nature" treatises of some pre-Socratics. But he also had Parmenides' and Empedocles' poems, Heraclitus' aphorisms, and perhaps most important, the rich tradition in Athens of comedy and tragedy. It is fair to assume, then, that Plato's choice of the dialogue form was much more considered and self-conscious than, say, our own choice to write essays. We are therefore justified in asking, as I am, what the philosophic import of his choice of format might be.[23] Finally, Plato surely cannot be blamed for the subsequent historical fact that so dominant did the treatise format become that not only did almost all philosophers adopt it, but that they would read its conventions back into writings such as Plato's dialogues.

I have been arguing that the dramatic aspects of the dialogue form entail that we be much more wary than we usually are about making generalizations regarding Plato's theory of this or that.

---

22. Aristotle, *Metaphysics*, book 1, 983b, ff. For an interesting account of this issue which, on the one hand, recognizes that Aristotle's criticisms of his predecessors must be read skeptically, yet on the other hand, argues at length for a certain consistency between his criticisms of Plato and the content of at least the "late" dialogues, see Kenneth Sayre,'s *Plato's Late Ontology: A Riddle Solved* (Princeton, N.J.: Princeton University Press, 1983). I shall address the question of Aristotle's reading of Plato in more detail in my final chapter.

23. In an earlier article, "Why Plato Wrote Dialogues," *Philosophy and Rhetoric* 1, no. 1, (1968): 38–50, I develop at length a response to this question which focuses on the criticism of writing in the Phaedrus.

Am I then saying that Plato's views are missing from the dialogues, that what we get in each case is a collection of relativistic, merely parochial discourses from which no more general lesson can be taken, other than the architectonic lesson about the philosophic significance of place? Not at all. But surely the determination of those more general teachings will be rendered more complex than in the case of treatises. How can we begin making that determination?

In the case of most treatises, we have the philosophic speech and nothing else. The author's teaching, we are invited to assume, is contained in that speech. The Platonic dialogues, by locating each speech in a given place and a given existential context, offer us a richer field of interpretation, more akin to the richness of our own lived philosophic discussions. We still have philosophic speeches, to be sure, and those speeches (*logoi*) will always be decisive in philosophy. But we can now compare them, balance them, perhaps modify them, in the light of what we can call the *local action* of the dialogue. Perhaps "Plato's view" on this or that is located not simply in the specific speeches of this or that person (including Socrates), but also in the interstices, the ironic contrasts, even the contradictions, between speech and action, between what is said in one place, and to one kind of person, and what is said in another place, to another. If Socrates refutes Polemarchus' definition of justice as "helping friends and harming enemies" in book 1 of the *Republic*, yet later employs that very principle as the guideline for the conduct of his "guardians" in the "city in speech," that ought to provoke us to a reflection on the relation between those two scenes. Perhaps a core part of "Plato's teaching" lies in the provocation to reflect on tensions such as these.

We must take note briefly of two other important aspects of the dramatic context of Platonic dialogues. I refer to the very ambiguous presence/absence of Plato, and a parallel presence/absence of the reader. In one sense, Plato, as writer of every dialogue, is always present. Yet, with the curious exception of the *Apology*, where he is said to be present (but silent!), he is never portrayed as actually present at the dramatic place of the dialogue.[24] In a similar way, the reader is in one sense present at every dialogue, yet in the dramatic sense, always absent.

This raises the possibility of a "hierarchy of places" in the hermeneutics of the Platonic dialogue. There is the place of the dramatic context. But there is also the place of Plato himself as he writes the dialogue, about which we know very little that is helpful. And third, there is the place of the reader, who must always contribute something of the significance of his or her own place in the way the dialogue is interpreted.[25]

The fact that every dialogue occurs in a specific place and with specific people suggests that every philosophic occasion is limited by its place and those present; yet those very limitations also offer the possibility of the particular dialogue. That finitude, limitation, is inseparable from possibility, that the very factors of limitation are also the factors of possibility, offers, I suggest, at least one larger lesson that we can draw from an examination of the dialogue, one that Plato reiterates in numerous ways. To show this, let me develop this issue further, through a reiteration of the general remarks made in the introduction, in a way which I hope will make clear the crucial role of place in Plato's larger teaching.

In dialogue after dialogue, as I have argued, Plato suggests dramatically that the occasion of philosophy, and perhaps the human occasion altogether, is almost always one in which we are forced to confront a situationally specific form of finitude, of limitation. In the *Crito*, Socrates is limited by the fact that he is in jail, and that he is confronted by Crito, a nonphilosophic friend who has arranged for him to escape illegally. In the *Phaedo*, he is limited decisively by his impending death, and by the fact that at the beginning of the dialogue everyone present but Socrates himself is wallowing in sorrow—a powerful inhibition indeed to the possibility of philosophy. In the *Republic*, he is limited in part

---

24. Indeed, in the *Phaedo* he is explicitly mentioned as being absent (*Phaedo*, 59b). I shall develop the significance of this point more fully in the penultimate chapter of this book.

25. Again, since many, if not most, readers of the Platonic dialogues are "placed" in the academy, a critique of the way in which its conventions have confined and limited fruitful reflection could be given here.

by having been constrained to stay when he wished to go home, by the specific character of the individuals who are present, and, especially in book 1, by the necessity of overcoming the dominance of Thrasymachus and his aggressive assertion of the truth of sophistic relativism. In the *Euthyphro*, he is limited by the impending trial, the charge for which he is on the way to answer, as well as by the complacent self-certainty of Euthyphro.

As was adumbrated in the introduction, when we are confronted by finitude, there are a number of ways in which we can respond. One is to try to demolish the limiting condition, to conquer or overwhelm it, to remove its limitation from our lives. In the dialogues, it is often the Sophists who exhibit and even espouse this strategy, and there is no better exemplar of it than the conduct of Thrasymachus in the *Republic*, whose rhetorical strategy, an attempt to intimidate and overpower, is a consistent reflection of the position he espouses that "justice is the advantage of the stronger." Or, by way of a second example, consider the striking optimism of Eryximachus in the *Symposium*, whose confidence that human techne in its various forms can control not only the "healthy" but even the "diseased" eros, and not just in the human body but throughout the cosmos, is at once the informing theme and the decisive defect of his speech. But as Plato has the dialogues make clear, such a belligerent strategy toward finitude is rarely successful.

A second strategy, no less appealing on occasion, is simply to submit to the finitude, to capitulate to it and be dominated by it. In the dialogues, this standpoint is represented often by interlocutors who are unwilling to engage in dialogue with Socrates, who prefer to "stand pat" with their position, neither to question it nor bother to defend it. Philebus is one such person, as are Cephalos and Cleitophon in the *Republic*.[26] In more moderate form, Theodorus, so anxious to avoid the challenge of dialogue with Socrates in the *Theaetetus*, or Phaedrus, who seems delighted with any speech whatsoever, or Agathon in the *Symposium*, who

---

26. As David Roochnik has recently argued, such passivity makes them, in fact, next to impossible to refute; see his "The Riddle of the *Cleitophon*," *Ancient Philosophy* no. 4, (1984): 132–45.

seems not in the least distressed when Socrates convinces him that he didn't know what he was saying, exhibit this standpoint as well. No less obviously, Plato presents such a strategy as usually unsatisfactory, however pervasive it might be.

There is a third strategy, however, one that on the one hand does not pretend that our finitude can be comprehensively overcome, yet does not on the other hand passively capitulate to it. This is to acknowledge and understand the finitude as what it is, to recognize it in its depth and complexity, but to respond to that limiting condition by transforming it into possibility, to engage in what we may call "finite transcendence."

We see this phenomenon arise in the dialogues in a number of ways, some as explicit aspects of an argument, some in the existential drama of the dialogue. When Glaucon, in his account in *Republic*, book 2, of the origins of the city, characterizes our natural situation as one of radical injustice, of "a war of all against all," he suggests that the "social contract" wherein we agree to be just is a transforming and transcending response to that limitation.[27] Even more explicitly, Socrates, in reply, begins his own, very different account of the origins of the city by asserting that "none of us is sufficient for our own needs, but each of us lacks many things."[28] Here we see an explicit acknowledgment of our finitude, to which the developing of the city is a transforming, positive response.

Again and again, I suggest, Plato writes his dialogues in such a way that these three strategies or stances are presented, indeed, often, as in book 1 of the *Republic*, in such a way as distinctly to confront each other. So ubiquitous is this presentation, and so consistently is the third option presented as the more fruitful, that it is plausible to suggest that it is an informing theme of Platonic philosophy. As subsequent chapters will show, irony, comedy, and tragedy are all topics whose presence in the dialogues reflects a similar structure, as is, more particularly, the effort to construct a just city out of human incompleteness in the *Republic*.[29]

---

27. Plato, *Republic*, 359a–b. See the next chapter for an extended analysis of this and the next point.

28. Plato, *Republic*, 369b.

29. I treat these themes in depth in subsequent chapters.

But surely the most pervasive instance of this theme in the dialogues is the dramatic situation itself. The place in which and the people with whom we find ourselves almost always present us with limitation. Faced with the alternatives of dominance and submission, we are sometimes able to see the situation for what it is, and to make of it a possibility of significance and meaning. When we do, by and large, we live well. Plato again and again brings home to us this lesson by placing his characters in such a limiting situation, and allowing us to watch the effort to transform it into possibility. Let me elicit two examples to which I have already alluded, which I think bring home this point with special force.

Consider again the situation faced by Socrates in the *Crito*. Crito wakes him from what the businessman characterizes as a remarkably comfortable sleep to inform him of the arrangements he has made to assure Socrates' escape. Two massive limitations here confront Socrates. First, he is in jail, and soon to die. Second, his non-philosophic friend, Crito, has made arrangements to accomplish precisely what, as is clear even from the *Apology*, Socrates has decided not to accomplish: his avoidance of death. Given this situation, a number of responses are available. He could, of course, in spite of his better judgment, simply capitulate to Crito's pleas. He could allow himself to be spirited away and spend the rest of his days, not in nearby Thebes or barbarian Thessaly, but in distant, civilized Crete. In so submitting, he would avoid having to persuade Crito otherwise, not to mention avoid suffering an imminent death. Second, Socrates could refuse even to consider the matter; he could retire into one of his well-known intellectual trances, refusing to speak, or he could curtly dismiss Crito, as he soon will curtly dismiss his wife, Xanthippe, on the day of his death, or he could, in the manner of Thrasymachus, hurl a torrent of insults at Crito for interrupting his sleep.

Instead, as we know, Socrates does something very different. Confronted with this twofold limiting condition, he transforms it into a twofold possibility, the possibility, first, of restoring to his friend his lost sense of what is just and what is unjust, while at the same time, second, engaging in one more philosophic dialogue, one more effort to question the foundations of one's beliefs and one's actions. The *Crito* is the actualization of that possibility, of that finite transcendence of a limiting situation.

As a second example, consider again the opening scene of the *Republic*. Socrates, wanting to go back up to Athens from the Piraeus, is detained from behind by the slave of Polemarchus and a number of others, and ordered to stay for a party and a horse-back race. Once again, a number of paths are open to Socrates, which he does not take. First, as always, there is submission. He could accede to the request, have a good meal, see the race, and then, perhaps, be free to go home. (He would surely have gotten home earlier than he in fact does, given the length of the ensuing dialogue that obviously extends throughout the night.) Second, there is the path of mastery or dominance. He could try refusing to stay, or convincing them to let him go. Indeed, he pretty clearly entertains this possibility at 327c, asking Polemarchus, who had playfully threatened Socrates with the force of their numbers, "what if I persuade you to let me go?" The reply, however playful, is striking given the theme I am invoking: "How can you persuade us if we will not listen?"

What Socrates does, instead, is to transform this limiting condition into the possibility of philosophic dialogue which becomes the *Republic*. He indeed goes to the house of Cephalos, thereby superficially acceding to the demands of Polemarchos and the others.[30] But they never make it to the horse race, and the party itself is transformed into a monumental dialogue on justice by the philosopher who had just been unjustly detained from going back up from the "cave" of the Piraeus. For it is unmistakable that it is Socrates himself who determines the course of the discussion. Cephalos, innocently responding to Socrates' penetrating query as to what he thinks the chief benefit of his wealth is, allows that it is the ability to avoid doing injustice by

---

30. Does Socrates *provoke* the desire for his presence by pretending to be such a reluctant guest, as Mitchell Miller has suggested to me? Consider a similar scene at the beginning of the *Symposium*, where Socrates, by remaining behind on a neighboring portico, seems to provoke the desire for his presence all the more intensely by his sustained absence.

not having to lie and by paying one's debts. Socrates seizes upon this innocent reply as a *definition of justice*,[31] and the great dialogue begins. Once again, Socrates has transformed what might be considered an inherently unphilosophic situation into yet another occasion for philosophy. Finitude has been turned into possibility, an unphilosophic presence into the potentiality for philosophy.

So, it might be objected, is Plato's thought no longer relevant to us, since what he portrays is limited to situations and issues as they might have arisen in fifth-century Athens? That would be so only if the philosophical predicaments that humans face today are so radically different from those in ancient Athens that there was literally nothing that was said out of those ancient situations that transcends the limitations of specific context and would be applicable to similar situations today. I certainly believe no such thing, nor, surely, did Plato, or why would he have written dialogues for posterity? Again, as I have insisted, we are not merely limited to parochial discussions. It is always possible to transcend the specific situation out of which philosophic discourse arises, to, as we say, generalize from this or that instance; but that transcendence is always *finite*. Part of one's understanding of a given "theory" must always be a consideration of the kind of situations out of which and in terms of which it might arise. But a totalizing or "absolute" theory is impossible.

Then what about the "theories" that have made Plato famous, the theory of forms, Plato's criticism of art, Plato's theory of the state, and so on? We can certainly talk of forms, as characters in Plato's dialogues do. But we must remember that it is we who come to speak of it as an abstract "theory." Plato never does. We do not know whether Plato had such a "theory." We do know that his characters speak from time to time of the necessity of forms, or now of the weaknesses, now of the positive possibilities of art, in response to specific problems and predicaments, and in different ways to different people. I suggest only that we do not forget that reality of the Platonic texts.[32]

---

31. Plato, *Republic*, 331c.

32. In the last chapter I shall address in detail the issue of the transformation of the various discussions of forms in the dialogues into the "theory of forms" of classical scholarship.

Philosophy in our time may have become a largely abstract "discipline," whose task is to solve or dissolve an equally abstract set of "philosophical problems." But we must recognize that it was not always so, and it was especially not so for Plato. Plato's dialogues suggest that place and the presence of others constitute the limiting condition, but also the potentiality, of philosophic discourse. Plato brings home to us this conviction by showing it to us in every philosophic dialogue he creates. In so doing, he teaches us that philosophy can never be reduced to the assertion of a collection of abstract theories spoken, to paraphrase Nietzsche, "to everyone and no one," everywhere and nowhere.[33] The finite presence conferred by place and by others always qualifies the universality of what can be said and the way it is said. But it also confers on us the potentiality, the always finite potentiality, of philosophy.

---

33. *Thus Spoke Zarathustra* is announced as "a book for everyone and no one."

2

REPUBLIC, BOOK 2, AND THE ORIGINS OF POLITICAL PHILOSOPHY

In chapter 1, I claimed that one of the many places where the theme of finitude and transcendence is exhibited in the dramatic action of the dialogue is in book 1 of the *Republic*, in Socrates's being constrained to stay in the Piraeus, in his transformation of this situation into the possibility of philosophy, and in his confrontation with the belligerent Sophist, Thrasymachus. Very soon after that—indeed, at the beginning of book 2—Socrates encounters the theme much more explicitly as part of the topic of discussion.[34] This occurs when Glaucon and Adeimantus again prevent Socrates from leaving and demand that he more adequately defend his claim that the just person is happier than the unjust. Glaucon sets out, as a challenge to Socrates, his own version of the origins of the polity and of justice, to which Socrates responds with his vision of the "healthy" or "true" city. In both cases, as I hope now to show in this chapter, we see that the political situation in the literal sense, the conditions that lead us to gather together in polities, is an explicit instance of a confrontation with finitude that must somehow be transcended. Book 2 presents us with two fundamental possibilities of such a transcendence, only one of which is developed in the rest of the *Republic*. Let us turn, then, to a study of the theme as it arises in book 2.

As has often been observed, book 1 of Plato's *Republic*, if taken in isolation from the rest of the work, reads remarkably like one of the earlier "aporetic" dialogues, such as the *Charmides*,

---

34. An earlier version of this chapter was published as "*Republic* Book II and the Origins of Political Philosophy," *Interpretation* 16, no. 2 (1988–1989): 247–61.

Lysis, Laches, or *Euthyphro.*[35] The topic in the *Republic* is "justice," a number of "definitions" are asserted by Socrates' interlocutors, each definition is in turn subjected to Socrates' elenchus, and the dialogue does not "succeed," in the sense of finding an acceptable definition. Nevertheless, at the conclusion, the interlocutors (and the readers) are better off than they were at the beginning, since now, at least, they do not "think they know what they do not know," but instead realize their ignorance; they are left in philosophic aporia, itself a striking instance of the finite transcendence of the limitations of ignorance. Moreover, as often happens, Socrates closes book 1, in an apparent effort to make the interlocutors feel better, by taking the blame himself for the failure to achieve a successful definition (*Republic,* 354b–c). So far, so aporetic, so "early," so "Theaetetan."

What makes the *Republic* virtually unique among such dialogues is that the interlocutors—or at least two of them—do not let Socrates go home at this juncture, but insist that he stay and defend more adequately his refutation of the preceding assertions of Thrasymachus. Glaucon and Adeimantus, brothers of Plato, transform a typically short aporetic dialogue into the monumental *Republic* by asserting their recognition that Socrates' elenchus was inadequate and by demanding that he do a more adequate job of defense. They thus accomplish the notoriously difficult task, which more famous rhetoricians such as Thrasymachus and Protagoras find next to impossible, of turning the tables on Socrates and making him speak positively, forcing him to develop and defend a view of his own. To be sure, he does so in his usual context of a "dialogue" with the two brothers, but no one fails to see that the setting out of the "city in speech" (369a) of the *Republic* is primarily Socrates' doing.

---

35. It should not be forgotten that it is also similar to the "later" *Theaetetus,* reminding us that Plato did not "abandon" this possibility in his later writing. Nevertheless, this similarity has led some scholars to the rather curious speculation that book 1 is an "early dialogue," to which, during his "middle period," Plato tacked on the ensuing nine books. See, for example, Vlastos, *Socrates, Ironist and Moral Philosopher,* 250.

Book 2, however, belongs at least as much to Glaucon and Adeimantus as it does to Socrates. Not only are they the efficient cause of the continuation of the dialogue, but they establish the terms, the context, in which Socrates will have to develop the more positive view of the succeeding books. They do so, with Glaucon taking the lead, by developing a more adequate defense of a position similar to that of Thrasymachus, and by grounding that defense in an account of the origins of justice, of the polity, and indeed of human nature itself. Because that account is so clearly determinative for the rest of the *Republic*, it will be worth our while to examine it and Socrates' initial response to it more closely than is often done. For, I shall argue, book 2 contains to a remarkable extent a statement of many of the fundamental controversies of political philosophy.

Glaucon begins by distinguishing three kinds of goods and asking Socrates to say to which class he believes justice belongs. The distinction Glaucon draws is both subtle and not especially clear.[36] The first class is "a kind of good that we would choose to have not because we desire its consequences, but because we delight in it for its own sake—such as enjoyment and all the pleasures which are harmless and leave no after effects other than the enjoyment in having them."[37] The second class "we like both for its own sake and for what comes out of it, such as thinking and seeing and being healthy" (357c). The third kind of good, examples of which Glaucon lists gymnastic exercise, medical treatment, and the other activities from which money is made, are "drudgery but beneficial to us; and we would not choose to have them for themselves but for the sake of the wages and whatever else comes out of them" (357c–d). The distinction, especially between the first two classes, is made somewhat obscure because in each case the standard of measure, enjoyment or delight, would

---

36. David Sachs, "A Fallacy in Plato's *Republic*," in *Plato's Republic: Interpretation and Criticism*, ed. Alexander Sesonske (Belmont, Calif.: Wadsworth, 1966), 66–81. See esp. 70–72.

37. *Republic*, 357b. Unless otherwise noted, I shall throughout follow the translation of Allan Bloom, *The Republic of Plato*, (New York: Basic Books, 1968).

itself seem to be an "effect" and so belong to the second class. It has been plausibly suggested that the first class must refer to goods whose good effects are "in themselves" and exerted within the soul of the possessor, whereas the second class includes goods which "in conjunction with other things, have additional good effects."[38]

While the distinction itself may be somewhat vague, the point toward which Glaucon drives is relatively clear. He asks Socrates to which of the three classes he supposes justice to belong, and when Socrates predictably puts it in the second class of things "liked both for itself and for what comes out of it" (358a), Glaucon notes that most people, on the contrary, would put it in the third class of goods that are drudgery in themselves but pursued for their good consequences. The challenge for Socrates therefore is to show that justice is indeed in the second class. However, since the second and third classes, wherein the disparity between Socrates' and the common view lies, agree on the good consequences of justice, the real challenge to Socrates lies in showing that justice "in itself" is a good and not drudgery. This is the force of Glaucon's otherwise extreme demand that Socrates show that the just man, *stripped* of the good consequences of justice, that is, with the reputation for great injustice, will nevertheless be happiest (358a, 361a–d). In any case, it is questionable whether, in the ensuing books, Socrates even takes up this precise challenge, much less whether he successfully meets it. What he does do is dictated by the way in which Glaucon now presents the thrust of his position.

Glaucon develops his challenge in three ways (358c–d). First, he sets out "what kind of thing they say justice is, and where it came from" (358c). That is, he presents us with what we shall see is an extraordinary account of the origins of justice and the polity. Second, he supports the common view that justice belongs to the third class of goods, that "all those who practice it do so unwillingly, as necessary but not good" (358c). Third, he argues that they are right to do so, for "the life of the unjust man is, after all, far better than that of the just man, as they say" (358c).

---

38. Sachs, "A Fallacy in Plato's *Republic*," 71–72.

Glaucon's stunningly compact account of the origins of justice is worth quoting at length:

"They say that doing injustice is naturally good, and suffering injustice bad, but that the bad in suffering injustice far exceeds the good in doing it; so that, when they do injustice to one another and suffer it and taste of both, it seems profitable—to those who are not able to escape the one and choose the other—to set down a compact among themselves neither to do injustice nor to suffer it. And from there they began to set down their own laws and compacts and to name what the law commands lawful and just. And this, then, is the genesis and being of justice; it is a mean between what is best—doing injustice without paying the penalty—and what is worst—suffering injustice without being able to avenge oneself. The just is in the middle between these two, cared for not because it is good but because it is honored due to a want of vigor in doing injustice. The man who is able to do it and is truly a man would never set down a compact with anyone not to do injustice and not to suffer it. He'd be mad. Now the nature of justice is this and of this sort, and it naturally grows out of these sorts of things." (258e–359b)

We can begin by noting the profoundly alienated and negative character of the teaching Glaucon sets out. As the first line makes clear, the *natural* order of things is radical injustice; justice is an imposition on this natural order by those incapable of flourishing within its context. The natural order, what we might call Glaucon's "state of nature," is truly a "war of all against all," and more than one commentator has noted the affinity with the position subsequently set out and made famous in Hobbes's Leviathan.[39] Glaucon's view implies, in accordance with Thrasymachus's, that justice is indeed a human convention, that it is

---

39. E.g., R. E. Allen, "The Speech of Glaucon in Plato's *Republic*," Journal of the History of Philosophy, 25, no.1 (1987): 3–11; 5. Leo Strauss, *The City and Man* (Chicago: Rand McNally, 1964), acknowledges the connection but qualifies it; see esp. 88.

functionally identical to legality, that "the strong" will not feel themselves bound by its strictures, and that it originates as the negation of, and so is defined by, "natural" injustice.

Perhaps more light can be shed on Glaucon's position if we think through the conception of the human situation implicit in it. I begin with an outline of two fundamentally different characterizations of this situation, which I shall call respectively the relational and the atomistic.[40] According to the first view, our very nature is determined by the quality of our relations with the world and other humans. What I *am* is a given set of relations, or the potentiality thereof. If I say, for example, that I am a teacher, husband, father, American, these are words naming the specific relations that constitute who I am. One of the most famous instances of this conception of the human situation is Aristotle's "definition" of human being as "the political animal."[41] The thrust of this characterization is that humans do not merely *happen* from time to time to gather in polities, but that it is part of our essential nature to do so. We would not be the beings we are if we were not political. The same is true of Marx's famous formulation of us as "species beings,"[42] or of Buber's assertion early in *I and Thou* that "There is no I taken in itself, but only the I of the primary word I-Thou and the I of the primary word I-It."[43] In each case we see a characterization of our very natures as relational. This view is almost always presented positively by its proponents, as in the three cases mentioned; but it is worth noting that such an under-

---

40. For a more detailed formulation of these two standpoints and their significance, see my *The Question of Play* (Lanham, Md.: University Press of America, 1984), esp. chaps. 4 and 5.

41. Aristotle, *Politics*, book 1, chap. 2, 1253a.

42. Examples of this notion can be found in T. B. Bottomore, *Karl Marx: Early Writings* (New York: McGraw Hill, 1963); see esp. "Bruno Bauer, 'Die Judenfrage,'" 13, 26, 31, and "Economic and Philosophic Manuscripts of 1844," 127. Perhaps the most explicit and succinct formulation is in the famous sixth "thesis on Feuerbach": "But the essence of man is no abstraction inherent in each separate individual. In its reality it is the ensemble of social relations."

43. Martin Buber, *I and Thou*, trans. R. G. Smith (New York: Charles Scribner's Sons, 1958), 4.

standing of human nature can be criticized by proponents of the "atomistic" view as entailing an excessive dependence on others, a lack of autonomy or self-reliance.

According to the second, "atomistic" view, a human being is naturally an autonomous, independent, radically self-interested "monad" or "atom," who, to be sure, may enter into relations with others, but where such relations will never be essential to, literally definitive of, the individual. Our nature, that is, is entirely intrinsic. Probably the best example in all of philosophy of the atomistic conception of the individual is the "ego" of Descartes's "ego cogitans" who, at least originally, does not even know whether it has a body, much less whether an external world exists to which it might be essentially related. But its pre-dominance in the thought of Thoreau, Emerson, and certain representatives of the "existentialist" tradition suggest the strong appeal of this conception in our tradition. In its positive versions, such a conception of the individual emphasizes autonomy, independence, "self-reliance," and as such is often presented as a desirable way to be, indeed as a situation toward which we should strive. Its negative possibilities, however, point toward a sense of isolation and a self-interest so radical as to imply an indifference toward and even a fundamental alienation from other humans.[44]

As I hope my examples suggest, these two views have exerted a strong influence on our tradition, and a worthwhile study could be done of their "dialectic" in the history of Western culture. But we can return to book 2 by noting that Glaucon clearly presents a prototypical version of the atomistic view, including within it the negative consequence of radical alienation from others.[45] Human beings "naturally" are alienated and selfish; the establishing of the conventions that lead us "not to do

44. Marx draws out these implications especially well; see "Bruno Bauer, 'Die Judenfrage,'" 13, 25, 26.

45. R. E. Allen, "Speech of Glaucon," sees this in passing; he remarks that Glaucon "tends toward a view of human intercourse which is remarkably atomic and isolated" (6).

injustice" are impositions on the natural order of alienation.[46] I want to emphasize here that, according to Glaucon, the political situation arises out of a situation of fundamental negativity or limitation; there exists a "natural" injustice, alienation, and self-interest, all of which are founded in a deeply atomistic conception of the individual. The transcendence of this original limitation is the forming of polities. It is thus to counter this initial negativity, to turn limitation into possibility, that Glaucon develops his understanding of the "social contract," the origins of the polity and conventional justice. If humans were not limited by our atomistic alienation and natural injustice, we presumably would not need a social contract, not need a polity, not need conventional justice. "Justice" is thus a response to a specific version of human nature and a transcendence of a specific form of negativity and limitation. It is not part of our original nature, not "natural" in that sense.

Glaucon's second thesis is that those who do justice do so unwillingly and only for the good consequences that accrue from a reputation for justice, that is, that justice belongs to the third category of goods outlined earlier. His chief support for this claim is the myth of Gyges. The ancestor of Gyges is presented as an archetypical human being. Thanks to the acquisition of a magical ring that enables him to become invisible whenever the collet is turned inward, he is placed in a situation where he can do injustice without risking the negative consequences thereof. Freed from those consequences, he does all manner of injustice with a vengeance. The clear implication is that we would all behave

---

46. It is worth noting that Glaucon's is hardly the only version of an originally atomistic state of nature. For the most challenging alternative, consider Rousseau, who characterizes human being in the state of nature as radically atomistic but *not* alienated, and construes the movement from the state of nature to civil society as necessitating a change in human nature from the atomistic to the relational. In my judgment, Rousseau is deeply ambivalent about this change. See "The Second Discourse" in R. D. Masters, ed., *The First and Second Discourses: Jean-Jacques Rousseau* (New York: St. Martin's Press, 1964), 106, 110, 127–35, esp. 133–34; *Of The Social Contract*, trans. Charles Sherover (New York: Harper & Row, 1984), book 1, but esp. 18.

accordingly, and therefore that the only reason we are just is because we fear the consequences of getting caught doing injustice. Thus justice is in the third category of goods, not at all a good in itself (359d–60d).

The point of the Gyges story is clear enough. If Gyges's ancestor can be taken as typical of humans, then Glaucon is surely right that justice is not something that we would do without fear of punishment for our unjust acts. We thus really are, as his account of the origins of the polity suggested, atomistic beings, alienated from each other and naturally unjust. The Gyges story is consistent with the earlier account of our origins.

Glaucon's third point is an elaboration of the second. The people who are just, who control under duress their natural tendency to do injustice and do so only from the fear of punishment, are right. Justice really is in the third category, drudgery in itself, something pursued only for its consequences. To bring this out and to seal his challenge to Socrates, Glaucon develops his two "statues," one of the utterly just man who not merely misses the rewards usually associated with a reputation for justice but, to the contrary, has a reputation for the greatest injustice and is therefore subjected to the harshest of punishments, and the other of a massively unjust man whose injustice is accompanied by clever intelligence, so that he both avoids the usual penalties for injustice and enjoys the benefits of a reputation for justice. Having not only stripped away the usual consequences of justice and injustice but reversed them, Glaucon asks Socrates to show that notwithstanding, the just man would be happier than the unjust (360e–62c).

The import of Glaucon's powerful images is again fairly clear, but a number of points should be underlined. First, the two "statues" dramatically emphasize the thesis that justice is usually pursued, and injustice eschewed, exclusively because of the consequences associated with them respectively, and that, freed from those consequences, the thesis of the Gyges story, and of the account of the origins of the social contract, would be sustained. Our natural, unconstrained tendency is to be unjust and alienated from each other. Glaucon's three theses hold together coherently, and are grounded in the crucial account of the origins of the polity and conventional justice.

Second, the fact that Glaucon not only strips away the consequences usually associated with justice and injustice, but also reverses them, makes the challenge to Socrates more extreme than its earlier statements suggested. The account of the three classes of goods suggested only that Socrates needed to establish that justice was a good in itself, that is, that it was desirable *without* appeal to its consequences. After the presentation of Glaucon's two statues, Socrates is asked to show further that even if the men's respective reputations were reversed, and in particular that if the just man not only did *not* enjoy the usual consequences of justice (all that was required by the earlier formulation of goods) but in addition was saddled with the negative consequences of a reputation for utter injustice, he would nevertheless be happier that the unjust man with a reputation for justice. Perhaps an indication of the utter extremity, indeed the unreasonableness, of this challenge is that, arguably, Socrates never even attempts to meet it, but rather proceeds to alter the expectations of Glaucon and Adeimantus. On the other hand, it should be noted that he might fail to meet *this* challenge but succeed in meeting the earlier one that informed the discussion, to show that justice was indeed a good "in itself" and therefore not desirable merely for its good consequences. It is not obvious that the only way to do that is to meet the extreme challenge of the two statues.

Third, as Bloom nicely points out, Socrates himself might be the exhibition of just such a just man with a reputation for injustice who is nevertheless happy.[47] He may thus be a sort of existential proof that renders a dialectical one unnecessary. There is surely some plausibility to this thesis. On the other hand, it should be noted that the kind of justice that Socrates seems to exhibit is significantly different from the justice that supposedly will be exhibited subsequently by the philosopher-rulers. Their justice will presumably be accomplished by ruling with perfect justice in the light of their comprehensive knowledge of the ideas; they will be wise, and rule in the light of that wisdom. Socrates, however, "minds his own business and does not interfere with the business of others" in a very different way, by avoiding politics as

---

47. Bloom, *The Republic of Plato*, 347.

much as possible and by pursuing the life of a questioner and questor after wisdom, who recognizes his lack thereof and seeks after it, in a word, a "philosopher" in the literal sense.

Glaucon's account of the origins of the city emphasized that people agree to obey the law out of fear of suffering injustice; once established, the efficacy of the laws, he supposes, will depend on their success as a deterrent. His story of Gyges showed that the shepherd, and by implication most humans, if freed from the fear of punishment, will do almost any manner of injustice. And his two statues again place strong emphasis on the dreadful consequences of having a reputation for injustice. In short, his account generally emphasizes the idea that the chief motivation to do justice is the dire consequences of being caught doing unjust acts. His brother, Adeimantus, now enters and supplies the converse emphasis, but with the same final point, that justice belongs not in the second but in the third category of goods. People praise justice and are just not for its inherent qualities, but for the various rewards that come with having a reputation for being just (363a ff). He thus is most impressed by how pleasant the reputation for justice is, and wants Socrates to show that in fact justice is no less pleasant in itself than is the reputation for doing justice.[48] Whereas Glaucon wanted to be shown that justice in itself is "worth the trouble," Adeimantus demands that Socrates show that justice in itself, without reference to the benefits of good reputation, is *no trouble at all*, but intrinsically pleasant. In a sense, his demand is even more extreme than Glaucon's. Together, the task may well be so formidable (or even unreasonable) as to be impossible, and Socrates twice indicates that he believes it is impossible to meet the demands set before him (362d, 368b).

In truth, he does not, at least not explicitly. What he does is change the expectations of Glaucon and Adeimantus. Through a masterful rhetorical stroke, Socrates shifts the brothers' attention to a project even more intriguing and finally more revealing than a possible response to their explicit, extreme challenge: he invites

---

48. Both Strauss (*City and Man*, 90) and Bloom (*The Republic of Plato*, 342–43) point out the differing emphases of Glaucon and Adeimantus, and connect them plausibly to differences in their respective characters.

them to found a city. By introducing the famous city-soul analogy (368d), Socrates shifts the focus of the discussion to the nature of the city and the justice to be found in it. The *Republic* thereby becomes the monumental work of political philosophy that it is.

This tack enables Socrates to respond explicitly to Glaucon's earlier account of the origins of the city with a very different account of his own. He constructs "in speech" (369a) the "healthy" or "true" city (372e). This construction presents an altogether different version of the nature of human being and the origins of the polity than that presented by Glaucon, and the differences, when made explicit, reveal some of the decisive controversies in political philosophy.

Socrates begins his account as follows:

> "Well, then, I said, a city, as I believe, comes into being because each of us isn't self-sufficient but is in need of much. Do you believe there's another beginning to the founding of a city?"
>
> "None at all," he said.[49]
>
> "So, then, when one man takes on another for one need and another for another need, and since many things are needed, many men gather in one settlement as partners and helpers, to this common settlement we give the name city, don't we?" "Most certainly."
>
> "Now, does one man give a share to another, if he does give a share, or take a share, in the belief that it's better for himself?"
>
> "Certainly."
>
> "Come now, I said, let's make a city in speech from the beginning. Our need, as it seems, will make it."
>
> "Of course." (369b–d)

---

49. Adeimantus here either forgets, or quietly indicates his disagreement with, his brother's utterly different account of the origins we have just discussed.

The city originates, according to Socrates, because of something about human nature, our *lack* of self-sufficiency, our *need* of each other. That is, and explicitly contrary to Glaucon's account, we are *relational* by nature. We see posed in the contrast between Glaucon's and Socrates' accounts those two conceptions of human nature as atomistic and relational that I outlined earlier. Moreover, and, crucially, from the very beginning, human beings encounter each other not in alienation, as Glaucon insisted, but in the spirit of cooperation.

If we take the two pairings, atomistic and relational, alienated and nonalienated, we can see that there are four possible accounts of the origins of the city, the two extremes of which Plato presents in the mouths of Glaucon and Socrates. Those accounts would be:

1. A state of nature in which human beings are atomistic and, when they do encounter each other, alienated; Glaucon's position.
2. A state of nature in which human beings are atomistic but, when they do encounter each other, unalienated; possibly the best example we have of this view is that set out by Rousseau, and made famous in his notion of the "noble savage."
3. A state of nature in which human beings are relational but alienated; something like this seems to be Marx's view, where the conditions of scarcity bring about the necessity of alienation, which must in turn be overcome as we move toward the telos of history, where we will be relational and non-alienated.
4. A state of nature in which human beings are relational and non-alienated. This is the account that Socrates formulates.

Socrates' position is thus the opposite of Glaucon's as an account of that fundamental human condition that might give rise to the city, to politics. Plato puts into the mouth of Glaucon the most pessimistic and into the mouth of Socrates the most optimistic account of the human situation and the origins of the city.

Still, in both cases we see the confrontation of an original experience of limitation or negativity that must be turned into possibility by the founding of the city. We see, that is, the coming together into cities as an instance of a finite transcendence of an originating experience of finitude. For Glaucon, the original limitation or negativity was our natural alienation that led us, in the state of nature, to do all manner of injustice to each other. The city, the social contract, is a construct to ward off this original tendency. With Socrates, the limitation, the negativity, is quite different. We *lack* autonomy; we are *not* self-sufficient; we *need* each other. Our response to this reality, our effort to turn limitation into possibility, is to gather together into cities so that, in the spirit of cooperation, we may enhance each others' lives.

We lack; we need; we seek ways to overcome those lacks and needs. We need only recall Plato's *Symposium* to recognize the phenomenon to which Socrates here alludes as that aspect of human nature that leads us to be political; it is our eros. Not just the formulation of "laws and institutions," to which Diotima called our attention in the *Symposium* (209b), but the very impetus to gather in cities, is founded in our nature as erotic.

But it is an eros which, at least until Glaucon breaks in at 372c, is portrayed by Socrates as strikingly easy to satisfy. If we are simply furnished with the necessities of food, clothing, and shelter (369d), that is, if we are furnished with reasonable, even rustic comfort, we will be content, or so Socrates seems to suggest. To accomplish this comfort, this enhancement of our lives together, Socrates introduces the crucial principle of the division of labor at 369e:

"Now, what about this? Must each one of them put his work at the disposition of all in common—for example, must the farmer, one man, provide food for four and spend four times as much time and labor in the provision of food and then give it in common to the others; or must he neglect them and produce a fourth part of the food in a fourth part of the time and use the other three parts for the provision of a house, clothing, and shoes, not taking the trouble to share in common with others, *but minding his own business for himself?*

(*all' auton di' hauton ta hautou prattein*; 369e–70a; my emphasis)

According to Socrates, the principle of the division of labor, that most decisive of events in the economic history of the world, arises not out of an original alienation but out of the cooperative effort to enhance each others' lives. Once again, an initial limitation is confronted and transformed into possibility, done not as a control over our capacity to commit injustice, as Glaucon would have it, but in the spirit of cooperation.

But Plato has chosen his words carefully here, and anyone who is reading the *Republic* for at least the second time cannot fail to note in the passage just quoted the first occurrence in the book of the phrase that I emphasized, "minding one's own business." This phrase will, of course, become the core of the subsequent "definition" of justice (433a, 433b, 433d, 434c) which is to inform the dialogue. But we also cannot fail to note that here it is used in a sense opposite to the one that will be given to it as the principle of justice. Justice, that is, will be formulated as "each one minding one's own business and not interfering with that of others" in the sense founded on the *first* of the alternatives suggested by Socrates in the above quotation, to wit, that in accordance with the principle of the division of labor, or "one person, one job," each person will pursue one's own designated activity, presumably do it well since it will accord with one's particular abilities, contribute that activity to the whole, and receive the other necessities of life from the work of the other citizens who will be following a similar principle. Justice, construed on this interpretation of "minding one's own business," thus makes each citizen radically, indeed irrevocably *political*, contributive to the welfare of others but also utterly dependent on the help of others for sustenance.

By contrast, the sense of "minding one's own business" quoted above at 370a is entirely different. Here, minding one's own business implies doing everything for oneself, that is, making one's *own* food, clothing, shelter, and whatever else, and therefore neither contributing to the welfare of others nor depending at all on the help of others for sustenance. This latter interpretation of minding one's own business thus would make one radically *apolitical*, that is, would make one a fundamentally autonomous, atomistic being for whom any relations with others would be entirely extrinsic to one's nature and welfare. It is hardly surprising therefore that this interpretation is not the one pursued in the "city in speech" of the *Republic*[50] (though Socrates himself seems in some ways to be a virtual instance of it). But that should not blind us to the provocation Plato here presents us. For in the two possible interpretations of "minding one's own business" we see reiterated precisely the two fundamental conceptions of human being earlier discussed, the one that makes us fundamentally relational, the other that characterizes us as naturally atomistic. The *Republic* will now pursue the relational interpretation, as presented by Socrates in its various modifications, in great detail. But we should not forget its important, and

---

50. Rousseau would seem to agree. Consider *The Social Contract*, part 2, section 7:

> He who dares undertake to give institutions to a people ought to feel himself capable, as it were, of changing human nature; of transforming each individual, who in himself is a complete and independent whole, into part of a greater whole, from which he receives in some manner his life and his being; of altering man's constitution in order to strengthen it; of substituting a social and moral existence for the independent and physical existence which we have all received from nature. In a word, it is necessary to deprive man of his native powers in order to endow him with some which are alien to him, and of which he cannot make use without the aid of others. The more thoroughly those natural powers are deadened and destroyed, the greater and more durable are the acquired powers, the more solid and perfect also are the institutions; so that if each citizen is nothing, and can be nothing, except in combination with all the rest, and if the force acquired by the whole be equal or superior to the sum of the natural forces of all the individuals, we may say that legislation is at the highest point of perfection which it can attain. (Rousseau, *The Social Contract*, trans. Charles Sherover [New York: Meridian Books, 1974], 65.)

I suggest that the ambivalence present in this paragraph is reflected in the *Republic* itself.

unrefuted, alternative.[51] To put the point differently, justice in the explicitly *political* sense of "minding one's own business" will now be emphasized in the *Republic*. However, we should not forget that its *apolitical* sense is limned, but passed over for the most part in silence. Socrates will speak in behalf of the political version while himself exhibiting the alternative.[52] Or is it quietly suggested by Plato that somehow we must be both monadic and relational at once? Perhaps that is the model of the Platonic philosopher.

The relational interpretation that is pursued is acknowledged, if tentatively, by Adeimantus (370a), and then supported by Socrates with a strikingly strong statement of the uniqueness of each human being's talents:

> "I myself also had the thought when you spoke that, in the first place, each of us is naturally not quite like anyone else, but rather differs in his nature; different men are apt for the accomplishment of different jobs. Isn't that your opinion?"
>
> "It is." (370a–b)

The principle of the division of labor is thus said to be founded in the natural differences in human nature rather than, say, in economic conditions. But the principle Socrates here articulates has other important ramifications as well, not the least of which is that it offers us our first clue as to why the later "noble lie," that there are three kinds of souls, gold, silver, and bronze, each suited for different activities (415a ff), *is* in fact a lie; it simply fails to take adequate account of the genuine complexity and diversity of

---

51. In the *Charmides*, at 161b ff, *sophrosyne* is defined, first by Charmides and then supported by Critias, as "doing one's own business," and Socrates refutes it by interpreting it as an extreme version of the *atomistic* thesis, that it means doing and making everything for oneself. For a longer discussion of this passage, see my *The Virtue of Philosophy: An Interpretation of Plato's Charmides*, 71 ff.

52. This tension continues through the *Republic*. For example, the philosopher-rulers, once their education is complete, will *want* to be "monadic," to engage in apparently solitary contemplation of the forms. They will be *compelled* to be "relational," to rule the city.

human nature. The later "city in speech" will therefore be founded on principles (the lie of metals in particular) that ignore the realities of human diversity, ignore, one might say, the complexity of human eros. Can it therefore be genuinely just?

Socrates proceeds to build his "healthy" city (370b–72c) on the "one person, one job" principle established on the basis of the division of labor and the agreement regarding the diversity of human abilities. It is an idyllic, peaceful, cooperative city, comprised of craftsmen, farmers, tradesmen, merchants, sailors, and wage-earners. Those activities absent from the city are perhaps more striking than those present in it; there are no doctors, which may be related to the implication that this will be a city of vegetarians. There are no soldiers; apparently the spirit of cooperation that informs the internal functioning of this city will extend to other cities as well. There are no educators, and certainly no philosophers. There is no government; the simple principle that informs the city seems to be something close to "from each according to his ability, to each according to his needs." The state has not so much withered away as failed to arise. There is no competition, no alienation, it is a classless society.

I use these phrases not only accurately to describe this rustic and idyllic city, but also to invoke the spirit of Marx, since there are clear similarities in Socrates' city to some of Marx's aspirations. But Marx, I think, would be entirely in sympathy with Glaucon's strongly worded objection to the city which the more austere Adeimantus seemed to find acceptable; this is a city of pigs:

> "If you were providing for a city of sows, Socrates, on what else would you fatten them than this?"
>
> "Well, how should it be, Glaucon?, I said."
>
> "As is conventional, he said. I suppose men who aren't going to be wretched recline on couches and eat from tables and have relishes and desserts just like men have nowadays." (372d–e)

Socrates' response to Glaucon's bold interjection is remarkable. In order to appreciate this, we need only consider what his usual response to this sort of interjection might be. "A bold idea, you best of men. But let us examine what you say to see whether it is true." Whereupon, we might predict, the usual Socratic elenchus would ensue, showing Glaucon that he thought he knew what in fact he did not know. But nothing of the sort occurs here. Instead, strikingly, Socrates *accedes immediately* to Glaucon's objection:

> "All right," I said, "I understand. We are, as it seems, considering not only how a city, but also a luxurious city, comes into being. Perhaps that's not bad either. For in considering such a city too, we could probably see in what way justice and injustice naturally grow in cities." (372e)

What, we must now ask, could be so important, so powerful, about Glaucon's objection that Socrates, that famous questioner of all opinions, does not so much as call Glaucon's view into question but accepts it immediately?[53]

However boisterously, Glaucon here introduces into the discussion a decisive notion; the city so far constructed by Socrates and Adeimantus is founded on an idle, and idyllic, pretense, that human erotic striving is so simple, so easily satiated, that if only we meet our elemental needs for food, clothing, and shelter, we will be satisfied, no longer erotic in the sense of experiencing other forms of incompleteness and striving to overcome them. Glaucon knows better. Human eros is far more complex, more manifold. Our eros is not such that we experience a determinate number of "incompletenesses" which, if only they can be overcome, we will be satisfied, no longer erotic. Instead, eros is indefinitely expanding. The satisfaction of certain needs only leads to the development of others. Because our eros will not be so easily satisfied as Adeimantus and Socrates pretend, because, as Glaucon implies, our eros continually seeks new objects, sooner or later our individual efforts to satisfy our desires will come into conflict; the satisfaction of one person's desires will only be

---

53. Perhaps, as Mitchell Miller has suggested to me, Socrates accedes so readily because it was precisely his intention to provoke such a response by his exaggeratedly rustic account of the healthy city.

accomplished by the suppression of someone else's, and there will be a *problem* of justice in the luxurious city. For there is no problem of justice in the healthy city. When, at 371e, Socrates asks Adeimantus where in the healthy city justice is to be found, Adeimantus cannot find it,[54] and we now see, for a good reason. On the pretense of an easily satisfied eros our desires will never come into conflict. There will thus be no *need* for justice, and, if it is present at all, it will be virtually invisible. Justice arises as a need, as a demand, and so becomes visible, only when human desires expand sufficiently that they come into conflict. By recognizing the greater complexity of human desire, Glaucon prepares us for a turn to the real human situation in which justice is a problem, in which it arises as needful.

We thus learn from a comparison of the healthy and luxurious city that justice arises as an issue, as a need, only out of a condition where desires are sufficiently complex that they conflict. As the eventual "definition" of justice, "minding one's own business and *not interfering with the business of others*" attests, justice necessarily involves the *control* of one's natural desires or impulses when the satisfaction thereof involves the suppression of others. Justice arises in a situation where eros must be suppressed, either my eros or the eros of others. There is thus an inherent conflict between justice and human nature, or at least, that aspect of human nature which is our eros, and we begin to see why the *Republic* as a whole leaves us so skeptical that a "perfectly just city" could ever come into being.

From this standpoint, there is no such thing as a just city that is characterized by the unconstrained pursuit of all one's desires and aspirations. Justice, again, requires the control of one's eros; *sophrosyne* is an inseparable requirement of justice, and we can see why the eventual "definition" of *sophrosyne* seems so closely related to that of justice (430d, ff.).

In response to Glaucon's challenge, Socrates develops what he calls the "luxurious" or "fevered" city, which, in the subse-

---

54. Even though, it should be noted, the members of this polity are obeying the letter, without effort as it were, of the later "definition" of justice as "minding their own business and not interfering with the business of others."

quent books of the *Republic*, will itself have to be purged (399e). A brief contrast of the healthy and the luxurious city will enable us to see some of the consequences of an acknowledgment of the indefinitely expanding character of human eros.

The luxurious city will grow much larger due to the introduction into it of all those activities, pastimes, and products "beyond the necessary." Predictably there will be a plethora of artists and artisans of the unnecessary, such as beauticians, barbers, and cooks. More surprisingly, teachers head a list that includes "wet nurses, governesses, beauticians, barbers, relish-makers, and cooks" (373c) as unnecessary but luxurious additions to the city. Meat will be added to the diet of the citizens, and—perhaps related—doctors will now become more important members of the community (373c–d). And now, in a decisive passage at 373d, Socrates recognizes that a consequence of the pursuit of unnecessary desires will be scarce resources. The city will be unable to produce enough to meet not just the necessary but the continually expanding needs of its citizens. It will have to go to war against its neighbors:

"Then must we cut off a piece of our neighbors' land, if we are going to have sufficient for pasture and tillage,and they in turn from ours, if they let themselves go to the unlimited acquisition of money, overstepping the boundary of the necessary?"

"Quite necessarily, Socrates," he said.

"After that, won't we go to war as a consequence, Glaucon? Or how will it be?"

"Like that," he said.

"And let's not say whether war works evil or good, I said, but only this much, that we have in turn found the origin of war—in those things whose presence in cities most of all produces evils both private and public." (373d–e)

In his earlier account of the origins of the city, Glaucon had described an original, prepolitical situation characterized by a "natural" tendency to injustice toward each other. Socrates' "state of nature," the healthy city, had been much more idyllic, more peaceful. He now indicates that alienation and injustice are not part of an original situation with humans but a consequence of the pursuit of luxury, or, as I have put it, of the pursuit of the indefinitely expanding desires generated by eros, which Glaucon had insisted upon and Socrates had accepted. Socrates seems to assume, plausibly, a natural world sufficiently bountiful to supply us adequately with the necessities of life without doing injustice to others, but not sufficient to meet our indefinitely expanding desires without conflict. Our greed for the unnecessary, he implies, can only be satisfied by injustice and war.

To fight these wars, an army will be needed. Utilizing the now established principle of "one person, one job," Socrates easily persuades Glaucon of the necessity of a professional army (374a ff.) and launches into the elaborate task of training and educating first the soldier class, then the "philosopher-rulers" who will rule the city, a task that will take up the next several books. Socrates' rhetoric immediately shifts to emphasizing the necessity, first, of an army to *defend* the city against invasion (374a) and subsequently, an army that functions as an internal police to its own citizens (410a, 415d). But we must not forget that the originating impetus for an army is to wage wars of aggression against other cities.[55] *Within* the city in speech, justice as "minding one's own business and not interfering with the business of others" may be pursued. But it is clear from the beginning that this city will be indifferent, indeed straightforwardly unjust, toward the citizens of other cities.[56] We again ask, can such a city be called just?

As I have tried to show, book 2, and especially the challenge to Socrates by Glaucon and Adeimantus and his initial response to them, is in a fundamental way determinative for the rest of the *Republic*. A number of alternative accounts of the origins of

---

55. Bloom, *The Republic of Plato*, 348.

56. The consequences of this for the individual soul, if we apply the "city-soul" analogy, are troublesome indeed. See the following chapter for some of the implications. Diskin Clay recognizes the importance of this originating act of injustice in his "Reading the *Republic*," in *Platonic Writings, Platonic Readings*, ed. Charles Griswold (New York: Routledge, 1988), 27.

political things are offered, alternative accounts of that context of limitation or negativity to which the city is a transcending response. One of those possibilities is pursued in the rest of the *Republic*, without, however, a corresponding refutation of the alternatives. Those unrefuted alternatives are simply left behind, in silence. As such, the problematic of book 2 is never resolved in the *Republic*; it remains as a provocation.[57] Only by ignoring that provocation can we say that this great book is intended as Plato's "solution" to the problem of politics. By accepting the provocation and attempting to rethink the development of the dialogue in the light of the set of alternatives presented in book 2, we may hope to plumb some of the depths of the political problematic, presented as such by Plato, and without solution.

But this inference flies in the face of the conventional interpretation of the *Republic*. After all, does not Socrates go on in the subsequent books to develop his "ideal city," that is, his "solution" to the political problem established in book 2? Is not this eventual "utopia" completed by philosopher-rulers who are not lovers (and so lackers) of wisdom but wise people, ruling the city in perfect knowledge of the forms and even the idea of the Good? And does not such a city overcome any notions of "finite" transcendence which I have entertained and constitute an "absolute" solution to the political problem, and therefore an "absolute" transcendence?

To sustain my thesis, we must next look more closely at the supposedly utopian character of the "city in speech" of the *Republic*. For if indeed Plato genuinely believes in the possibility of such a comprehensive solution to the political problem, then in this instance at least, the finite character of any transcendence on which I have so far insisted is decisively overcome. In the next chapter, we shall take up this problem in greater detail.

---

57. I borrow this very apt term from Mitchell Miller, "Platonic Provocations: Reflections on the Soul and the Good in the *Republic*," in *Platonic Investigations*, ed. Dominic J. O'Meara (Washington, D.C.: Catholic University of America Press, 1985), 163–93.

3

PLATO'S "THREE WAVES" AND THE QUESTION OF UTOPIA

One of the important contemporary controversies over the interpretation of Plato's *Republic* centers on the question of utopia.[58] Was Plato, in setting out his "city in speech" (*Republic*, 369a) or "city in heaven" (592b), constructing a city whose realization as an earthly city he considered genuinely possible? If so, the *Republic* may be interpreted as a realizable utopia, and Plato interpreted as a radical political thinker in at least two senses. On the one hand, he invites us, given the real possibility of a perfectly just city, to be radically dissatisfied with any city— every city—that fails to live up to that realizable standard of perfection. He invites us, that is, to become revolutionaries. Second, on this view Plato would clearly hold to the possibility of a radical or "absolute" transcendence of the political problem, rather than the finite transcendence for which I have been arguing. Or is the real teaching of the *Republic* quite the reverse, intended to reveal the impossibility (and perhaps undesirability) of the conditions for perfect justice, thereby teaching us that the standard of perfection is inappropriate in the realm of politics, that there is no "solution" to the political problem, and thus that we should be political moderates? On this view, any transcendence of our political predicaments would be partial and finite.

Both sides of this controversy, which is important not only for the interpretation of Plato but as a core question of political

58. I wish to thank Professors Charles Griswold, Helen Lang, and David Roochnik for their helpful comments on earlier drafts of this chapter. One earlier version was published as "Plato's Three Waves and the Question of Utopia," in *Interpretation* 18, no. 1, (1990): 91–109.

philosophy, have well-known representatives.[59] Their disagreement is based in part on the fact that, as we shall see, the evidence
in the *Republic* itself is deeply ambivalent. The crux of the issue
would seem to hinge on the contents of books 5–7, where the
famous "three waves" are presented by Socrates as the most
formidable obstacles to the establishment of the perfectly just city.
The general procedure of most commentators has been to consider the three waves together as a unity and to make their
judgment on the possibility and desirability of such a city's
coming into being. This procedure only adds to the confusion,
since what is said about each of the three waves is hardly the
same. I shall argue that by looking at what Socrates says of each
of the waves separately, we shall discover that he has very
different attitudes regarding the questions of possibility and
desirability for each of them. This will lead us not only to a
reassessment of the perfectly just city, but also to a reconsideration
of its significance for the meaning of the *Republic* as a whole. In
order to accomplish this task, a careful examination of what is
said of each of the three waves will be necessary.[60]

---

59. For the former view, see T. L. Thorson, ed., *Plato: Totalitarian or
Democrat?* (Englewood Cliffs, N.J.: Prentice Hall, 1963), a compendium of
six essays, all of which, with the noteworthy exception of Leo Strauss's,
assume that Plato argued seriously for the possibility of his "ideal
state". The essays of R.H.S. Crossman, "Plato and the Perfect State,"
and Karl Popper, "Plato as the Enemy of the Open Society," are the most
explicit examples of this widely held view, a view which, as this volume
attests, does not preclude vigorous disagreement on other issues among
its defenders. For representatives of the view that the *Republic* is an
antiutopian work, see Leo Strauss, *The City and Man*, Allan Bloom, *The
Republic of Plato*, and Stanley Rosen, "The Role of Eros in Plato's
Republic", *Review of Metaphysics* 18, no. 3, (1965): 452–75. For a discussion
of the history of Platonic interpretation, I remind the reader again of E.
N. Tigerstedt, *Interpreting Plato*, and the excellent critical discussion of it
by Alan Bowen, "On Interpreting Plato," in *Platonic Writings, Platonic
Readings*, ed. Charles Griswold (New York: Routledge, 1988), 49–65.

60. It might be objected that, on the surface, Socrates seems to affirm
the possibility and desirability of all three waves. To call this surface
appearance into question demands reading between the lines, taking

Let us briefly recover the context. At the end of book 4, Socrates has completed an outline of the just city, and wants to turn next to a delineation of the types of inferior cities, which he finally gets to only in book 8. He is interrupted in this enterprise because he has, in his outline, slipped over some extremely controversial issues, on which, at the beginning of book 5, Adeimantus and Polemarchus catch him up. They insist that he make explicit and defend these proposals. Books 5–7 are his defense, and constitute the long setting out of the three waves. The first wave, which entails the equal education and treatment of women and men, extends from 451d to 457b. The second wave, which lasts from 457c to 473c, includes the communality of wives and children, the abolition of private property, the abolition of the family, and the establishment of extraordinary laws for sexual intercourse in the name of eugenics. The third and much the longest wave, from 473d to 541b, that is, from the end of book 5 through all of books 6 and 7, concerns the establishment of philosopher-rulers.

Let us now begin our tracing of the argument at the beginning of book 5. The first noteworthy fact is that when Adeimantus and Polemarchus catch Socrates up at 449c, the issue they focus on is in fact what is later called the second wave, having women and children in common.

> "In our opinion you're taking it easy," he said, "and robbing us of a whole section of the argument, and that not the least, so you won't have to go through it. And you supposed you'd get away with it by saying, as though it were something quite ordinary, that after all it's plain to everyone that, as for women and children, the things of friends will be in common." (449c)

---

serious account of the possibility of irony, and construing Plato as not necessarily always intending that the reader of the dialogue accept as Platonic doctrine everything that Socrates says. For an extended hermeneutic of irony in the Republic which addresses these themes, see the following chapter. For a different but compatible statement of the complexity of interpreting Platonic dialogues, consider the seminal notion of "Platonic provocations" set out in Mitchell Miller's "Platonic Provocations: Reflections on the Soul and the Good in the Republic."

At 450c, in his reiteration of the charge, Glaucon adds to the community of wives and children "their rearing when they are still young, in the time between birth and education, which seems to be the most trying" (450c). This is still the second wave, since the first wave treats of the guardians' education when they are older. In short, there is no predisposition on the part of those present to view the first wave as problematic. It is what becomes the second wave that initially troubles Socrates' interlocutors. Socrates himself introduces the first wave. It is not surprising, therefore, that there is less resistance to it.

The next point of importance to our topic occurs at 450d, where Socrates introduces the criteria of decision for the ensuing argument concerning the three waves: possibility and desirability in the sense of "what is best".

"It's not easy to go through, you happy man," I said. "Even more than what we went through before, it admits of many doubts. For, it could be doubted that the things said are possible; and, even if, in the best possible conditions, they could come into being, that they would be what is best might also be doubted. So that is why there's a certain hesitation about getting involved in it, for fear that the argument might seem to be a prayer, my dear comrade." (450d)

Henceforward, these are the two standards by which the three waves, and so the city in speech, will be judged.

The first wave begins at 451d, though it is not named as such until its completion at 457b. It is bounded by references to "the female drama" at 451c, and "the woman's law" at 457b. The gist of it is that women and men should be reared, educated, and treated as equally as possible.[61] We might thus be tempted to call it the first "Equal Rights Amendment," although given the rigorously Spartan lives this class will have in the city in speech, it

---

61. For a comprehensive and instructive discussion of the history of scholarship on the proposals for women in book 5, as well as the attitudes toward women generally in the dialogues, see Natalie Harris Bluestone, *Women and the Ideal Society: Plato's Republic and Modern Myths of Gender* (Amherst: University of Massachusetts Press, 1987). Bluestone

might more accurately be described as the first "Equal Responsibilities Amendment". It is introduced by analogy to dogs:

"Do we believe the females of the guardian dogs must guard the things the males guard along with them and hunt with them, and do the rest in common; or must they stay indoors as though they were incapacitated as a result of bearing and rearing the puppies, while the males work and have all the care of the flock?"

"Everything in common", he said, "except that we use the females as weaker and the males as stronger." (451d–e)[62]

We might note this one proviso on absolute equality. When physical strength is at issue, such as in battle, concessions will be made to the generally superior strength of men. We can acknowledge that, given the nature of warfare at this time and the fact that the rulers are to excel both at philosophy and the waging of war (543a), this qualification is a significant one. But it is no less important to recognize that it is the only qualification on equal treatment granted in the first wave, and it is repeated at 456a, and at 457a–b.[63] It is therefore a fair inference, especially for us today,

---

includes the suggestion, which she does not develop, that "although the co-equal proposals (the three waves) are connected as Plato presents them, the justice of each can be considered separately" (106).

62. The words employed here, *asthenesterais....ischuroterois*, both have as their primary senses *physical* strength and weakness, although both can also be used with broader connotations (Liddell and Scott, *Greek-English Lexicon*, 256, 843). Both the immediate context of their introduction (the analogy with dogs) and the absence of explicit suggestion to the contrary suggest that they should be used in their primary, physical meanings. Especially given what Socrates is presently to say regarding equal treatment, it is most plausible to limit his meaning here to relative physical strength and weakness.

63. The apparent qualification at 455d in fact deepens the point. Socrates appeals to Athenian cultural sexism by inviting the affirmation that the class of men excels that of women in all pursuits, which elicits from Glaucon the decisive qualification which will establish the principle of equal treatment: "However, many women are better than many men in many things."

that should conditions be such that physical strength is not at stake, there would be no exceptions to the principle of equal education and treatment of men and women. In any case, and this is the crucial point, since the men are to be educated through the two foundations of Greek education, music and gymnastic, "Then these two arts, and what has to do with war, must be assigned to the women also, *and they must be used in the same ways*" (452a; I emphasize the last clause to bring out the point that women are not to be given the same education and then treated differently, as is so often still the case).

This equal treatment will be so thoroughgoing, Socrates continues, that women and men will even exercise naked together in the gymnasium. This, he insists, is "the most ridiculous" aspect of the first wave (452a–b), a point that should be noted. If this aspect can be justified, we may infer, the first wave will be relatively unproblematic. It is justified by an appeal to Athenian provincialism; once, the Athenians thought the idea of *men* exercising naked together was laughable, but now it is accepted as quite natural (452c). So there is no reason to suppose that the present attitudes could not be overcome.[64] But perhaps, against Socrates' argument and the evidence of such practices as nude beaches and nudist colonies, one might regard the problems with mixed nudity, conventional or not, as insurmountable. Nevertheless, it is worth noting that if one slight concession to convention were made, that is, allowing the guardians to exercise clothed, such a step would resolve this "most ridiculous" aspect of the first wave, and nothing would stand in the way of the core of its proposal, the equal treatment and education of women and men.[65]

---

64. Although the convention against men and women exercising naked together might seem even more difficult to overcome than that regarding men alone, Socrates' point remains well taken; the problem is one of convention, and *could* be overcome, as our more modern experience with nude beaches, not to mention the customs of many so-called primitive cultures, attests.

65. Bloom, in his *The Republic of Plato* (380 ff), among others, has suggested that the first wave is written in the jesting manner of Aristophanes's *Lysistrata* and *Ecclesiazusae*, but the analogy is more mis-

Socrates now employs a strategy which he applies in the first wave alone; he presents the counterargument to the position he espouses and refutes it (453b–56b). Let us recognize that this is reasonable strategy when one is arguing seriously for a position. The most persuasive arguments often present the positive evidence for the position espoused and then present the counterarguments and show their inadequacy. I emphasize this because the very structure of the argument suggests a tone of seriousness which, as we shall see, is lacking in the second wave.

The gist of the counterargument will be immediately familiar as the most common argument used against defenders of equal rights and equal treatment of women today: men and women have different natures, and therefore should be treated differently and should do different things (453b–d).

Socrates replies by distinguishing what *aspects* of male and female nature are different, and whether and to what extent those differences are relevant to rearing, education, or fighting. To make his point, he uses, as a reductio ad absurdum, the analogy of the bald shoemaker:

> "Accordingly," I said, "it's permissible, as it seems, for us to ask ourselves whether the nature of the bald and the long-haired is the same or the opposite. And, when we agree that it is opposite, if bald men are shoemakers, we won't let the longhaired ones be shoemakers, or if the longhaired ones are, then the others can't be."
>
> "That," he said, "would certainly be ridiculous." (454c)

The point is clear enough; only when it can be shown that the differences between men and women *make* a difference in regard to education and treatment will it be acknowledged as relevant. As we have already seen, only one difference has been so

---

leading than helpful. In those plays, the point of the women's scheme is not to achieve *equal treatment* and therefore justice, but to replace the dominance of men by the dominance of women, one form of injustice for another. If anything, the first wave should be *contrasted* to Aristophanes' plays.

acknowledged, that of physical strength, which will have a certain relevance to the duties assigned in war. Socrates states this principle nicely at 454e:

> "Then," I said, "if either the class of men or that of women shows its excellence in some art or other practice, then we'll say that art must be assigned to it. But if they look as though they differ in this alone, that the female bears and the male mounts, we'll assert that it has not thereby yet been proved that a woman differs from a man with respect to what we're talking about; rather, we'll still suppose that our guardians and their women must practice the same things." (454e)

The positive statement of the criteria of selection for a given activity is set out briefly at 455c: some people learn better and more easily retain the information necessary for a given enterprise. This is what determines whether a person has the right nature for each activity. Since, with regard to ruling, none of the crucial information to be learned is necessarily tied to gender, Socrates draws the following important conclusion:

> "Therefore, my friend, there is no practice of a city's governors which belongs to woman because she's woman, or to man because he's man; but the natures are scattered alike among both animals; and woman participates according to nature in all practices, and man in all, but in all of them woman is weaker than man." (455d–e)

Women and men will participate equally in everything from music and gymnastics to medicine, philosophy, and ruling (455e–56a), with again the sole concession being made to relative physical strength.

Socrates begins his summing up of the argument for the first wave at 456c:

> "Then we weren't giving laws that are impossible or like prayers, since the law we set down is according to nature. Rather, the way things are nowadays proves to be, as it seems, against nature." (456c)

The first wave is *desirable* because it is according to nature. "Nature" is here taken clearly in the teleological sense. For something to be "according to nature" is for it to be the *best* that it can be, a view that seems to inform almost all of Greek intellectual life with the exception of sophistry, which argued for the superiority of convention. The first wave is according to nature since in all but one of the requirements for ruling (physical strength), men and women are equally likely to be qualified. Indeed, as Socrates notes, the present practice of discrimination against women is against nature. It is *possible* because, as has been shown, the present strictures against equal treatment are themselves conventional rather than natural. Thus, Socrates concludes at 457a, the first wave is both possible and beneficial. The escape from the first wave is announced at 457b.

Especially because of its contrast to the next wave, it is worth reviewing the structure and content of the argument for the first wave. The criteria of possibility and desirability are established. The counterargument, that women and men have different natures and therefore should be treated differently, is presented and refuted on the grounds that the only difference that *makes* a difference when it comes to the tasks the guardians will be assigned, including ruling and philosophy, is physical strength, which is easily accommodated. Equal education and treatment is defended as *desirable* because it is natural (in the teleological sense) and as *possible* because the present prescriptions against it are merely conventional. In short, the arguments for the first wave seem structurally and substantially plausible, and I find no reason to hold that Socrates is not quite serious in his optimism about its possibility and desirability.[66]

---

66. *Contra* Bloom, *The Republic of Plato*, 380–84, who calls the first wave, together with the second, "absurd conceits" (380), "absurd considerations" (381), and "nonsense" (382) and describes Socrates as "fabricat[ing] a convention about the nature of women," and "admit[ting] that the best women are always inferior in capacity to the best men" (383). Bloom is surely right, however, when he asserts that part of the teaching here is that "Full humanity is a discrete mixture of masculinity and femininity" (384), a position on which I shall comment further in my

The second wave is announced at 457d:

> "All these women are to belong to all these men in common, and no woman is to live privately with any man. And the children, in their turn, will be in common, and neither will a parent know his own offspring, nor a child his parent."

Glaucon acknowledges immediately that this wave is far bigger than the first (it is, after all, the one to which he and Adeimantus originally objected), and that it is far more dubitable as regards its possibility or benefit (457d), and well he might. For as it is developed, the second wave gets expanded to include not only the communality of women and children and the systematic ignorance of parentage, but also, among its more startling proposals, the abolition of private property (458d), the abolition of the family (460d), and the assurance of eugenics through the control of sexual encounters by the fixing of lots drawn to see who can have sex at the sacred times (459a). Clearly, just in so far as the second wave is more dubious, its defense, both in structure and content, will have to be all the more powerful than the defense of the first wave. As we shall see, the exact opposite is the case.

While the structure of the argument for the first wave was sensible and plausible, that of the second is bizarre. Socrates begins by trying to evade the argument for desirability, hoping that its benefit will be assumed, though its possibility disputed.

> "As to whether it is beneficial, at least, I don't suppose it would be disputed that the community of women and the community of children are, if possible, the greatest good," I

---

conclusion. For a view closer to my own, see Dale Hall, "The *Republic* and the Limits of Politics," *Political Theory* 5, no. 3, (1977): 293–313. In reference to the first wave, Hall argues against Bloom and Strauss that "There are none of the familiar signs of irony or comedy in Plato's discussion of equality. Socrates does not appeal to absurd premises, nor reason fallaciously, nor contradict himself" (296). Hall goes on, unfortunately, to make the same claims for all three waves, and Bloom, in his reply ("Reply to Hall," *Political Theory* 5, no. 3, [1977]: 315–30) is able to raise serious and plausible objections to Hall's overall thesis.

said, "But I suppose that there would arise a great deal of dispute as to whether they are possible or not." (457d)

When Glaucon plausibly insists that both would be in dispute, Socrates immediately takes the reverse tack; he asks that its possibility be assumed while he proves its desirability, and then— he says here—he will go on to prove its possibility. Claiming that he is "idle" and "soft," he requests,

"I too am by now soft myself, and I desire to put off and consider later in what way it is possible; and now, having set it down as possible, I'll consider, if you permit me, whether their accomplishment would be most advantageous of all for both the city and the guardians. I'll attempt to consider this with you first, and the other later, if you permit." (458a)

Though perhaps strange, such a strategy, were it followed faithfully, would probably be acceptable; after all, it is not obviously important which of the two criteria, possibility or desirability, should be satisfied first. However, if we now, for the sake of seeing the structure of the argument, leap to the end of the second wave, we see that after having presented his evidence for the desirability of the extraordinary proposals of the second wave, and now forced by Glaucon to turn to the evidence for its possibility (471c), Socrates responds with the following strategy, or perhaps better, strategm, which I quote at some length:

"Do you suppose a painter is any less good who draws a pattern of what the fairest human being would be like and renders everything in the picture adequately, but can't prove that it's also possible that such a man come into being?"

"No, by Zeus, I don't," he said.

"Then what about this? Weren't we, as we assert, also making a pattern in speech of a good city?"

"Certainly."

"Do you suppose that what we say is any less good on account of our not being able to prove that it is possible to found a city the same as the one in speech?"

"Surely not," he said.

"Well, that's the truth of it," I said. (472d–e)

Socrates goes on, in a complex way to be examined subsequently, to develop the third wave as the simplest and best way to attain an *approximation* (473b) of the second wave. Here it is important to recognize that even prior to our examination of the explicit content of the argument for the second wave, its very structure is suspect, and in a way of which the author of the text must surely have been aware. Its possibility is never established. We shall have to see about its desirability. Let us turn to the details of the second wave.

As previously mentioned, the second wave calls initially for the communality of women and children and the systematic ignorance of who one's natural relatives are among the guardians. As the implications of these ideas are developed, private property and the family are abolished. Most stunning of all, however, are the steps recommended regarding sex. The men and women, exercising naked together, will be sexually attracted to each other (458d). In order to control this attraction, "geometric necessity" must be imposed on "erotic necessity,, to borrow Glaucon's phraseology (458d). Strict rules will be imposed on sexual encounters, rules whose connection to "geometric necessity" is eventually expressed in the notoriously complicated and playfully ironic "nuptial number," introduced at 546b.[67] The secret principle of these rules will be eugenics, which is introduced by a comical analogy with Glaucon's dogs and cocks. Just as Glaucon watches over their "marriages and procreation" (459a) and allows only the best to mate with the best and at the best time, so shall the same principle be followed with the guardians. Now, as we saw, the analogy with animals had been plausibly used in the first wave to suggest that men and women should be

---

67. See Stanley Rosen, "The Role of Eros in Plato's Republic," *Review of Metaphysics* 18, no. 3, (1965): 462. For an imaginative account which apparently takes the number quite seriously, see James Adam, *The Nuptial Number of Plato: Its Solution and Significance* (London: C. J. Clay & Sons, 1891).

treated as equally as possible. Here we must ask, is it also plausible to treat human eros with the same calculated utilitarianism that we apply to animals? Is there no reason to believe that human erotic feelings are deeper and more complex than we assume to be the case with animals? If Plato had never written the *Symposium* or *Phaedrus*, it might be plausible to entertain this possibility as a serious position. But it is, to say the least, dubious that the author of the *Symposium*—where erotic attraction is characterized as the source of creative inspiration (206c ff) and the first decisive step to philosophy (210a ff)—and of the *Phaedrus*—where eros is called one of the four forms of "divine madness" (245b ff)—really thinks so. To the contrary, as these texts attest, Plato is one of the first thinkers of our tradition to genuinely appreciate the profundity, the complexity, and so the deep significance of human eros. His total abstraction from this significance in the present passage therefore cannot be intended literally. The abstraction from eros throughout the *Republic* has been noted by a number of commentators.[68] The present passage is surely one of its most striking instances. It is the first serious flaw in the argument for the second wave, and it is decisive.

Nevertheless, the principle of eugenics is to include:

1. Lies and fixed lotteries to deceive everyone into thinking that it is just by chance that the "best" people keep drawing the winning lots, and so being selected to have sex, again and again (459d-460a).
2. Temporary "marriages", apparently lasting only long enough for copulation to occur, so that women and children will be held in common and natural parentage will remain unknown (460c).
3. The exposure of defective children (460c).
4. Incest prohibitions with rather obvious loopholes (461e).

At 462a, with the details of the structure of the second wave now apparently established, Socrates turns to the defense of its

---

68. Rosen, "The Role of Eros in Plato's *Republic*"; Strauss, *The City and Man*, 128; Bloom, *The Republic of Plato*, 313, 376, 382.

desirability. The gist of his argument is this: the greatest good for the city is unity, the greatest evil that which divides it (462b). If people have private concerns, desires, and possessions, these might at times come into conflict with the concerns of the city and so cause divisions (462c–d). By eliminating all privacy, therefore, including private property, the family, and even the recognition of who one's natural children are, one could eliminate the cause of divisions in the city. If the city *is* my parent, or more generally, my family, there can be no conflict between my concerns for my family and for my city. I shall be the perfect patriot.[69] So the second wave will be beneficial because the community of wives and children will be the cause of the unity of the city.

A number of serious flaws can be noted in this argument. First, it assumes that political unity, or patriotism, is not just a good but the highest good. More fully, it assumes that what may—problematically—be the highest *political* virtue should straightforwardly be instituted, thereby implying that there are no goods that might supersede even the highest political ones. Most of us might agree that political unity is one of the desiderata in a political community. But should we simply accept without argument, as Glaucon does at 462b, that it is the highest good? Are we not all too familiar with situations in which the demand for political unity seems more to undermine justice than to encourage it? One need only consider the case of Socrates himself, against whom the charge of corrupting the youth is clearly tantamount to the claim that he undermined the unity of the city. Even within the project of the *Republic* itself, the claim that unity is the highest good is problematic. One might argue (though Socrates does not) that the primacy of unity is implicit in the earlier definition of justice as each one minding one's own business and not interfering in the business of others (433a–b), but

---

69. The infamous "noble lie," announced in book 3 at 414c ff and now apparently abandoned, was meant to accomplish the same end. There is a tension between the noble lie, which entails the belief that I am born not of human parents but of the earth beneath my city (414d), and the second wave, which entails the belief that all guardians of a certain age are my parents, brothers and sisters, and so on.

this is hardly obvious or unproblematic. In any case, what about the other cardinal virtues, or the knowledge necessary to rule? Quite especially, what about the Good itself, which would seem to be the leading candidate in the *Republic* for the highest thing? At 504d, Socrates clearly asserts that the Good is *greater* than justice, and so that even the highest political virtues are not the highest altogether.[70] In sum, it is hardly self-evident that political unity is the highest good. If it should turn out not to be, then other goods might conflict with and even supersede it. Then it would be even less obvious that the extreme measures suggested in the second wave would be justifiable in the light of these other goods. In any case, the supremacy of the principle of political unity, a crucial premise in the defense of the desirability of the second wave, has not been argued for.[71]

Second, there is a flaw in the quest for the abolition of privacy, an absolute limit on the possibility of communism, which is subtly admitted by Socrates at 464d: the *body* is irreducibly private.

---

70. It should be clear here that the objection is not against the association of unity with the Good at some higher level, but against the identification of *political* unity with the highest good. Thus even if one assumes that when Aristotle refers to some who believe in unchangeable substances as holding that "the One itself is the good itself" (*Metaphysics*, 1091b13–14), he is referring to Plato, and moreover, that he is correct, it is hardly obvious that *political* unity is identical with the Good itself. Still further, if we do identify political unity with the Good, stunning consequences would follow. Since we are told that the Good is "beyond being" and intelligibility (*Republic*, 508e–9c), it would seem to follow that we could not in principle comprehensively understand unity/good, nor could we establish it within "being." By this argument, then, the perfectly just city would be manifestly impossible. For an extended discussion of the connection of unity and the Good, see Stanley Rosen, *The Question of Being: A Reversal of Heidegger* (New Haven: Yale University Press, 1993), especially part 1, "Platonism."

71. For an interesting discussion of the issue of political unity with reference to the *Symposium*, see Arlene Saxonhouse, "The Net of Hephaestus: Aristophanes' Speech in Plato's *Symposium*," *Interpretation* 13, no. 1 (1985): 15–32.

"And what about this? Won't lawsuits and complaints against one another, in a word, vanish from among them thanks to their possessing *nothing private but the body*, while the rest is in common?" (464d; my emphasis).

Is this a small qualification, as Socrates, here, obviously wishes it to be taken? Or is it not rather a decisive limit on the possibility of communism, and so on the guarantee that I shall never experience "private" desires that conflict with the public good? Are not "bodily," and so private, desires one of the primary sources of injustice? Once again, no argument is presented in support of this claim that the privacy of the body is not decisive. It is passed over in silence.

Third, it is hardly plausible to assert that simply by believing that we are all of one family, divisions and discord will be eliminated. As Greek tragedy demonstrates beyond doubt, Greek culture was profoundly aware that arguments and discord among family members can be among the most bitter and violent.[72]

Fourth, in any case, it is only the guardians, apparently, who will have this communism. The entire class of workers and artisans in the city will presumably continue to have orthodox families and private property. Will they not continue to have the same old problems, perhaps even exacerbated by the now enormous differences between their lives and those of the guardian class? Socrates assures Glaucon at 465b that nothing of the kind will occur, but his assurance is hardly consoling, especially without any argument.

There follows (467a–71c) a long discussion by Socrates concerning the training for and conduct of war by the guardians, which includes such policies as bringing the children to watch battles from a safe distance (467e), erotic rewards for valor (468b–c), and the different treatment of Greek enemies than barbarian ones (469c–71b). Glaucon finally catches Socrates up on this at 471c, but in an unfortunate way. Indicating that Socrates is

---

72. Especially considering what we are given to believe about Socrates' marital situation, we can hardly expect him to be naive about this!

likely to go on and on, Glaucon demands that he turn now to whether such steps as the second wave requires would be possible. But in so doing, he *grants* its desirability:

> "Is it possible for this regime to come into being, and how is it ever possible? I see that, if it should come into being, everything would be good for the city in which it came into being." (471c)

As we have seen, its desirability has hardly been adequately established. Especially compared to the power of the arguments for the first wave, those for the desirability of the second wave are critically deficient.

Socrates responds to Glaucon's challenge by admitting that he has been stalling, but for the reason that establishing the possibility of the second wave requires the third wave, which threatens to be overwhelming:

> "All of a sudden," I said, "you have, as it were, assaulted my argument, and you have no sympathy for me and my loitering. Perhaps you don't know that when I've hardly escaped the two waves, you're now beginning the biggest and most difficult, the third wave." (472a)

The logical structure of the connection between the second and third waves is thus somewhat complex, and needs to be clarified. The *desirability* of the second wave is founded on the principle of the supremacy of political unity and the presumption that human eros can be treated in roughly the same way as the sexual desire of animals (we have seen the flaws in these arguments). The *possibility* of the second wave, we are now told, requires the third wave, the establishment of philosopher-rulers. Thus, it would seem that *if* the third wave proves possible, and *if* we were to accept the arguments for the desirability of the second wave, then the second wave would have been shown to be both possible and desirable. However, Socrates' next steps throw this whole situation into question.

For his very next step, as we have seen earlier in the chapter, is simply to deny that the possibility of the second wave as it stands can be proved. I have already quoted the passage at 472d–e where he admits this. However, he qualifies this impossibility in a subtle and important way. If we pick up his speech at the point of his denial of its possibility, we find Socrates saying:

> "Well, then, that's the truth of it," I said. "But if then to gratify you I must also strive to prove how and under what condition it would be *most possible* [*kata ti dunatotat an eie*], grant me the same points again for this proof."
>
> "What points?"
>
> "Can anything be done as it is said? Or is it the nature of acting to attain to less truth than speaking, even if someone doesn't think so? Do you agree that it's so or not?"
>
> "I do agree," he said.
>
> "Then don't compel me necessarily to present it as coming into being in every way in deed as we described it in speech. But if we are able to find that a city could be governed in a way *most closely approximating* what has been said, [*hos an eggotata ton eiremenon polis oikeseien*], say that we've found the possibility of these things coming into being on which you insist." (472e–73b; my emphasis)

Here a number of crucial points must be reiterated. First, Socrates admits that he cannot prove the real possibility of the second wave as it stands. This is already a crucial limitation on the original project of proving the possibility and desirability of all three waves. In the strictest sense, it is an admission of defeat. Second, only an *approximation* of the second wave can be established, and Glaucon must accept that. Recall that there was no such talk of a mere "approximation" regarding the first wave. In the case of the first wave, presumably, we can have the real thing. Third, the smallest step required even for this approximation of the second wave is, as we see at 473d, the third wave, the establishing of philosopher-rulers.

A moment's reflection on this situation makes clear that everything would seem to depend on precisely *how* the city established with philosopher-rulers would *differ* from the city of the second wave. What, after all, is and is not possible in deed as well as in speech? Will the fixed lotteries and rules for eugenics still be in effect? Will parents know their natural children? Yet we are never told anything about how the two cities would differ. Nevertheless, we must remember that what is being established in the third wave is *not* the precise city of the second wave but some *undetermined modification* of it, with philosopher-rulers at its head. By implication, the third wave presents us, however quietly, with a different city from the city of the second wave.[73]

We must conclude of the second wave, therefore, that a defense of its possibility is admittedly impossible and the arguments for its desirability manifestly inadequate. We can turn now to the third wave, which, I emphasize again, is introduced as the smallest step necessary to render possible some undetermined modification of the second wave.[74]

The formulation of the third wave occurs at 473d:

"Unless," I said, "the philosophers rule as kings or those now called kings and chiefs genuinely and adequately philosophize,...there is no rest from ills for the cities, my dear Glaucon, nor I think for human kind."

The working out of this wave, however, takes more than two books (the end of book 5, plus all of books 6 and 7) to accomplish.

---

73. To this may be added the evidence of book 8, at 546–47. There, in Socrates' account of how the city in speech, even if established, must fall, he attributes its inevitable failure explicitly to the failure to sustain the conditions of the *second* wave: the sex laws will inevitably be disobeyed. This is tantamount to an explicit admission that even if an approximation of the second wave were somehow established, it would not endure.

74. Since, as we have seen, the first wave is possible and desirable, and, as we shall see, the third wave is called unlikely but not impossible (499b–c, 499d, 502a–b, 502c, 540d), the second wave, as admittedly impossible in the strict sense, would seem to be the most extreme. It is puzzling, therefore, that Socrates calls the third wave the biggest (473c). The explanation of this will lie in the extreme complexity of the third wave.

It is full of philosophically important discussions, including the Good, the divided line, and the image of the cave. We shall be concerned here only with those aspects of the argument that directly concern the establishing of the desirability and possibility of philosopher-rulers. It is, as one might expect, exceedingly complex. Suppose we begin, as does the actual argument (474d ff) with the question of desirability. Why is it even problematic that having rulers who are philosophers would be desirable? Because philosophers are in ill-repute in most cities, regarded as at best harmless but useless, at worst harmful to the cities (487c–d). To deal with this problem, which Socrates acknowledges is a real one (487d), he must distinguish between the reputed philosophers and the true philosophers. The elucidation of this distinction involves the introduction of the themes of being and becoming, opinion and knowledge, and the forms (474d ff; see especially 476–80), as well as a long discussion of the extreme difficulty and unlikeliness of actually developing such philosophers (487d ff; see especially 496b–e). This includes the enormously problematic recognition that such philosophers, were they to come along, would not *want* to rule and so would have to be *forced* to do so (519c ff). Throughout these passages, Socrates regularly reiterates his contention that the development of such philosophers, and so of philosopher-rulers, would be very unlikely, but not impossible (499b–c, 499d, 502a–b, 502c, 540d). So far, so good, at least by the order of the argument. The problem arises for the issue at hand because Socrates' account of the "true" philosopher suggests a man or woman (540c) who, by the standards of the other dialogues, is less a *lover* of wisdom, lacking and therefore striving after wisdom, than a *wise* person, with a comprehensive knowledge not only of the forms and their relation to phenomena, but even of the idea of the Good itself (see especially 484b, 484c–d, 506a).[75] Thus the philosopher-rulers are described as people who "grasp what is always the same in all respects" (484b), who "not

---

75. Again, how could the Good be known comprehensively by anyone if it is "beyond" truth, intelligibility, and even being (*Republic*, 508e–9c)?

only know what each thing is, but also don't lack experience or fall short of the others in any other part of virtue" (484d), and who will know the just, the beautiful, and the Good (506a). In short, the apparent assumption of this section of the *Republic* is that the philosopher-rulers will in fact be *wise* people, with a comprehensive knowledge of the whole, in the light of which they will, reluctantly, rule the city.

But the whole thrust of most other Platonic dialogues, and even of the discussion of the Good in the *Republic*, is that such a situation is humanly impossible. Wisdom of this sort is for the gods alone, indeed, is the principal difference between the gods and humans. In the *Apology*, Socrates is called by the Delphic Oracle the wisest of humans, and his wisdom is precisely the recognition of his lack of knowledge (*Apology*, 20 ff). In the *Symposium*, human being, as erotic, is characterized by a radical *incompleteness* and the constant *striving* for completeness, including the completeness of wisdom (see especially the speeches of Aristophanes and Socrates),[76] and in the *Phaedrus*, only the gods are portrayed as being able to sustain a contemplation of the "hyperouranian beings" (247–48), whereas the souls of mortals are constantly dragged down, and get only partial glimpses of these higher entities (248a–c). Human beings are, like the eros which is our nature, ontologically "in the middle" between the mortal and the divine (*Symposium*, 202d–e), between ignorance and wisdom (*Symposium*, 203e–4a). Indeed, at *Symposium* 204b, philosophers are explicitly singled out as being in this intermediary state between ignorance and wisdom. All of this is, obviously, prima-facie evidence for the necessary finitude of all human transcendence. Philosophic aporia *is* a transcendence of ordinary ignorance, but it is not an "absolute" transcendence to wisdom. The philosopher-rulers of the *Republic* are thus portrayed as having achieved an epistemological status elsewhere

---

76. Diotima's discussion of our "sudden" "glimpse" of Beauty Itself might seem to qualify this. But Diotima is a priestess, not a philosopher. I shall develop at greater length in later chapters how this fact must qualify what she says about our possibilities for such a complete or radical "transcendence."

reserved for the gods.[77] Not for nothing is this city referred to as "in heaven" (592b). Indeed, even within the *Republic* itself, as the previously cited passage at 546a–b attests, the ultimate incompleteness or partiality of the philosopher-rulers' wisdom is admitted. They will fail in their efforts to adhere consistently to the complex sex laws.[78]

This makes the question of the possibility of the philosopher-rulers all the more problematic. If, as it certainly seems, the philosopher-rulers are not people like Socrates who lack wisdom, recognize their lack, and strive for wisdom, but rather are wise people, then there is next to no evidence in the dialogues as a whole that Plato believes such an achievement is possible for humans. Considering the question from the standpoint not of *philosophers* but of *wise people*, the third wave is almost certainly impossible. On the other hand, by this (impossible) standard, it is also more plausible that it would be desirable. Do we not all wish for political leaders who genuinely and comprehensively know what they are doing?

But suppose we consider the possibility not of *wise* rulers as entertained in the *Republic,* but, more realistically, of genuine philosophers of the Socratic stripe becoming rulers. Certainly it would be possible for people like Socrates, who recognize their lack of wisdom but spend their lives striving for it, to take the rule of a city. No doubt it would be, as the *Republic* itself suggests, extremely unlikely, since precisely those philosophers would not

---

77. See Jean-François Mattei, "The Theater of Myth in Plato," in *Platonic Writings, Platonic Readings,* ed. Charles Griswold (New York: Routledge, 1988): "Philosophers will never reach the shores of absolute knowledge" (71).

78. Compare *Euthydemus,* 291b ff, for the impossibility of the "kingly art." Even if one were to ignore such evidence as 546a and adopt a version of the "chronological hypothesis," arguing that although "the early Plato" held to the impossibility of comprehensive wisdom," "the mature Plato" (of the *Republic*—ignoring 546a) thought that wisdom was achievable, one would still have to explain away such crucial "mature" dialogues as the *Theaetetus,* which ends in aporia, not to mention the discussion in the *Republic* itself of the impossibility of comprehensive knowledge of the Good.

want to rule (the case of Socrates himself is apt here). Nevertheless, such a person would fairly fit the *Republic*'s contention that it would be "unlikely but not impossible" to find such a ruler. But then, would it any longer be desirable? If it would be relatively unproblematic to desire as a ruler someone with a genuinely comprehensive knowledge of the political realm and of the whole, it is, to say the least, less obvious that the best of all possible regimes would be ruled by a *Socratic* philosopher, always questioning, never accepting on faith conventional beliefs, caring more for the individual souls of citizens than for the political whole, and so on. Perhaps one could generate what would no doubt be a long and involved argument in behalf of such a ruler. But no such thing is presented in the *Republic*.

At the very end of book 7, bringing his argument to a conclusion, Socrates reiterates once more his insistence that the rule of philosopher-rulers is hard but not impossible:

"Do we agree that the things we have said about the city and the regime are not in every way prayers; that they are hard but in a way possible; and that it is possible in no other way than the one stated: when the true philosophers, either one or more, come to power in a city..." (540d)

Glaucon, altogether reasonably, as we now see, asks how. Socrates responds with the following striking conclusion as to how such a situation, the conditions of the third wave, might be brought about:

"All those in the city who happen to be older than ten they will send out into the country; and taking over their children, they will rear them—far away from those dispositions they now have from their parents—in their own manners and laws that are such as we described before. And, with the city and the regime of which we were speaking thus established *most quickly and easily*, it will itself be happy, and most profit the nation in which it comes to be." (541a; my emphasis)

Are we to believe that Plato seriously held that it would be possible to convince the parents of an entire city (presumably including artisans as well as potential guardians and philosophers) to leave that city, leaving their children under ten behind in the hands of the founders of a new city who would raise them according to the austere measures set out by Socrates earlier in the dialogue? I suggest that it is altogether more likely that the claim that such a city is possible is ironic, that the conditions for bringing it about, far from being accomplished "most quickly and easily," are effectively impossible.

Let us briefly summarize where we stand so far. We have seen that significantly different judgments are made regarding the first, second, and third waves. To review briefly, the first wave, equal treatment and education of men and women, was plausibly argued to be both possible and desirable. The second wave, radical communism, abolition of the family, eugenics, and their sundry implications, turned out to be indefensible as regards its possibility, and desirable only on the dubious premises that, first, political unity was the highest of all goods (an assumption decisively undercut by the claim in book 6 that the Good is the greatest thing), and second, that human eros could be fairly treated with the same cold calculation as that of dogs. Only a vague and undetermined modification was allowed, and that only on the hypothesis that the third wave would be proved possible and desirable. For all intents and purposes, we can conclude that the second wave in the strict sense is neither possible nor desirable. The third wave, the establishment of philosopher-rulers, proved to be structurally the most complex. If we take "philosophers" in the sense outlined in books 5–7, namely, as *wise* persons with comprehensive knowledge of the structure of the whole, then philosopher-rulers would be quite plausibly desirable but almost certainly impossible. If, more realistically and more in keeping with the conception of philosophy regularly *exhibited* by Socrates, we take the philosopher to be someone who lacks wisdom, recognizes that lack, and strives to overcome it, then a philosophic ruler seems possible, though hardly probable, but its desirability becomes much more debatable, and in any case is not defended in the *Republic*. What conclusions can be drawn from this?

First and most obviously, we see that we should no longer speak simplistically of the possibility or impossibility, desirability or undesirability, of the three waves taken together, at least not without first recognizing that different judgments must be made on each separately. If we do take all three waves together, especially considering the extremely problematic character of the second wave, we may fairly conclude that the weight of the evidence is on the side of those who argue that the city in speech in not intended as a real possibility. But this judgment must always be moderated by the recognition that very different conclusions are drawn for each of the three waves taken singly.

But another, perhaps more far-reaching conclusion can be drawn regarding the connection of the three waves to the teaching of the *Republic* as a whole. To see this, we must remind ourselves that the construction of a perfectly just city was not the originating project of the dialogue. The originating project was the concern to answer the questions generated by the discussions in book 1, especially between Socrates and Thrasymachus: what is justice, and who is happier, the just or the unjust person? The concern with the city arose as a consequence of the famous "city-soul" analogy, introduced in book 2 (368d–69b) in order to get a "better look" at justice.

Keeping this in mind, let us leap ahead to the apparent conclusion of the whole issue of the "city in speech," which occurs at the very end of book 9. Socrates has been arguing in conclusion that the philosophic person should be concerned with the health of one's *own* soul, the "regime within." Glaucon comments:

"Then," he said, "if it's that he cares about, he won't be willing to mind the political things."

"Yes, by the dog," I said, "he will in his own city, very much so. However, perhaps he won't in his fatherland unless some divine chance coincidentally comes to pass."

"I understand," he said. "You mean he will in the city whose foundation we have now gone through, the one that has its place in speeches, since I don't suppose it exists anywhere on earth."

"But in heaven," I said, "perhaps, a pattern is laid up for the man who wants to see and found a city within himself on the basis of what he sees. *It doesn't make any difference whether it is or will be somewhere. For he would mind the things of this city alone, and of no other.*" (592a–b; my emphasis)

The real issue, we are told in conclusion, is not whether such an actual city is possible, which now seems to be rather unimportant, but whether such a city can be established in Glaucon's, and in each of our, souls. About this striking conclusion a number of observations may be made.

First, Socrates' last exhortation at 592b (which I emphasized in the quotation) is in striking tension with the whole thrust of the setting up of the city in speech, where we were regularly reminded that the happiness of the individual must be deferred to the happiness of the city as a whole (for example, 420b, 466a), and that in particular the philosopher-rulers must be made to see that they have a duty precisely *not* to "mind the things of this city alone" (that is, the individual soul), but rather to make their concern the ruling of the larger city (519c–20a). Yet here, at the end of book 9, we are told that even if such a real city were established, the true philosopher would mind the concerns of the city within his soul alone, "and of no other" (592b). In short, this crucial conclusion of the *Republic* flies in the face of a central contention, a central requirement, of the city in speech.[79]

Second, the conclusion clearly invokes again the issue of the city-soul analogy. An analogy, of course, is never an identity; it must always be examined to see where the analogy works, and where it breaks down. Let us do that with particular reference to the relevance of the three waves to the city-soul analogy. What do we discover?

The first wave, equality of men and women, might seem at first to have no correlation when we turn to the individual soul, and perhaps that is the simplest way to take it. What, after all, would be the literal correlation to men and women within the individual soul? Moreover, the principle has already been estab-

---

79. Diskin Clay recognizes the importance of this qualification of the whole project in his "Reading the *Republic*," 29.

lished in the discussion of the first wave that gender is irrelevant to the issues of ruling and philosophy. However, one might speculate that a correlation is possible if we take such equality to refer to the "masculine" and "feminine" characteristics of the individual soul. We could then say that the point of the first wave, applied to the individual soul, is that, first, there are both "masculine" and "feminine" elements in each soul, and, second, that the "masculine" and "feminine" elements in the soul must be treated and nurtured equally, and that this is especially true for the philosophic soul.[80] The conclusion of the application of the first wave to the city-soul analogy would thus be that equal treatment and nurture of the "masculine" and "feminine" elements in the individual soul is both possible and desirable.

The second wave, radical communism of women and children, and the like, simply has no specific correlation when we turn to the individual soul. Questions regarding sex laws, who should have sex with whom and when, rigged lotteries, and how to keep people from knowing their natural family members, have no correlate in the relations between parts of the individual soul. I suspect that this is no accident. Recall that the second wave was of the three the most unambiguously problematic regarding its possibility and desirability. It proved impossible as it stands and arguably undesirable as well. But because the second wave is irrelevant when applied to the soul, it need not affect negatively our conclusions regarding the soul, though it certainly must when applied to the city. With regard to the individual soul, then, we can dispense with the morass of problems regarding the second wave.

The third wave, however, the rule of philosophy, does seem manifestly relevant. Given the triadic structure of the soul (580d ff.), it clearly appeals to the desirability of reason ruling over the

---

80. "Full humanity is a discrete mixture of masculinity and femininity" (Bloom, *The Republic of Plato*, 384). One might also note *Symposium* 203b ff, where Eros' parentage is delineated—*contra* Pausanias—as the *heterosexual* couple, Poros and Penia, and where, thus, the erotic aspect of the soul is portrayed explicitly as partaking of both the "masculine" and "feminine" parents.

spirited and desiring parts of the soul, which is precisely the point Socrates seems to be appealing to in his conclusion at the end of book 9. It is tantamount to the rule of philosophy in the individual soul.

If we now recall the ambiguity of our conclusion regarding the third wave and apply it to the individual soul, we get, as our final conclusion, something like this: If comprehensive wisdom were possible for an individual, it would certainly be desirable to live one's life by the dictates of that wisdom; but it seems that such an achievement is not possible for humans. If, however, we take philosophy, more realistically, in something like the Socratic sense, we get, as the real conclusion to the *Republic* on this issue, that living a life under the rule of philosophy, that is, living the sort of interrogative life exhibited by Socrates, is possible, though unlikely, and problematically desirable. For women and for men. That seems a fair conclusion.

The clear force of my arguments, then, is to support the position that the three waves taken as a whole are insurmountable for a polity, and thus that Plato does not intend the *Republic* as a realizable utopia but as an antiutopian work, designed to show that utopias are impossible and even undesirable. This, once again, is to support as well the view that what transcendence is possible out of the finitude of our human situation is always and necessarily partial.

But this view also entails the conclusion that the *apparent* claim that the perfectly just city ruled by philosopher-rulers is both possible and desirable is itself ironic. This is turn forces on us a more serious consideration of the presence and significance of Platonic irony. In the next chapter, I shall develop the significance of irony in the dialogues not just as an important dramatic trope regularly employed by Plato, but as itself an instance of the confrontation with negativity and the finite transcendence thereof.

4

IRONY AS FINITE TRANSCENDENCE

Early in book 10 of the *Republic*, Plato has Socrates set out his famous, or rather infamous, criticism of poetry and by implication, of all art.[81] In a series of clearly problematic arguments, Socrates begins with the implication that all art is an imitation of artifacts. His guiding example here is that of a couch; the painter imitates in his painting the couch made by the carpenter (*Republic*, 597a ff). But in turn, the couch made by the carpenter is itself an imitation of the "idea of the couch" which the carpenter uses as a model. Art, then, is an imitation of an imitation, or "three removes from reality" (597e). On the basis of this understanding, Socrates easily persuades the pliable young Glaucon that art is dangerously misleading, that its claims to revelation are usually fraudulent, and that no one who had the choice would concern oneself with distant imitations when the reality, the idea itself, is accessible through philosophy (599a ff).

For those who take their Plato straight, who assume that what Socrates says in the dialogues is more or less what Plato believes, and moreover, that the possibility of irony, though it may be mentioned in prefatory remarks (or at most, an introductory chapter) as an indication of one's literary sensitivity, need not be incorporated as an integral part of the presentation of Plato's genuine philosophic teaching, this argument in book 10 is proof positive that Plato is an intractable enemy of art. After all, in book 10 itself he writes of the "long-standing war between poetry and philosophy" (607b). Moreover, earlier in the *Republic*, Socrates

---

81. An earlier version of this chapter was published as "Taking the Longer Road: The Irony of Plato's *Republic*," in *Revue de Metaphysique et de Morale* no. 3, (1988): 317–35.

had played the role of a general in this war through his severe censorship of the kind of art that would be allowed in the perfectly just city in speech that he was founding (377a ff). Add to that the traditional account that before he came under the influence of Socrates, Plato was an aspiring poet, and it is hardly surprising that he, like so many converts, should become an exaggeratedly severe critic of his former and now repudiated aspiration.[82]

But consider: Plato did not, as he could have, write "A Theory of Justice," in the first person, in which he set out his views on the topic; he wrote a dialogue, in which Socrates has a rather long conversation with the likes of Thrasymachus, Glaucon, and Adeimantus. He thus formulates a written imitation of the conversation that Socrates had.[83] The *Republic* itself is therefore an imitation. But the first line of the dialogue begins, "I went down yesterday to the Piraeus with Glaucon, son of Ariston, to pray to the goddess...."(327a). The actual dramatic setting of the *Republic*, then, is a portrayal of Socrates telling the story of, and so imitating, the conversation that constitutes the dialogue, which actually took place "yesterday." In short, the *Republic* itself is a written imitation of a spoken imitation, an "imitation of an imitation," or precisely the characterization of art which gets so severely criticized within its own pages. As if this were not strange enough, Plato, as the writer of the dialogue, "imitates" the words not only of Socrates, but also of Glaucon, Adeimantus, Thrasymachus, Polemarchus, and Cephalos. He thus imitates a variety of character types, both good and bad, which is again just the practice that Socrates outlaws in his development of the censorship of poetry in book 3, where he argues that such diverse imitation at best confuses the soul and at worst corrupts it (392d ff). In the very structure of the *Republic*, then, we are faced with a

---

82. See Alice Swift Riginos, *Platonica: The Anecdotes Concerning the Life and Writings of Plato* (Leiden: E. J. Brill, 1976), 43–51. Riginos argues— unpersuasively in my view—that the anecdote concerning Plato's early poetic interest "has no historical basis" (48).

83. I am in no sense claiming that the conversation was historical, but only that dramatically we are to suppose that it took place.

massive example of Platonic irony, a phenomenon as well known as it is seldom taken seriously by philosophers. Part of my intention in this chapter is to show that irony in the *Republic* (and elsewhere in the dialogues) is not just an aspect of Plato's "literary style" but a central aspect of his philosophic position; in brief, irony is one of the primary manifestations of Plato's teaching on negativity[84] and finite transcendence.

What is irony? We can begin with what I take to be an orthodox understanding of the concept, although I shall want subsequently to modify it in order to elucidate the specific character of Platonic irony. Ironic speech is speech wherein the truth is significantly other than, and in strong cases the opposite of, what is said.[85] Unlike lying, however, in which success depends upon the concealment of this opposition from the hearer, ironic speech intends that the listener, or at least the more subtle listener, understand and appreciate the opposition.[86] As Paul Friedlander puts the point in his study of Platonic irony, "Yes and no are peculiarly intertwined in the words of the ironic man."[87] Thus in the *Republic* when Thrasymachus first breaks in angrily on the discussion, Socrates pretends to be terrified of him and begs him not to be hard on his poor self. Thrasymachus recognizes the irony of Socrates' remark and retorts, "Heracles! Here is

---

84. More pervasive, and perhaps more fundamental, than the explicit remarks of the Eleatic Stranger in the *Sophist* (237c ff).

85. Aristotle, who, at least on the surface, has a considerably lower opinion of irony than either Socrates or Plato, speaks of it primarily as a form of dissembling where one understates the truth about oneself. It is the other extreme from boastfulness, of which the mean is telling the truth. See the *Nicomachean Ethics*, 1108a19–22, 1124b29, 1127a22, 1127b22; *Rhetoric*, 1379b32, 1419b32, 1420a1. A thorough study of Aristotle would, of course, have to consider the extent to which he himself practiced irony.

86. R. Schaerer, "Le Mecanisme de l'ironie dans ses rapports avec la dialectique," *Revue de Metaphysique et de Morale* 48 (1941): "[L'ironie] n'existe que pour etre demasquée....L'ironiste ne trompe pas pour tromper, mais pour qu'on devine qu'il trompe" (185).

87. Paul Friedlander, *Plato: An Introduction*, vol. 1, trans. Hans Meyerhoff (New York: Pantheon Books, 1958), 139.

the habitual irony of Socrates. I knew it, and I predicted to these fellows that you wouldn't be willing to answer, that you would be ironic and do anything rather than answer if someone asked you something" (337a). To which Socrates replies, no less ironically, "That's because you are wise, Thrasymachus."[88] Socrates' words are ironic because he says he is afraid of Thrasymachus but he is not, and he says that Thrasymachus is wise though he believes, and will presently demonstrate, that he is not.

Ironic acts and events, derivatively, are such that in them the outcome is significantly other than what was anticipated or predictable. In the purest or simplest cases, the outcome may be the direct opposite or contradiction of what is expected; but as we shall see, irony is regularly attributed to speeches and events where the outcome is significantly other than anticipated rather than directly opposite. One would expect that a work that criticizes art as being an imitation of an imitation would not itself conform to the conditions it criticizes; in doing so, the *Republic* becomes ironic.

Irony can also occur, and often does in the dialogues, through the juxtaposition of speech and act. In fact, this is often the locus of some of the deepest irony. When Socrates in particular says one thing but acts quite differently, we can suspect Socratic or Platonic irony. At the opening of the *Charmides*, for example, Socrates claims to be "inflamed with passion" at a glimpse inside the handsome young Charmides' cloak, and unable to speak (*Charmides*, 155d); he responds with a dialogue on *sophrosyne*. Within the *Republic*, the contrast between the demands laid on the putative philosopher-rulers and the actual conduct of Socrates raises the question whether Socrates himself would have been allowed to live in the city he is establishing, and whether, as the previous chapter discussed, the philosopher-rulers are even human or rather wise gods.

---

88. Vlastos, in his otherwise interesting discussion of this passage, seems to miss the irony that the real locus of the irony is not Thrasymachus' accusation but Socrates' reply; see *Socrates, Ironist and Moral Philosopher*, 24 ff.

It may be appropriate at this point to say a few words about the distinction between Socratic and Platonic irony. The distinction between Socrates' views and Plato's is always an obscure one in the dialogues, in my opinion intentionally so.[89] For our purposes, however, a simple and relatively clear difference in their respective ironies can be stated, at least in a preliminary fashion. Let Socratic irony be those instances of irony where the words and intentions are attributable, dramatically if not historically, to Socrates. The episode with Thrasymachus described above is an apt example. Platonic irony, on the other hand, is that irony that occurs in that action or structure of the dialogue which Socrates could not be supposed to control.[90] The aforementioned connection of the structure of the *Republic* with the criticism of art internal to it, which Socrates could not have controlled, would thus be an example of Platonic irony. For the most part, I shall be concerned with issues that are true of both Socratic and Platonic irony, although if the occasion demands I shall distinguish them.

Why would Plato have written ironically? There are a number of answers to this question now prevalent in the scholarly literature, and I shall presently rehearse some of the most important. Two things, however, can be said about them in general. First, the various explanations are for the most part compatible. It is entirely possible and indeed likely that elements of each explanation can find support in the irony of the dialogues.

---

89. Ralph Waldo Emerson puts the point well when he comments, "Socrates and Plato are the double star which the most powerful instruments will not entirely separate"; quoted in Friedlander, *Plato: an Introduction*, 144–45. The implication of the metaphor, that, however difficult to determine, there still *is* a difference, also holds. Scholars such as Vlastos, on the other hand, are curiously optimistic that they can easily tell the difference. See again Vlastos's *Socrates, Ironist and Moral Philosopher*, esp. chap. 2, "Socrates *contra* Socrates in Plato." Vlastos comes close to acknowledging that this distinction is primarily of historical rather than philosophical importance on page 45.

90. Charles Griswold makes the same general point in his "Irony and Aesthetic Language in Plato's Dialogues," in *Literature as Art: Essays in Honor of Murray Krieger*, ed. Douglas Bolling (New York: Haven Press, 1986). 71–102.

Second, however, they share the common defect of stopping short of an explanation that attributes genuine philosophic intentions and significance to Plato's use of irony. This defect will lead me to suggest an alternative account that would make Platonic irony part of his philosophic teaching.

The first and most prevalent account of Plato's irony derives from those who distinguish between "Plato the artist" and "Plato the philosopher." On this view, irony is to be understood as a literary device, and like the other "literary" elements in the dialogues, such as the dialogue form itself, the intertwining of action and speech among the various characters, and the placing of each dialogue in a specific setting, irony is interpreted as a kind of hangover from Plato's poetic youth, before he came under the presumably sobering influence of Socrates. Put most positively, Plato is both a great artist and a great philosopher. A. E. Taylor, in his well-known work, *Plato: The Man and His Work*, puts the point clearly: "Lovers of great literature have every reason to be whole-heartedly thankful that once in the world's history a supreme philosophical thinker should also have been a superb dramatic artist."[91] Taylor adds immediately that this gain for literature is at the expense of the metaphysician, who must now with great difficulty separate the philosophy from the literature. It is here that the defect of this explanation lies. The "and" in the epithet, "great artist and great philosopher" is by implication disjunctive rather than conjunctive; the two can and must be separated. The upshot of this view, therefore, is that it gives its adherents licence, when speaking of Plato's philosophy, effectively to ignore all those aspects of the dialogues that are judged to be "literary," and that has certainly included irony. For this reason, these writers have failed to consider the possible philosophical significance of irony. I emphasize that this view is the dominant one among English-speaking writers on Plato.[92]

---

91. A. E. Taylor, *Plato: The Man and His Works* (New York: Meridian Books, 1959), 23.

92. As so often, Vlastos is one of the best examples. His account, as the title of his book suggests (*Socrates, Ironist and Moral Philosopher*), concentrates on Socrates' irony more than Plato's. But it describes irony

A second explanation of irony, which is far more provocative and at least begins to connect irony with philosophic intentions, argues that the motive for irony is political or prudential. One of its most articulate recent spokesmen was Leo Strauss. According to Strauss, Socratic and Platonic irony are founded in their recognition that philosophers will necessarily speak to people of varied character and intelligence, to whom one ought to say different things. The philosopher, then, recognizing both his own superiority and the varied abilities of the hearers, will speak and write in such a way as to take account of those differences in the audience, and that way is irony: "Irony is then the noble dissimulation of one's worth, of one's superiority. We may say, it is the humanity peculiar to the superior man: he spares the feelings of his inferiors by not displaying his superiority."[93] Moreover, "If irony is essentially related to the fact that there is a natural order of rank among men, it follows that irony consists in speaking differently to different kinds of people."[94] The irony of Socrates, of Plato, and therefore of Plato's *Republic*, will thus consist in the fact that that their own views will not be utterly clear, and that they will seem to say very different things to different readers. To say the least, the *Republic* is ironic in this sense.[95]

Strauss's political or prudential account of irony is superior in that it implies a connection between Plato's use of irony and his philosophical convictions, mediated, as it were, by political or prudential considerations. In the presumption of a natural order

---

as a characteristic of the (historical) man, and does not connect it directly to his actual philosophical position.

93. Strauss, *The City and Man*, 51.

94. Ibid.

95. One need cite as evidence for this only one well-known text, *Plato: Totalitarian or Democrat?*, ed. T. L. Thorson (Englewood Cliffs, N.J.: Prentice-Hall, 1963), a series of essays by a number of authors attributing to Plato a whole range of places on the political spectrum, from protocommunist to liberal democrat to protofascist. Or even within a given "school" of interpretation, consider the debates, say, among Vlastos, Terence Irwin, and others, who agree on all hermeneutical principles but *still* can't agree on what "Plato" is saying, much less on whether he is right.

of rank among people and the implied connection between rhetoric and the knowledge of the souls of one's readers lie a number of important and controversial issues about human nature. Its limitation is that of partiality; by confining the significance of Platonic irony to the prudential level, it overlooks the possibly richer philosophical significance that irony might have as part of Plato's account of the human situation.

There are a number of variations and elaborations on this Straussian position, often developed by those who have benefitted directly from Strauss's writings. One very important elaboration, which includes the recognition that the presence of rhetorical or political irony in the dialogues means that one cannot gain access to Plato's philosophical teaching without including the significance of irony in one's interpretation, distinguishes between "hard" and "gentle" or "pedagogical" irony.[96] Perhaps the first and best statement of hard irony appears in Plato's own dialogue, the *Symposium*, in Alcibiades's encomium to Socrates which turns out to be as much criticism as speech of praise. Speaking of Socrates' oft-professed love of others, especially handsome or talented youths, Alcibiades says:

> "You should know that if anyone is noble and good looking it means nothing to him; but he looks down upon this as no one would ever believe, nor if anyone is wealthy nor if they have any of the other honors which the many consider most blessed. But he believes all these possessions to be worth nothing—and we ourselves to be worth nothing, I tell you— but he spends his whole life being ironic and playing with mankind."[97]

---

96. Friedlander, *Plato: an Introduction*, 145; Stanley Rosen, *Plato's Symposium* (New Haven, Conn.: Yale University Press, 1968), xiv, xx; René Schaerer, *La Question Platonicienne: Etudes sur les rapports de la pensee et de l'expression dans les dialogues* (Neuchatel: Memoires de l'Universite de Neuchatel, 1969), 54–59; Bloom, *The Republic of Plato*; Drew A. Hyland, *The Virtue of Philosophy: An Interpretation of Plato's Charmides* (Athens: Ohio University Press, 1981).

97. *Symposium*, 216e; my translation.

According to Alcibiades, then, one source of Socrates' irony is his arrogance and contempt for others. This kind of irony is clearly present in book 1 of the *Republic*, in Socrates' encounter with the polemical Sophist, Thrasymachus. Socrates' pretended awe of Thrasymachus and his attribution of wisdom to that Sophist drip with contempt for the fraudulence of his claims to knowledge. The significance of such hard irony for our understanding of Plato is at least twofold. On the one hand, it is Plato, after all, who put this critical account of Socratic irony into the mouth of Alcibiades; to the extent that it constitutes at least an implied criticism of Socrates, we must ask to what extent it is well founded. Insofar as it is, we must begin to understand the dialogues as at least in part a critical evaluation of Socrates. This in turn would furnish yet more evidence that we cannot naively assume that Socrates is Plato's "ideal philosopher," and certainly no longer interpret whatever Socrates says as what Plato believes.[98] Second, the recognition of hard irony as a characteristic of Socratic irony should lead us to ask whether it is also sometimes characteristic of Platonic irony, and if so, what that implies for our understanding of Plato.

But clearly, Alcibiades' accusation is only part of the complex story of Socratic irony. At least part of the time, Socrates' irony seems to have a more philanthropic source; it is a gentle or pedagogic irony. The regularly recurring presence of this irony occurs whenever Socrates is conversing with young men and pretends to know nothing about the issue under discussion, but seems to want to inquire with the young man and to draw out the youth's wisdom, to act, that is, as "midwife." In the *Republic*, Socrates takes this stance to some extent with the bright young brothers of Plato, Glaucon and Adeimantus.[99] The irony in these instances, easily visible to the reader, is that Socrates does know

---

98. Contra Vlastos and others in his hermeneutical camp; see *Socrates, Ironist and Moral Philosopher*, 117. See my discussion of this point in the introduction.

99. And even, to a certain extent, with Thrasymachus, with whom, despite the rancorous exchange, Socrates claims to become "friends." It is obviously possible to engage in "hard" and "gentle" irony at the same time, if one is subtle.

much more than he indicates and does lead the discussion pretty much in the direction that he wants. The significant point here is that the apparent motivation for this irony is Socrates' conviction that the best way to educate most people is not to dispense knowledge through lectures but to draw out their own nascent understanding through judicious questioning. But if this is true of Socratic irony, might it not also be true of Platonic irony? Might it too have a pedagogical intention, but this time directed toward the reader of the dialogue? If so, we hardly act as good students by simply recognizing its presence from time to time and ignoring its implications. We must rather make the recognition of that irony an integral part of our interpretation of the dialogue's philosophic significance.

Evidently, this account of Socratic and Platonic irony takes steps toward giving that irony genuine philosophic significance. Still, it does not go far enough, and I would like, in the spirit of Kierkegaard's *The Concept of Irony: With Constant Reference to Socrates*, to take some further steps toward establishing the thesis that Platonic irony must be understood as central to his philosophic teaching. In turning to this development, let me restate as succinctly as I can my dissatisfaction with the previously discussed accounts of Platonic irony. It may be true that part of the attraction of irony for Plato derives from his literary sensibilities; it may be true that he sometimes employs irony out of political prudence, that sometimes there may be an element of playful contempt in it, and that he sometimes employs it to educate his readers to begin to think philosophically for themselves. But in each case, Plato (or Socrates) would be using the device of irony for some end external to the philosophic content of the dialogue, and an end that is not itself ironic: educating the reader, being prudent, and the like. He would thus be imposing irony on his writings not as a reflection of what the dialogues themselves are about, but for ends exterior to that explicitly philosophical content. I repeat that all of these explanations may be true. However, I wish now to show that there is another source that is internal to the actual philosophical content of the dialogues, that irony is at the core of Plato's philosophical teaching.

Return for a moment to the standard formulation of irony cited earlier in this chapter. Irony is understood to have two aspects or "moments." First, an assertion is made. But that assertion is considered ironic only if, second, the truth is to be understood as significantly other than what is said. Let us take as our example probably the most famous instance of irony in all the dialogues, Socrates' oft-reiterated claim that he is not wise. This claim is ironic, of course, because we know that the truth is virtually the opposite, that Socrates *is* wise, indeed one of the wisest of humans. This means, however, that there is inherent in every instance of irony negation, or more generally, negativity. Kierkegaard, in his work on irony, sees this point perhaps too well, emphasizing that Socratic irony is entirely negative, its complete negativity being finally, in Kierkegaard's eyes, a defect.[100] I shall want to modify that judgment presently, but Kierkegaard is surely right to see in irony the presence of, and recognition of, negativity. Negativity should here be taken, with Kierkegaard, in as wide a sense as possible, ranging from straightforward contradiction through opposition to simple otherness. Irony can exhibit this entire range of negativity. Let us then take this first point in its "positive" significance: irony is one pervasive way that Plato inserts into the dialogues the important philosophical issue of negativity. Perhaps we could say that Plato was a sufficiently attentive student of Parmenides that he did not write dialogues that speak positively of nonbeing. But the presence of irony testifies to his recognition of the decisive presence of negativity in human life and as a philosophic issue. That he presented it negatively rather than positively, as it were, may be testimony to his insight. Perhaps the irony of negativity in the world is best presented in, and as, irony.

Negativity, however broadly construed, is not identical with finitude. Nevertheless, the two are clearly akin; negation, especially experienced negation (as opposed, say, to merely logical negation), is usually a particularly powerful instance of finitude. Such negation/finitude can take a variety of forms, from denial (of one's desire, or just reward), to restriction (say, of one's freedom) to failure, all of which happen to Socrates. We can thus

___

100. S. Kierkegaard, *The Concept of Irony: With Constant Reference to Socrates*, trans. Lee Capel (London: Collins, 1966), 50, 72, 76, 77, 83, 92, et al.

say that in the irony through which negation is often expressed in the dialogues, we have found another important way in which Plato presents us with the manifold presence of finitude in human experience. We must see how and to what extent irony might also contain within its structure a mode of finite transcendence.

A further consideration of the very example of irony cited above, Socrates' famous claim that he is not wise, reveals that the situation is often more complex than a simple relation of opposition, the copresence of Yes and No, as Friedlander puts it. To be sure, Socrates asserts that he is not wise, whereas in fact he is wise. But what is his wisdom? It is his recognition that he is *not* wise in the divine sense of comprehensive knowledge; it is his recognition of this lack and the consequent striving to overcome it. Socrates' wisdom is his *aporia*. His initial denial of wisdom is, in a qualified and deeper sense, true. A look at the logical structure of this situation reveals that the irony is more complex by one step. Although on the surface the opposite of what is said is what is meant, at a deeper level we see by the conjunction of the two the sense in which each of the two earlier moments, notwithstanding their partiality and apparent opposition, is true, though not equally so.[101] To post-nineteenth century philosophers, the general structure of this movement will be familiar. At the risk of anachronism, we might say that the deeper or third "moment" is the *Aufhebung* of the opposition between the earlier moments. One might thus suggest that we find in the structure of Platonic irony an important precursor to Hegelian dialectic.

Let us see to what extent this protodialectical structure is present in other instances of Platonic irony, with special reference

---

101. See Berel Lang, *Philosophy and the Art of Writing: Studies in Philosophical and Literary Style* (Lewisburg, Pa.: Bucknell University Press, 1983), 67: "irony both incites conflict and discloses the subordination of one side to the other in that conflict without, however, reconciling them." Vlastos's account of Socrates' "complex irony"(see *Socrates, Ironist and Moral Philosopher*, 31), that in it "what is said both is and isn't what is meant: its surface content is meant to be true in one sense, false in another," is therefore true as far as it goes, but does not go far enough, as I hope to show in the following pages. Lang's account already captures more of the richness of irony in the dialogues.

to the *Republic*. I shall choose just a few of the seminal examples of irony therein, beginning with the first case mentioned earlier, the irony of Socrates' criticism of art. In the first moment, Socrates, using primarily the example of a couch, characterizes art as an imitation of an imitation. But second, this characterization is turned into a criticism or negation of all art as something three removes from reality, and as such misleading and far inferior to philosophy, which concerns itself with the reality itself. However, and this moves us toward the third moment, the dramatic structure of the *Republic* itself is such that it is an imitation of an imitation, and so conforms to its own portrayal of art. What is the significance of this irony? Consider the following:

Philosophy, as literally the love of wisdom, strives to achieve knowledge of the whole. If it were possible, this wisdom would be articulated in a single, homogeneous speech, a "logic," which successfully incorporated within it the heterogeneous parts, from natural science to history, art, and religion, that make up the whole of knowledge. Hegel's dialectical logic, as exhibited and given content in his *Encyclopedia of the Philosophical Sciences*, is arguably the most monumental claim to have achieved such a homogeneous speech, or absolute knowledge, in the history of philosophy. In his dialogue, the *Charmides*, Plato has Socrates characterize such a putative complete speech about the whole as "the science of itself and of the other sciences and of the absence of science."[102] Hegel and Plato would thus seem to share the conviction that this is what wisdom, if achievable, would be. But they differ in that, as the *Charmides*, *Apology*, and the other dialogues regularly demonstrate, Plato seemed to hold that such a complete, homogeneous speech about the whole, or wisdom, is impossible.[103] The dialogues themselves are ample demonstration of this. They are, to be sure, Plato's "speech" of philosophy. But since they employ myth, drama, poetry, and even visual aids as well as logical argument, they are all heterogeneous speeches. The heterogeneity of the speech of the dialogues indicates the

---

102. *Charmides*, 166e ff.

103. For an extended discussion of this point, see my *The Virtue of Philosophy*, chaps. 6–8.

impossibility of the single homogeneous speech of wisdom, yet at the same time constitutes Plato's best attempt to articulate the heterogeneous nature of the whole. The dialogues are a heterogeneous attempt to articulate the heterogeneous whole. But this means that such dialogues, the heterogeneous speech of philosophy, *imitate* the irreducible heterogeneity of the whole, or are *art*. As Plato has Socrates say on his dying day, "Philosophy is the highest music."[104] More explicitly, the *Republic*, as an imitation of Socrates' philosophic conversation with the others present, is indeed an imitation of the speech of philosophy that by its own heterogeneity imitates the heterogeneity of the whole. The irony of the *Republic*, then, the third moment of this ironic triad, is that it shows that philosophic writing is indeed art: the highest art, now transformed into a positive moment.

A second area of massive irony in the Republic has to do with the conditions required for setting up the "city in speech" (369a), the perfectly just city. Recall that early in the formulation of that city, Socrates urges on Glaucon the daring suggestion that in order to get its citizens to believe what is necessary to establish perfect justice, it will be necessary to tell a lie, a "noble lie," as he calls it:

> "Could we," I said, "somehow contrive one of those lies that come into being in case of need, of which we were just now speaking, some one noble lie to persuade, in the best case, even the rulers, but if not them, the rest of the city." (414c)

So startling, even appalling, is this suggestion to modern ears that translators have gone to extraordinary lengths to avoid facing up to its consequences. F. M. Cornford, in his famous and widely read translation of the *Republic*, translates *gennaios pseudos* as "a convenient fiction...a single bold flight of invention," and even warns us in a footnote against entertaining the translation "noble lie," which might suggest that Plato would countenance such an ignoble thing as propaganda.[105]

---

104. *Phaedo*, 61a.

105. F. M. Cornford, *The Republic* (New York: Oxford University Press, 1956), 106.

Cornford might have done better to translate the passage as it was written and consider the possibility of irony. As it happens, there are not one but two lies that will have to be told, the lie of autocthony, that we spring not from our biological parents but from the city itself, which is our true mother, and the lie of metallic souls, that there are three kinds of souls, bronze, silver, and gold, each of which is naturally intended for working, fighting, and ruling, respectively (414d–15d). It is not difficult to see what the political significance of these lies is. The lie of autocthony, if believed, will establish that one owes to one's city the kind of allegiance, love, and sacrifice usually accorded to one's parents. That is, it is a lie intended to establish patriotism as the highest duty and virtue, and, moreover, a lie that will eliminate the natural tension between patriotism and familial loyalty; if my city is my parent, my political duty to my city and my private affections for my family can never conflict. The lie of metals will establish a belief in a "natural" order of rank originating not in environment but by birth. If I believe that I am "by nature" bronze souled and therefore destined for manual labor, I will be more likely to accept my station in life without complaint.

It is important to reiterate at this point that Socrates calls these "noble lies." Plato could have had him call them "noble myths." A myth, as Socrates had told us earlier, is a truth couched in fiction (377a). If these were noble myths, then the fundamental allegiance to the city or *polis* and the natural order of rank among humans would be the "truths" couched in the "fictions" of autocthony and metallic souls. But they are lies, not myths. We must therefore construe the Platonic Socrates as meaning that in order for a perfectly just *polis* to be possible its citizens must become convinced of two lies: that they owe a "natural" allegiance to the city and that their station in the city is established "by nature." We must understand and take seriously the implication that Socrates regarded these beliefs as untrue. The truth would thus seem to be that there is a natural difference or tension between the private and the public, and that differences in human abilities, though real, are not necessarily "by nature."

We begin to see the irony in this situation when we wonder about the implication that perfect justice must be founded on lies.

A straightforward, nonironic interpretation of this passage would ask us to believe that Plato thought, first, that it would be possible to convince people that they originated not from their human parents but from the earth beneath their city, and that they are by nature either golden, silver, or bronze souled, and second, that it would be desirable to do so. But we are told that these are lies, that is, that the truth is the negation of these assertions. If this is an instance of irony in the more complex sense that I have been setting out, then there should be a third moment, a deeper sense in which these lies do have at least a kernel of truth. If we take the issue to be not the explicit formulation of the lie but its political significance, the ironic upshot of the need for a noble lie, its third moment, might be something like this: Plato is suggesting that the establishment of perfect justice would be possible only if people came to believe that they owed their most fundamental allegiance to the city or public rather than to the private or familial, indeed, that the two could never come into conflict, and, moreover, that they are destined by nature to whatever occupation they are assigned. But he further intends to suggest that such beliefs are false, and therefore that there is an inevitable tension between the ideal of perfect justice and the truth about the human situation. He thus suggests that the establishing of perfect justice is both impossible and undesirable, because incompatible with its citizens' knowing the truth about themselves and their city. A "solution" to the political problem, the radical or "absolute" transcendence of this mode of finitude, is impossible and undesirable. Once again but for different reasons, the thesis of chapter 3 is substantiated: the *Republic* is Plato's antiutopian work.

Such complex irony might seem far-fetched were it not repeated in other episodes in the *Republic*. In book 4, Socrates arrives at his famous definition of justice as "each man doing his own business and not meddling in the business of others" (433b, 443d). Yet later, as the constituency of the just city is built up, we learn that the critical class, without which justice will be impossible, is the class of philosopher-rulers, who will rule. What is their "business"? They have not one but two jobs: to be philosophers and to rule, thus violating the "one man-one job" principle that has, under Socrates's guidance, informed the city in speech to this point. Worse than that, their job as rulers is to oversee—in sometimes astonishing detail—the lives of the other classes and especially the guardians, from their education, to their preparations for war, to the most intimate details of their sex lives (412b, 415d, 423 ff, 459c ff, 467 ff). In short, the job of the philosophers is precisely not to "mind their own business"— which is to concern themselves with knowing the forms (479a ff, 496d)—but to oversee everyone else's business. In the perfectly just city the occupation of the rulers is definitive of injustice.[106] Yet, and here again is the third moment of irony, it may well be true that someone must, in any reasonably complex political system, occupy a capacity as overseer, and that in a just city the overseers should be the ones most qualified. The irony thus is that the establishing of justice would require that the decisively important class of overseers embody the conditions of injustice. Once again, Plato leads us, through his irony, to call into question the possibility and desirability of such a utopia, such a radical transcendence of the finitude of our political situation.

The predicament of the philosopher-rulers is in another way even more ironic. As philosophers, they want nothing so much as to pursue their search for wisdom and contemplation of the ideas. That is their "business," and they want to mind it. Consequently, because, as Socrates himself puts it in book 6, they have seen "that no one who minds the business of the cities does anything healthy" (496c), they do not want to rule. But the establishing of justice requires that the ones best qualified to rule do so. The philosophers must be forced to rule:

> "Then our job as founders," I said, "is to compel the best natures to go to the study which we were saying before is the greatest, to see the good and to go up that ascent; and when they have gone up and seen sufficiently, not to permit them what is now permitted."

---

106. Rosen, "The Role of Eros in Plato's *Republic*," 460. One might formulate the point differently but no less ironically: the "business" of the philosopher-rulers is to watch over everyone else's business, and so to contain within their "justice" the very definition of injustice.

"What's that?"

"To remain there," I said, "and not be willing to go down again among those prisoners or share their labors and honors, whether they be slighter or more serious." (529d)

The establishing of the conditions of justice requires not just that the philosophers embody injustice but that a radical injustice be done to them. Once again, the negativity present by virtue of irony in this situation suggests that the very enterprise of setting up a utopia, or "solving" the political problem, is misguided. According to an important modern political position, that political regime which is "the riddle of history solved and knows itself to be the solution"[107] will accomplish an abolition of alienation, the explicit politicoeconomic manifestation of negativity. Platonic irony, again, suggests that such an abolition, a radical transcendence of the finitude of the political situation which is the Marxian substitution for Hegelian "absolute knowledge," would be impossible. Moreover, even if possible, it could be accomplished only by an injustice so radical as to belie its claims to justice. One might suggest that the subsequent political history of the world has justified Plato's pessimism.

These interpretations, of course, are controversial in that many have argued that such assertions of Socrates—the criticism of art, the noble lie, the setting up of a utopia, the establishing of philosopher-rulers—are nonironic, and so are serious teachings of Plato. Inevitably, then, we must consider the question of how to assess ironic and nonironic claims. The first and central point to recognize is that there is no Platonic formula to determine the presence of irony. Conceivably, Plato could have placed an asterisk at the beginning of each sentence that contained irony, and there would be no problem of interpretation.[108] But he did

---

107. Karl Marx, *Economic and Philosophic Manuscripts of 1844*, in *Karl Marx: Early Writings*, ed. T. B. Bottomore (New York: McGraw-Hill, 1963), 155.

108. For example, Plato could have always used the "ironic particle," *ge*, when irony was present, and only used it when irony was present. But obviously things are not that simple.

not, and so there will always be a problem concerning irony: the issue of irony will always be a question of interpretation, never of certainty. Nevertheless, there are at least some clues, signposts along the longer road.

The first such signpost is plausibility. If a thinker of Plato's caliber makes an assertion that is so implausible as to be out-landish, we have good reason to suspect irony.[109] I am aware that what counts as plausibility and implausibility might be debated, but consider the following. At the end of book 7, nearing the completion of the city in speech, Socrates tries one more time, in apparent contradiction of the position I am defending, to convince Glaucon that such a city is indeed possible.

> "What then," I said, "Do you agree that the things we have said about the city and the regime are not in every way prayers; that they are hard but in a way possible...?" (540d)

Glaucon plausibly asks how it will be possible, to which Socrates replies, in a passage quoted earlier in chapter 3:

> "All those in the city who happen to be older than ten they will send out to the country; and taking over their children, they will rear them—far away from those dispositions they now have from their parents—in their own manners and laws that are such as we described before. And with the city and the regime of which we were speaking thus established most quickly and easily, it will itself be happy and most profit the nation in which it comes to be." (541a)

We are asked to believe that Plato seriously held that it would be possible to convince the parents of a city to leave that city, leaving their children under ten behind in the hands of the founders of a new city who would raise them ("most quickly and easily"!)

---

109. For recent versions of this general point, see Griswold, "Irony and Aesthetic Language in Plato's Dialogues," and Lang, *Philosophy and the Art of Writing*, 92–93. Perhaps the standard recent version of this principle is Leo Strauss, *Persecution and the Art of Writing* (Glencoe, Ill.: Free Press, 1952), 30.

according to the Draconian measures set out by Socrates earlier in the dialogue. I suggest that it is altogether more likely that the claim that such a city is possible is ironic.[110]

A second guideline is internal consistency in a given dialogue. If a thinker of Plato's stature contradicts himself so blatantly that even a student innocent of the subtleties of logic notices the contradiction, we would do well at least to consider the possibility that irony is at work. Again, I am aware that there is room for controversy here; we do not want to assume that no important thinker under any circumstances would unknowingly assert a contradiction. But I do suggest that we should conclude that it was an unwitting contradiction only after exhausting the possibility that the author was being ironic.[111]

A third signpost is an extension of the second. One can consider the consistency of positions asserted not just internally to the dialogue in question, but in relation to the positions presented in other dialogues as well. This signpost assumes that one of the things that makes great thinkers great is a certain coherence to their writings. When that overall coherence is flatly contradicted by a given assertion, we do well to consider the possibility of irony. Of course, it is possible that on at least some issues Plato changed his mind from one dialogue to another. A notorious example of this problem concerns Socrates' position on the immortality of the soul, which wavers between affirmation in the

---

110. It has been objected that I am assuming that the Greek commitment to the family was similar to the modern. One can acknowledge fully that the Greek family was not as close-knit as the modern (romanticized) family, but it remains well attested that Greek parents lamented the loss of their children.

111. For an excellent example of the use of this guideline, see Charles Griswold, "The Ideas and the Criticism of Poetry in Plato's *Republic*, Book 10," *Journal of the History of Philosophy* 19, no. 2, (1981): 135–50. Griswold resolves through the presence of irony the contradiction between the claim in book 10 that the ideas are created by the gods and the presumption throughout the earlier development of the *Republic* that the ideas are eternal. Vlastos's version of this guideline is his "principle of charity" (*Socrates, Ironist and Moral Philosopher*, 236), which, unfortunately, he does not employ as a clue to irony.

Phaedo, agnosticism in the *Apology,* and an almost straightforward denial in the *Symposium.* Was Plato constantly vacillating (or "developing") on this issue, or at least showing that Socrates was? Or is the apparent inconsistency explicable by a careful consideration of Socrates' audience in each case? I simply suggest again that such vacillation should be concluded only after having exhausted the other possibilities of interpretation, including, certainly, the possibility of irony.

I turn to one more instance of irony in the *Republic* in order to move to the final issue I want to raise in this chapter. As scholars such as Strauss, Rosen, and Bloom, among others, have observed, the *Republic* is extremely austere in its denigration of eros, from old Cephalus' expression of relief at having escaped the ravages of sexual desire through old age (329a), to the impossibly strict rules governing who shall have sex and when (460a, 546a ff), to the identification of eros with tyranny in the account of the downfall of successive regimes (573b, d). The *Republic,* it would be fair to say, recognizes the potential dangers of eros and responds to those dangers with its radical suppression. But philosophy, as the love of wisdom, is itself a manifestation of eros, as the *Phaedrus* and *Symposium* make abundantly clear. Indeed, the *Symposium* exaggerates the virtues of eros as much as the *Republic* exaggerates its dangers.[112] The two dialogues must be read together and allowed to moderate each other. Together, they teach that eros is the source both of the best (art, law giving, philosophy), and of the worst (tyranny) of human possibilities. If we allow a political environment that in an unmitigated way frees our eros for the best that we can be, as in democracy (577b ff), we also free it for the worst that it can be. Conversely, if we suppress eros so as to suppress the worst in human nature, we also suppress the best. The *Republic* falls prey to the latter danger. In radically suppressing eros in order to minimize the danger of tyranny, the city in speech would finally suppress genuine philosophy as well. But the possibility of philosophy is the very condition of justice. Once more, the irony of the *Republic* teaches us that the conditions for perfect justice are neither possible nor desirable.

---

112. I shall develop this example further in the next chapter.

The issue of eros offers us a clue to a question of great importance for an understanding of the philosophic significance of Platonic irony. It may be, as I have argued above, that one function of irony in the dialogues is to portray the presence of negativity in the world. But what is the source of that negativity? Why must an account of things include the role of negativity such that Plato might employ irony to reveal it? I would suggest that the central ontological source of negativity or finitude for Plato, and so of Platonic irony, is human nature itself: our nature as erotic.

According to the teachings both of Aristophanes and of Socrates in the *Symposium*, part of the nature of eros is that it manifests a lack or incompleteness. In Aristophanes' ribald myth, we were once double creatures, with four arms, four legs, and two heads, who, because of our *hybris*, had to be split in two by the gods as punishment for what we may call the Aristophanic version of Original Sin. Once split or rendered radically partial, we desired to join together, to become whole again, and this desire to attain wholeness out of our partiality is eros (*Symposium*, 191d). In Socrates' more sober account, love is always the love of something which it lacks (200e). In fact, then, our erotic nature has three moments. First is what we may call the ontological moment: we are as incomplete. But second, we experience or recognize that incompleteness, and third, we strive to overcome it. Any occasion in which we lack something, recognize that lack, and strive for a transcendence thereof is thus a manifestation of our eros, and this, for Socrates, includes sexual love and political ambition, artistic creativity and philosophy. To put the point differently, all human aspiration is a movement to negate an experienced incompleteness. But this negation is not merely negative. It is at once an effort to transcend that incompleteness, to achieve an *Aufhebung* of it. Eros makes human nature dialectical.

As Diotima's own myth of eros' parentage tells it, eros is the child of Poros and Penia, of Plenty, Overfullness, or Positivity, but also of Poverty, Want, or Negativity (203c). Human nature thus contains, in the incompleteness inherent in our eros, an irreducible element of negativity. To put the point in more modern terms, it is neither the world, Absolute Geist, nor economic history that is dialectical, but human nature itself.[113] But for a variety of reasons having to do with human finitude, this dialectical element in human nature is irreducible; it cannot be resolved in a final or totalizing *Aufhebung*. Our erotic natures are such that we will forever strive for a completeness that we can never attain, and which in any case, if achieved, would render us no longer erotic and in that sense no longer human. Philosophy itself, as the striving for wisdom or knowledge of the whole, is exemplary of this erotic condition. We are not wise; we recognize that incompleteness and strive to overcome it. Against a Hegelian optimism that would claim that the dialectical third in this triad is the achievement of wisdom or Absolute Knowledge, the dialogues suggest that such a final, totalizing *Aufhebung* is impossible and, even if it were possible, may not even be desirable. To say the least, human nature so construed, striving for an impossible goal, is ironic, an irony that the account of the political problem in the *Republic* imitates in considerable detail.

At the same time, the dimension of fullness or "plenty" in eros' nature also entails that eros, and the irony founded in it, is not merely negative. The paternal (Poros) side of our erotic parentage, our fullness, assures that we are not merely incomplete but overflowing; as we say in English, we "ex-press" ourselves. This "positivity" in eros is the foundation of the positive or third moment, the finite transcendence, in Platonic irony. Kierkegaard thus tells only half the story of Socratic or Platonic irony. It reveals negativity to be sure, but it also exhibits the positive transcendence of that negation. But that transcendence, to say it once more, remains necessarily finite.

---

113. There may, of course, be other sources of negativity in the world. The discussion of negation in the *Sophist* comes immediately to mind. Moreover, one might entertain the view that there may be negative forms, such as injustice or impiety. Again, appearances fall short of, and so are in a sense negative versions of, the forms they instantiate. All this is an apt subject for a longer study of the ideas, which I shall adumbrate in the final chapter. My point in this chapter is that the central focus of the negativity revealed through irony is human being itself. I wish to thank David Lachterman and Mitchell Miller for raising these important issues at an earlier presentation of this chapter at Vassar College.

To conclude this chapter: it has not been my intention to insist that every instance of irony in the dialogues conforms to this triadic, dialectical structure. Nothing prevents Plato from employing irony in its simpler, dyadic sense. Socrates' calling Thrasymachus wise in book 1 is probably an instance of this simpler irony. But I believe I have documented that in at least certain crucial cases, Platonic or Socratic irony is triadic and may even be called dialectical. This structure of irony is not merely literary but philosophical in that it is founded in and revelatory of Plato's teaching about human nature. Human life is therefore deeply and inherently ironic. Plato, I suggest, portrays this irony, this truth about the human condition, in the most appropriate and literally natural way imaginable: with irony. He thus imitates the truth about human nature. Philosophy is indeed the highest music (*Phaedo*, 61a).

5

THE WHOLE TRAGEDY AND COMEDY OF PHILOSOPHY

In this chapter I want to establish a number of points, the most general of which is that tragedy and comedy, notwithstanding the apparent "critique" of them in the dialogues, are in fact intimately connected to the movement of finite transcendence which I have been arguing informs Platonic philosophy in numerous ways.[114] Further than that, however, I want to begin the argument that philosophy itself is, or can be, an instance of that "tragicomic" movement. The first part of this chapter will therefore be devoted to eliciting the tragic element, after which I shall turn to a treatment of the comic element in philosophy.

Tragedy

In order to establish the source of the tragic character of the human situation and therefore of philosophy, I shall begin with some brief references to the *Republic* and turn then to a study of certain speeches in the *Symposium*, before returning to the *Republic* for confirmation.

The very suggestion that there might be a connection between Platonic philosophy and tragedy might seem at first strange. If the severe criticisms of tragedy in books 3 and 10 of Plato's *Republic* are taken as Plato's literal teaching on the subject rather than a provocation to the thoughtful reader, then it is hard to imagine how the question of whether there is a "tragic"

---

114. An earlier version of the first part of this chapter was published as "Philosophy and Tragedy in the Platonic Dialogues," in *Tragedy and Philosophy*, ed. N. Georgopoulos (London: Macmillan, 1993), 123–38.

dimension to Platonic philosophy could seriously arise. Unless we invoke explanations from psychopathology, how could a writer so harshly critical of tragedy knowingly include a tragic dimension within his own conception of philosophy? And indeed, many commentators, from very different schools of Platonic interpretation, have argued that the portrayal of philosophy in the dialogues is not tragic, and, according to some authors, even thoroughly antitragic. Thus Allan Bloom, in the "commentary" to his edition of Plato's *Republic*, characterizes that dialogue (it is less clear whether he would say the same for the dialogues altogether) as a "divine comedy"[115] and more recently, Martha Nussbaum, in her *The Fragility of Goodness*, devotes the central part of the book to arguing that Plato's philosophical standpoint abandons the tragic insight of his predecessors which only Aristotle restores.[116]

Yet clearly, the issue is more complex, for a number of authors have argued that notwithstanding the occasional surface teachings of the dialogues, Plato was much more sensitive to the tragic element in human life than might at first seem the case, and indeed, that there is a tragic element to his very conception of philosophy. David Roochnik, for example, argues the point superbly in his response to Nussbaum, and John Harman has recently argued that the portrayal of the philosopher in the *Republic* is a tragic one.[117] In this chapter I shall in part contribute

---

115. Bloom, *The Republic of Plato*, 381; see also 407–8.

116. Martha Nussbaum, *The Fragility of Goodness: Luck and Ethics in Greek Tragedy and Philosophy* (Cambridge: Cambridge University Press, 1986). See, for example, page 134, where the dialogues are characterized as "anti-tragic drama." Nussbaum's interpretation of Plato on this issue is successfully refuted by David Roochnik, "The Tragic Philosopher: A Critique of Martha Nussbaum," *Ancient Philosophy* 8, no. 2, (1988): 285–95. For his forceful presentation of the tragic dimension to philosophy, see his *The Tragedy of Reason* (New York: Routledge, 1991).

117. John Harman, "The Unhappy Philosopher: Plato's *Republic* as Tragedy," *Polity* 18, no. 4, (1986): 577–94. Stanley Rosen has argued consistently and persuasively that the Platonic portrayal of philosophy is somehow both tragic and comic. See, for example, his *Plato's Symposium*, 286.

to this debate by arguing, initially by appeal to the account of eros in the *Symposium*, that the account there of the human condition is indeed one with a strong tragic element (as well as a comic element, as we shall see later), and then appeal to the portrayal of philosophy in the *Republic* as confirmation of this interpretation.

I begin, strange as it may seem for one seeking tragic elements in philosophy, with a reconsideration of the hilarious account of eros presented in the *Symposium* by the comic poet Aristophanes (*Symposium*, 189c–93e). He begins his speech not with an account of the origins of eros but first with an account of the origins of human nature. We were originally very different than we are now. We were, by contrast to our present condition, double beings, with two heads, four arms, four legs, and more rounded bodies that enabled us to roll along the ground with great speed. We came, moreover, in three varieties, a double female, a double male, and a male/female pairing, divisions that Aristophanes will presently use to account for the three forms of sexuality in our present condition (189e–90c).

About this initial portrayal a number of points need to be observed. First, in an obvious sense, our original condition was "superior" to our present one; we were much more powerful and in a way more "complete." Our present condition is thus in some sense a "fall." If we keep in mind that Aristophanes begins his speech with a religious emphasis, arguing that Eros is not only a god but the god who loves mankind the most, and, moreover, that he emphasizes throughout the importance of our piety toward the god Eros (else we shall be punished by being split yet again), we can see how thoroughly Plato has had Aristophanes present a fundamentally religious portrayal of eros. For, as it turns out, though our original condition was indeed superior to our present one, it was not perfect.[118] We were characterized by a flaw, the familiar religious flaw of *hybris*, overweening pride. We desired, in what might be called the pagan version of Original Sin, to overthrow the gods (190b ff). The gods, once again consistent with the Judeo-Christian teaching, punished us by reducing our

---

118. *Contra* Nussbaum, *Fragility of Goodness*, who characterizes our original condition as "perfect and self-sufficient physical beings" (172).

condition and thereby rendering us as we are now. Zeus, with the consultation of Apollo, split us in two, and tied our skin in a knot at the front (now called the navel), so that we may look down upon it, be reminded of our former condition, and be humble (190e).

As Aristophanes tells it, Zeus' initial efforts to punish us were not entirely successful. He had three intentions: to punish us, to render us weaker so that we were no longer a threat to the gods, and to double our number, thereby increasing the number of sacrifices to the gods.[119] However, instead, we were dying off, since we spent our time doing nothing but trying to join together again with our original halves. Zeus, hardly omniscient, is portrayed as something of a comic fool. A second operation is necessary; Zeus moves our genitals around to the front so that when we attempt to join together we will procreate (at least, the male/female pairings will) and the race will be continued (191b–c).

There are a host of themes present here, some of them quite hilarious, which we can mention only in passing since they bear only indirectly on our theme of tragedy. Aristophanes here gives an account of the origins of the three forms of sexuality. Depending on what sort of original whole we were, we will, in our split condition, be either homosexual, lesbian, or heterosexual; sexual orientation is a function of genetics, not of environment! Moreover, given the significance of the episode where a second operation was necessary to ensure procreation, we can even see implicitly the traditional conservative bias in favor of heterosexuality.[120] It is only the unions of heterosexual pairings that will contribute to the continuation of our race. As for the homosexual

---

119. 190c. The Greek gods, somewhat more obviously than in the Judeo-Christian tradition, are strongly motivated by self-interest.

120. This is not contradicted by Aristophanes' later claim that "the best" of these types are the homosexual pairs, of whom the boys enter into politics when they grow up (192a). One need only look quickly at Aristophanes' plays and note the low opinion he has generally of politicians to see how thoroughly ironic this "praise" of homosexuality is. Note also that in his plays, tyrants are regularly portrayed as homosexuals.

pairings, says Aristophanes, "at least they will become satiated from the union, and stop, and turn to their work and the other concerns of life" (191c). Perhaps somewhat counter to this, it might be noted that Aristophanes, in opposition to what Diotima will later teach (206c), suggests that the urge to procreate is clearly subordinate to and, at least originally, an unconscious derivative of, the more primordial desire to join together (a priority, one might note, whose phenomenological accuracy is well attested).

Most importantly, however, Aristophanes has given us an account of the origins of eros and of our present human condition that makes them virtually identical. Eros is born out of our "fallen" condition as split, incomplete beings, and has three aspects or "moments." First, in what might be called the "ontological" moment, it is our condition as incomplete, partial. Humans are erotic because we are incomplete. But stones are incomplete too, and we do not call them erotic. The second moment in the structure of eros is that we experience our incompleteness as such, we recognize it. Third, we strive to overcome that incompleteness, to return to our original state of wholeness.[121]

Because Aristophanes is Aristophanes, he wants us to think of this triadic structure of eros primarily in terms of the sexual act itself, and so considered, it is ribald good fun. We take all those funny positions and get so passionately excited because we want to overcome our physical incompleteness and become whole again. That is what the sexual fuss is all about. But it is not difficult to see that the core of Aristophanes' teaching goes much deeper than that. In principle, all the myriad ways in which we are as incomplete, experience that incompleteness, and strive to overcome it, are manifestations of our erotic natures. This would

---

121. If this were Plato's literal view (which it is not), John Caputo's parody of the "Platonic" position (which Caputo does not seem to think is a parody) would be less egregiously in error. See his, *Radical Hermeneutics: Repetition, Deconstruction, and the Hermeneutic Project* (Bloomington: Indiana University Press, 1987). See esp. chap. 1, pp. 13–15. I cite Caputo as only one of a multitude of "continental" philosophers who completely misrepresent "Platonism" by ignoring the dramatic aspects of the dialogues. Especially given their commitment to "literary sensitivity," this misrepresentation is particularly deplorable.

certainly include political aspiration and, decisively, philosophy itself; precisely as Socrates understands it, philosophy exemplifies the condition of being incomplete (in regard to wisdom), recognizing that incompleteness (the clear pedagogical point of much of Socratic elenchus), and striving to overcome it.[122] Long before Socrates' speech, Aristophanes offers us the foundation for the erotic basis of philosophy.

Eros is not eternal; in our original situation before being split we were presumably not erotic. Eros is born out of the rendering incomplete of human beings. It is *our* nature as human. This is in clear tension with Aristophanes' explicit teaching, at the beginning and end of his speech, that eros is a god, a god who loves mankind, and one toward whom we should be pious (189c–d, 193b–d). Implicit within this religious presentation is a position that we today would call secular humanism. Eros is not a god but "alienated" human nature.

Already we can see clear implications for our theme of finitude and transcendence. For Aristophanes' speech suggests (and Socrates' speech will soon bear this out) that finitude, incompleteness, or limitation, is in fact part of our nature as human (recall the consistency of this with Socrates' account of the origins of the city in book 2 of the *Republic*). But so is the impetus to transcend it. Both our incompleteness and our desire to overcome it, says Aristophanes, are aspects or "moments" of eros. Since the ways that we are finite, and the ways we seek to transcend that finitude, are diverse, we can already see why Plato would portray this movement as occurring in such varied ways, as this book is trying to show. Nevertheless, just as we did in the last chapter in terms of the negative moment in irony, we have now located the

---

122. Why does Aristophanes fail to mention these two decisive manifestations of eros? His speech here purports to be a speech of praise. He would hardly cite in that context two modes of eros which, as his plays make abundantly clear, he considers most dangerous and the source of human disasters. But because his plays do treat political aspiration and philosophy so explicitly and critically, we can assume he is well aware of them, and that his "whole view" of eros would be considerably more qualified than the present encomium suggests.

ontological source (however mythically expressed) of our incompleteness and the "engine" of what transcendence is ours; it is our eros.

One more episode in Arisophanes' speech needs to be considered before we shall be prepared to elicit the tragic elements in Aristophanes' portrayal of the human situation. At 192d–e we are asked to suppose that Hephaestus were to ask us, as lovers, what we truly wanted. At first, we are told, we would not know, but would "speak cryptically and in riddles" (192d). If he inquired whether what we wanted was to be welded together so that we would live and die as one, we would reply that that is what we wanted all along, but could not articulate. The profound pessimism of this characterization, which Socrates's subsequent speech will take steps to qualify, should be noted. We as human beings cannot articulate our situation. We are not self-conscious; we do not have self-knowledge. We need the gods, and so religion, as a replacement for our inability to understand ourselves.

We can now turn to a consideration of the extent to which Aristophanes presents us with many of the elements of a tragic portrayal of human being. I begin with four dimensions to the human situation that are often associated with tragedy, and shall use the Oedipus story as my operative example.[123] First, a situation is tragic insofar as one is subject to a fate that is outside of one's control and for which one is not directly or entirely responsible. Oedipus is fated to kill his father and marry his mother, and as so fated, he can hardly be held straightforwardly responsible for those events. Second, part of what we are fated to is that we fight against, or strive to transcend, that destiny to which we are determined. Oedipus goes to extraordinary lengths,

---

123. I emphasize that I am not hereby claiming a "definition" of tragedy. I believe there is altogether too much emphasis by scholars on the supposed importance of definition in the Platonic dialogues. It should be noted that, with the bizarre and very superficial exception of the definitions of the four cardinal virtues in the *Republic* (428a ff), the attempts at definitions—of piety, courage, friendship, courage, *sophrosyne*, knowledge—nearly always fail. The real intent of the regular failure to "define" the virtues may well be to finally drive us away from an obsession with the closure of definition.

once he discovers his destiny, to avoid it. He leaves what he believes is his homeland and his parents, thereby, he supposes, assuring that he will be able to avoid the horrible prophecy. Third, the very activity of striving to overcome that fate in fact condemns the tragic figure to it. By leaving his "foster" home, Oedipus in fact returns to his true homeland, and the tragedy begins. Fourth, we do not understand this situation adequately. We understand our situation only darkly, at least until the very end, when our fate becomes manifest. Oedipus' slow, utterly painful awakening to self-knowledge is the substance of the ensuing tragedy.

A consideration of the human condition as Aristophanes portrays it shows at once how clearly it conforms to the tragic dimensions so far outlined. First, all humans, from the first generation of split people on, are fated to our situation as erotic: incomplete and experiencing that incompleteness. That situation is not one we can control, nor is it something for which we are directly responsible; it is the consequence of the "original sin" of our forebearers. Moreover, second, part of what we are fated to is that, as erotic beings, we are bound to strive to overcome the incompleteness we experience. That is precisely what the energy of eros is. Third, the nature of this erotic striving is such that it will never be finally successful. This is again fully obvious after the first generation of split people. The progeny of the original split generation, *born* split or incomplete, do not even have a true "other half" with whom to join. We are thus condemned not only to incompleteness but to a striving to overcome that incompleteness which is itself bound to fail. In a subtle but decisively pessimistic remark toward the end of his speech, Aristophanes says,

"Our race can become happy if we satisfy eros, and if each can find his proper beloved and return to his original, natural state. If this is the best thing, then, by necessity, what in our present circumstances comes closest to it is best for now. That is to find a love who is of like mind to oneself."[124]

---

124. *Symposium*, 193c. I follow, with some alterations, the translation of Suzy Groden, *The Symposium of Plato* (Amherst: University of Massachusetts Press, 1970).

Clearly, it is *necessary* (*anangkaion*) for us "in our present circumstances" to settle for a second best because our true aspiration, to
achieve our original wholeness, is no longer possible. Human
transcendence is necessarily finite.

Fourth, and finally, on this point, we do not fully understand
our situation, but can only "speak cryptically and in riddles"
(192d), as the episode concerning Hephaestus makes clear.

The preceding considerations have established, I hope, the
remarkable extent to which Aristophanes' portrayal of eros
presents us with an account of the human situation that contains
many of the elements of tragedy. That the comic poet presents a
portrayal that is in certain ways tragic is perhaps part of the
meaning of Socrates' insistence toward the end of the *Symposium*
that it is possible for the same man to write comedy and tragedy
(223d).

However, I have spoken cautiously of "elements" of tragedy
in Aristophanes' speech because we cannot say simply and
straightforwardly that Aristophanes' understanding of eros *is*
tragic. We cannot, because other elements of tragedy, and one
decisive one in particular, are missing from his portrayal. I am
thinking of the dimension of nobility. In Greek tragedy, it is not
simply that the tragic figure is fated to a situation wherein the
hero's efforts to overcome his or her fate are bound to fail; it is
further the case that the very effort to overcome that destiny,
notwithstanding and indeed in the midst of its failure, is nevertheless an effort that *ennobles* the hero. This is usually portrayed
symbolically by making the tragic hero be of royal lineage. But in
a deeper and more significant sense, the Antigones and Oedipuses
of Greek tragedy exhibit *noble character*. And it is this reference to
the nobility of erotic striving that is missing from Aristophanes'
account. For obvious reasons, he is much more impressed with
how foolish, how comical, eros, and so human nature, is. Notwithstanding the clear presence of tragic elements, then,
Aristophanes' speech remains a comic portrayal of the human
situation because he fails to see the element of nobility in our
tragic erotic striving. We are striving for a goal that we should
recognize is impossible to achieve, and that, as we shall later see,
is exemplary of the comic situation. To find that element of

nobility, and so to fulfill the tragic portrayal of human eros, we must turn to the speech of Socrates.

To a remarkable extent, Socrates' speech constitutes a proto-Hegelian *Aufhebung* of the previous speeches.[125] In the case of Aristophanes' speech, Socrates clearly goes beyond the comic poet's account and thus, as I shall presently argue, shows its inadequacy as a "complete speech" regarding the erotic nature of human being. But it is no less true that Socrates' speech lifts up and preserves crucial elements in Aristophanes' presentation, although, to be sure, in a different manner from the comic myth that Aristophanes sets out. Socrates begins his speech with a brief dialogue with Agathon, questioning Agathon's claim that eros both is beautiful and loves the beautiful (199c ff). The crucial premise in Socrates' refutation of Agathon establishes that eros is always eros *of* something, and moreover, of something which it *lacks*. The clearest formulation of this aspect of the argument occurs at 200e:

> "And now, said Socrates, are we agreed upon the following conclusions? One, that Love (Eros) is always the love of something, and two, that that something is what it lacks?"

It is not difficult to see that this point, established "logically," has its origin in Aristophanes' myth regarding our incompleteness. The core of Socrates' position here is that eros is founded in a "lack" or incompleteness, an incompleteness that, second, is experienced as such, and third, that eros is the impetus to overcome that lack; these are, of course, precisely the three "moments" of Aristophanes' portrayal of eros.

But Socrates goes further. Abandoning the elenchus with Agathon and turning to a recounting of the teaching that the priestess, Diotima, gave to him when, as a young man, he went to her to learn about eros, Socrates extends the significance of the essentially Aristophanic points established so far in a way that fulfills the tragic dimension to erotic striving. Indeed, Socrates,

---

125. See Stanley Rosen, *Plato's Symposium*, 2d ed. (New Haven, Conn.: Yale University Press, 1968), esp. the chapter entitled "Socrates and Diotima," 197 ff.

following Diotima, characterizes that manifestation of eros with which Aristophanes seemed exclusively concerned, personal love between individuals, as but a first, albeit necessary (210a: *dei*) and decisive step. Human eros is too complex, too multidirectional, to be exhausted or satisfied by one person, although love of an individual can certainly be part of the eros of a rich life. Still, there are other manifestations of eros, of experienced incompleteness and the striving to overcome it: the creation of laws, artistic creativity, and philosophy itself. By limiting the explicit manifestation of eros to individual love, Aristophanes, as we saw, construed eros primarily as a source of consolation for humans, and thereby failed to see in it the source of nobility. Socrates, by making explicit that eros has many other manifestations in addition to personal love, also makes more explicit than Aristophanes could the way in which erotic striving can be a source of nobility.[126] The desire for creativity or generation that eros inspires (206c ff) is the source not just of human children,[127] but of the creation of great legal traditions (Solon and Lycurgus are cited: 209d), of the creations of the great poets (such as Homer and Hesiod: 209d), and of philosophy itself, as the famous "ascent passage" at 210a ff makes clear.

What is the source of this more positive, potentially noble dimension to human eros? We are shown the source in a passage where Diotima seems to respond to Aristophanes' myth with one of her own. In answer to Socrates' strikingly strange question, "Who are eros's parents?", Diotima replies that eros is the child of Poros and Penia, of "Poverty" or "Lack," but also of "Plenty" or "Resourcefulness."[128] She goes on to describe how the child eros

---

126. I emphasize that eros can be a *source* of nobility, not that it is somehow noble "in itself." One of the ways in which Diotima establishes the status of eros as "in the middle" is that it is in the middle between nobility and baseness (202 ff). The point is that erotic striving *can* be noble, and therefore can take on this important dimension of tragic experience.

127. Although even of this creation Diotima insists there is "something divine" (206c).

128. *Symposium*, 203b ff. It is instructive that "Poros," in another of its possible meanings as "way" or "path," is the root word of the privative, "aporia," that recognition of his lack of knowledge so characteristic of Socrates' philosophic stance.

takes after both its parents, and so participates, however para-doxically, *both* in incompleteness or lack, and in a kind of over-fullness or resourceful power. If we contrast Diotima's myth to Aristophanes' (as we are clearly invited to do by the very fact that Diotima presents a myth of eros' origins), we could say that Aristophanes was far more struck by eros' maternal inheritance and failed to pay sufficient heed to its paternity. He emphasizes, and by its exclusiveness even exaggerates, the element of incompleteness in eros, but fails to recognize in the element of overfullness the source of creativity (206c ff) and nobility. Eros' parentage, according to Diotima, shows that there is something paradoxical about it; it is at once incomplete and overfull, the true child of Poros and Penia. That paradoxical character does not deny but rather makes it possible that human erotic striving could be, on the one hand, fated to fail, yet on the other hand, a revela-tion of the nobility of human aspiration; in a word, genuinely tragic.

We can thus formulate the crucial point for our argument. Human eros is not just a source of consolation for foolish humans; in its multiple manifestations, it is the source as well of the noblest of human aspirations.[129] As I have already suggested, this makes the human situation not less but more fully tragic. Not only are humans fated to a condition of incompleteness that they will never fully overcome, not only are they therefore fated to aspire toward a goal to which they are doomed to fail, but this aspira-tion, notwithstanding its fated failure, nevertheless can, in the striving, ennoble human being. The portrayal of eros in the *Symposium* therefore sets out in full richness the potentially tragic character of the human situation.

I know that this interpretation is controversial. Perhaps the most controversial point is my claim that the project of complete-ness, precisely in its manifestation as the love of wisdom, is itself

---

129. Diotima does not emphasize what is clearly compatible with this claim, namely, that eros can no less be the source of the worst of human aspirations. Plato shows his full cognizance of this by emphasizing in the *Republic* the connection between eros and tyranny (*Republic*, 573b, c, d). The *Republic* must thus be read in counterpoint to the *Symposium*, and not because Plato has "changed his mind" about eros.

uncompleteable. Could one not, after all, point to the "ascent passage," which culminates in a sudden vision of "Beauty Itself" (211a–b), and which Diotima claims is our achievement of immortality "if ever it is given to human being to be immortal" (212a) as clear evidence that the project of wholeness in the pursuit of wisdom is by no means uncompleteable but fully attainable? Could not one then turn to the *Republic*, in its development of the conditions for training philosopher-rulers who would be wise, who would comprehensively *know* the forms and rule in light of them, as further confirmation of this possibility of completeness? If so, what could possibly be tragic about a project of wholeness which is in principle fully achievable?

Such a position could be taken and has been taken, most recently by Martha Nussbaum.[130] Before leaving our consideration of the *Symposium*, then, I want to take up her interpretation of it briefly and indicate why I disagree with it so fundamentally, why, *contra* Nussbaum, I hold that the account of eros in the *Symposium*, and indeed Plato's account of the human situation, is deeply sensitive to its tragic dimension.

Nussbaum's interpretation of the *Symposium* concentrates on the speech of Alcibiades.[131] This is already noteworthy, since orthodox interpretations of the *Symposium* usually turn directly to the speech of Socrates, assuming that it will, of course, contain the core of "Plato's position." This, for example, is the strategy of Gregory Vlastos in his "The Individual as Object of Love in Plato's Dialogues,"[132] an article which, as so often is the case with Vlastos, establishes the prevailing opinion on the subject. His almost

---

130. Nussbaum, The Fragility of Goodness, esp. chaps. 5–7. A similar point is made more moderately (and implicitly) by Mitchell Miller in his *Plato's Parmenides: The Conversion of the Soul* (Princeton, N.J.: Princeton University Press, 1986). The full and "nonimagistic" access to the forms which Miller sees Plato as seriously arguing for would seem to make the project of wisdom completeable. Under these circumstances, it would be difficult to construe philosophy as "tragic." See esp. 18–25.

131. Hence the significance of the title of chapter 6 of *The Fragility of Goodness*: "The Speech of Alcibiades: A Reading of the *Symposium*."

132. Gregory Vlastos, *Platonic Studies*, 2d ed. (Princeton, N.J.: Princeton University Press, 1981), 1–34.

exclusive concentration on Socrates' speech, and his assumption that whatever is contained in that speech must be "Plato's view," leads him to criticize Plato for ignoring the significance of uniquely individual love in his concern with "universalizable" and therefore impersonal attributes. Nussbaum's recognition of the greater complexity of the dialogue form in ascertaining "Plato's view" enables her convincingly to call into question Vlastos's interpretation. Alcibiades' speech, which concentrates on the very personal, individual love of Alcibiades for that unique individual Socrates, shows clearly (as does Aristophanes' speech), that Plato was aware of the issue of, and the importance of, individual love.[133]

Nevertheless, in the final analysis Nussbaum virtually capitulates to Vlastos's central contention. While she insists that Plato was clearly *aware* of the attraction of personal love, she concludes that Plato in the *Symposium* is actually presenting us with the *choice* between *his own* view, embodied (here she concedes to Vlastos) in the speech of Socrates/Diotima, and the attraction of personal love with which he knows that he must contend:

We see two kinds of value, two kinds of knowledge; and we see that we must choose. One sort of understanding blocks out the other. The pure light of the eternal form eclipses, or is eclipsed by, the flickering lightning of the opened and unstably moving body. You think, says Plato, that you can have this love and goodness too, this knowledge of and by flesh and good-knowledge too. Well, says Plato, you can't. You have to blind yourself to something, give up some beauty.[134]

133. See Nussbuam, *Fragility of Goodness*, 167 ff, for the emphasis on individual love in Alcibiades's speech; see 173 for her recognition that Aristophanes' speech also exhibits this personal emphasis.

134. Ibid., 198. Nussbaum makes clear that she takes the teaching of Socrates' speech, consistent as it is with the "otherworldliness" of the *Phaedo* and *Republic*, as Plato's own view. See, for example, 152 ff and 192 ff. On 195 she characterizes "personal eros" as "the plague" which Diotima cures!

Having glimpsed something of the significance of the dramatic form of the dialogue, Nussbaum gives it up too soon and returns to the orthodox assumption that "Plato's view" is of course located in the speech of Socrates. I would contend that she needs to take her insight one massive step further, and see that "the Platonic view" is not contained in the speech of any single person in the dialogues, but is located in the elaborate tapestry of the dialogue as a whole. To which it may be objected with some plausibility that surely Socrates ought at least to have pride of place in our interpretations, even as he does in most (but again, not all) of the dialogues. To be sure. But then what are we to make of those dialogues, of which the *Symposium* is a good example, in which Socrates rather quickly departs from his characteristic mode of speech (for example, his brief dialogue with Agathon at 199c–201d) and instead reports what he has heard from someone else (in this case, his instruction on eros under Diotima)? At the very least, we ought to consider who it is whose speech Socrates is reporting and what effect that personnage might have on our construal of the speech. Who, then, is Diotima?

First and foremost, she is a priestess.[135] She speaks, therefore, with the authority of, but also from the finite standpoint of, religious revelation. Now this perspective is without doubt an important and thought-provoking one, but it is not identical with the philosophical standpoint. Perhaps, then, we should not facilely identify the two. We need to ask, what modifications might we have to make in order to render this dominantly religious presentation into a more straightforwardly philosophical one? That in turn forces us to ask, what is there about Diotima's speech that seems paradigmatically religious, perhaps even, from a philosophic standpoint, exaggeratedly so? One obvious candidate is the very strong "otherworldly" tendency of Diotima's position, her tendency to recommend that we "leave behind" (although she never puts it in exactly these terms, it is an easy inference from her position) the love of individuals, of the body, even of individual souls, in the name of more "universal" objects,

---

135. It is no less significant that she is a woman, though the importance of this is not directly germane to the issue I here address.

and ultimately, of "Beauty Itself" (210 ff). What is part of the exaggeratedly religious standpoint of the priestess Diotima's position, what needs to be modified in order to arrive at a more genuinely philosophic position, is precisely what Vlastos (and, finally, Nussbaum) take as Plato's own view.

The speeches of Aristophanes and Alcibiades, therefore, are not "alternatives" to Plato's own view but clues as to the direction in which Diotima's "otherworldly" tendencies need to be modified. And one thing that they both emphasize, as Nussbaum correctly sees, is personal, individual love, including, certainly, love of the body. I hasten to add, this is not to recommend going to the other extreme, repudiating entirely Diotima's position and opting instead for, say, an "existentialist" interpretation of Plato. Plato rather invites us, provokes us, to hold the positions together, to recognize and pursue the "higher," more "universal" objects of knowledge while at the same time preserving our concern for and even our love of individuals and the bodily. But, it will be objected with Nussbaum, is not preserving both concerns impossible? Precisely! The philosophic enterprise, through and through erotic, seeks to hold the whole together, as one. Without doubt that enterprise is doomed to failure. Yet even in that failure and precisely by striving to achieve the impossible, the pursuit may be the most noble of lives. And that is why philosophy, like the human erotic condition of which it is a high manifestation, is tragic.

But even if the portrayal of philosophy and the human situation in the *Symposium* is tragic, is not the portrayal in the *Republic* a clear and decisive refutation of a tragic element in philosophy? At the very least, will we not have to appeal to a "developmental" hypothesis and say that Plato "changed his mind" between the *Symposium* and the *Republic*? After all, the *Republic* presents us with an elaborate proposal, on the surface quite serious and straightforward, to educate a class of philosopher-rulers who will not be philosophers in the Socratic mode—lacking wisdom, recognizing their lack, and always seeking to overcome their aporia—but rather wise men and women, who comprehensively know the forms and who, however reluctantly, will rule with perfect justice in the light of their comprehensive wisdom. If such an education is possible, if such wise people are possible, if such a perfectly just city is possible, has Plato not decisively overcome the conditions that might lead us to view human life and philosophy as tragic? What could be tragic about living in a perfectly just city overseen by perfectly wise rulers?

In chapter 3, I have developed my position on the controversy regarding whether the portrayal of the "city in speech" of the *Republic* is to be taken as a real possibility, and to what extent. With crucial qualifications (regarding primarily the "first wave" of book 5: equal treatment and education of women and men), I concluded that the perfectly just city is not intended by Plato as a real possibility. To cite in review only the most striking evidence, the necessity of the successful implementation of the preposterous "noble lies" of autocthony and the metallic constitution of souls (*Republic*, 414b ff), the demonstrable incoherence of the arguments for the "second wave" of book 5 (the communality of wives and children, parents not knowing their true children, the bizarre sex laws, and so on), the manifestly ironic acknowledgment at the end of book 7 that the city can in fact be established "quickly and easily" by getting rid of everyone over ten years of age (541a), and the concluding remarks, at the end of book 9, that not only will the city not exist as a real city but that it does not even finally matter that it will not (592a–b)—all make clear enough that whatever the complex intentions of the *Republic*, its success does not depend on a claim that such a city is in fact possible. If I am right, then, the *Republic* does not contain, as a serious teaching, the antitragic optimism regarding the real possibility of a perfectly just regime. Indeed, part of the implausibility of such a regime is the necessity of hypostacized philosopher-rulers, who are portrayed not as philosophers in the literal sense elsewhere insisted upon and exhibited by Socrates—that is, as people who lack wisdom, recognize that lack, and strive for wisdom (and so are exemplars of our erotic nature)—but who are portrayed instead as wise people, with a comprehensive knowledge of the forms and how such forms are to be applied in governing. If such comprehensive wisdom were genuinely possible, philosophy would hardly be a tragic enterprise; but as the preceding considerations indicate, there is no reason to believe that such a possibility is real.

Why, then, present it? The concluding remarks at the end of book 9 point to the answer:

"But in heaven," I said, "perhaps, a pattern is laid up for the man who wants to see and found a city within himself on the basis of what he sees. It doesn't make any difference whether it is or will be somewhere. For he would mind the things of this city alone, and of no other." (592b)

Even though impossible, such a city is worthwhile *as a goal to be strived after,* within the soul of the philosopher. And this is just to confirm the tragic nature of the philosopher, pursuing a goal impossible to fully realize, but in doing so, indeed in ultimately failing, living the best possible life.[136] It confirms as well that tragedy is one other instance, a decisive instance, of the phenomenon that is the guiding theme of this book, that the human situation is one of experienced finitude that we are driven to overcome, but that that transcendence is always, and necessarily, finite, because human nature is always, and necessarily, erotic.

Comedy

In the *Philebus,* at 50b, Socrates speaks of "the whole tragedy and comedy of life" (*te tou Biou sumpase tragodia kai komodia*). Whatever else is meant by this intriguing phrase, it invites us to think of human life as at once tragic and comic, rather than deciding exclusively in favor of one or the other. And in turn, insofar as philosophic life is a species of life, it invites us to think of philosophy itself as containing a deeply comic dimension. That comic dimension, I shall argue in this section, is intimately tied to our guiding theme of finite transcendence.

Since Aristotle, almost everyone has agreed that comedy has something to do with the ridiculous. One of the ways that we sometimes make ourselves ridiculous, and thus become comic fools, is when we underestimate the depth or extent of our

---

136. For other ways in which the philosopher of the *Republic* is tragic, see John D. Harman, "The Unhappy Philosopher: Plato's *Republic* as Tragedy," *Polity* 18, no. 4 (1986): 577–94.

limitations and accordingly suppose that our transcendence of them can be relatively easy or even complete. The lesson that reality teaches us in this regard as it "puts us in our place" is often comic indeed. In this sense, as we shall see in detail presently, the paradigm comic situation in the dialogues is that of Socrates unmasking the pretence to wisdom on the part of his interlocutor, be he an arrogant Sophist, such as Thrasymachus, or a pompous know-it-all, such as a Euthyphro or Meno. But as we shall also see, there is a sense in which Socrates too is revealed as himself comic.

As we did with our treatment of tragedy, we might well begin with a brief general discussion of the important elements of Greek comedy. For help on this, let us turn first to Aristotle's *Poetics*, then to F. M. Cornford's *The Origins of Attic Comedy*.

We have unfortunately little text to go on from Aristotle, because book 2 of the *Poetics*, which presumably took up comedy in detail, has been lost. What he says about comedy, then, is mostly incidental and usually stated as a simple comparison to tragedy. Still, the few pronouncements we do have have been historically important. Comedy, Aristotle says, portrays people as worse than they are,[137] "worse, however, not as regards any and every sort of fault, but only as regards one particular kind, the Ridiculous, which is a species of the Ugly. The Ridiculous may be defined as a mistake or deformity not productive of pain or harm to others."[138] Thus, presumably, we are able to laugh at the (exaggerated) inferiority of the comic fool because it is portrayed in such a way as to avoid pain or harm to others. Socrates' unmasking of the claims to wisdom of the Sophists can be comic in that no harm (and possibly some benefit) is done to others and even to the Sophists themselves.

Cornford, in *The Origins of Attic Comedy*, fills in some of the blanks brought on by the loss of Aristotle's account with a much more detailed discussion of the origins of Old Comedy. In it, Cornford sets out a number of important elements distinctive of Old Comedy, including such aspects as a procession, a marriage/

---

137. Aristotle, *Poetics*, 1448a18.
138. Ibid., 1449a31.

feast, phallic elements, agons (he mentions four: the agon between death and life, summer and winter, youth and old age, good and evil), resurrection motifs, the parabasis, fertility themes, the unmasking of impostors, and ridicule.

Cornford notes that not even the comedies themselves always follow strictly the structure he outlines. We need not, therefore, discover every one of these attributes in the dialogues in order nevertheless to claim that there is a strong comic element therein. And indeed, several of these attributes are central aspects of the drama of the Platonic dialogues, especially the agonistic element and the unmasking of an impostor.[139]

It is striking how pervasive is the agonistic element in the dialogues. Of the four forms of agon Cornford explicitly mentions as characteristic of comedy, three are plainly present in various dialogues: the agon of life and death is central to the *Apology*, *Crito*, *Phaedo*, and even the *Theaetetus*; the agon of youth and old age is obviously present in those dialogues which Socrates has with youths, such as the *Lysis*, *Charmides*, and *Theaetetus*, but also in Socrates's youthful encounter with Parmenides in the *Parmenides*, and with Diotima in the *Symposium*; and the agon of good and evil is clearly if implicitly at work in Socrates' confrontation with the nihilistic doctrines of the Sophists.

No less manifest in the dialogues is the unmasking of impostors, whether they be Sophists such as Thrasymachus or Protagoras, pompous individuals such as Euthyphro or Meno, or even youths who may "think they know what they don't know," such as Charmides or Lysis. Clearly the function of the famed Socratic elenchus is precisely this unmasking, particularly the unmasking of pretended wisdom. Cornford himself makes the

---

139. Though other aspects of comedy are clearly present. Feasts are portrayed in several dialogues, such as the "feast of reason" which is the *Republic*, and the celebratory banquet which is the *Symposium*. In addition, Socrates characterizes his philosophic activity as midwifery in the *Theaetetus*, which invokes the theme of fertility in a novel—and comic—way. Third, the dialogues portray philosophy as arising out of everyday situations, which, says Cornford, is characteristic of comedy rather than tragedy; see *The Origins of Attic Comedy* (London: Edward Arnold, 1914), 204–5.

connection of comic unmasking and Socratic elenchus virtually explicit when he notes that one of the most common impostors unmasked in comedies was the "learned doctor," whom he explicitly associates with the Sophists.[140]

So by the standards of Greek comedy itself, there are clearly sufficient overlapping elements with the Platonic dialogues to raise the question as to what extent, at a deeper level, there is a significant comic dimension to the dialogues. As we turn explicitly to them, we must note two things; first, we must take account of at least the most important explicit references to comedy in the dialogues. But second, since, as I have argued throughout, those explicit pronouncements must always be taken in context and not necessarily as "Plato's theory of comedy," we must look even more closely at the dialogues themselves, at the way comedy arises within them and the way they portray the philosophic life as comic.

Many of the explicit references to comedy in the dialogues treat it as a rather dangerous phenomenon that may be used only with cautious censoring. Thus in the austere book 3 of the *Republic*, while outlining the censorship of the arts appropriate to the proper raising of children in the "city in speech," Socrates warns that the kind of foolishness portrayed in comedy encourages citizens to imitate it, and thus to act like buffoons.[141] And in the often even more austere *Laws*, we are told that comedy should be permitted in the city only if it is performed by slaves and aliens, never by citizens,[142] and moreover, that what comedy is allowed must never ridicule the citizens.[143] So if we take the Socrates of *Republic*, book 3 and the Athenian Stranger of the *Laws* out of context as simply "the voice of Plato," we could conclude simply and briefly that "Plato" is deeply suspicious of comedy and would permit it only in severely controlled and censored form.

---

140. Cornford, *The Origin of Attic Comedy*, 156–63. Cornford cites Aristophanes's *Clouds*, where Socrates is the "learned doctor" who is unmasked, as exemplifying this particular unmasking, and explicitly compares the *Euthydemus* to Aristophanic comedy (161).

141. *Republic*, 395–96.

142. *Laws*, 816e.

143. *Laws*, 935e.

The most extended explicit discussion of comedy in the dialogues, however, occurs in the *Philebus*, at 48 ff. Interestingly, even there it is not treated as a theme in its own right, but only as an example of the larger point Socrates is trying to make, namely, that pleasure and pain are often experienced together, strange as that may seem. Comedy, he suggests, is a good example of that copresence, since it is a combination of pleasure (the laughter at the ridiculous) coupled with pain (the malice, defined as "a pain in the soul" at 50a, of enjoying our friend's misfortune). In clarifying this rather curious example, Socrates suggests a number of instructive things about comedy. First, he ties it to a lack of self-knowledge (48d). Second, more explicitly, it is a lack of self-knowledge regarding the soul (48e). Third, and most explicitly, it is a lack of self-knowledge regarding the soul's wisdom (49a). To this Socrates adds that such self-ignorance is only comic if it is accompanied by weakness, so that the "fool" is unable to retaliate when laughed at (49b–c; if the ignorant one is strong, the ignorance becomes hateful and ugly).

If we were to take this as a serious "Platonic" analysis of the nature of comedy, we would probably want to say that it presents an excessively narrow portrayal of that form. Much more instructive is the fact that it fits perfectly the specific kind of "comedy" that is portrayed regularly in the dialogues. The Sophist or pompous know-it-all, ignorantly "thinking that he knows what he does not know," is shown up by Socrates' elenchus, and is unable to defend himself adequately in the face of Socrates' refutation. We might conclude, then, that the real force of the brief discussion of comedy in the *Philebus* is less to offer a general account of the genre than to point out the specific way in which Socratic elenchus, as well as other similar revelations of ignorance, should be considered as comedy. Let us turn, then, from the few explicit references to comedy toward the way in which comedy actually shows itself in the happening of the Platonic dialogues.

As we have seen, the most common and explicit manifestation of comedy in the dialogues is surely the unmasking of the pretense to wisdom. Such unmasking is often amusing to the spectators when it is done before a crowd, as in the *Gorgias,*

Euthydemus, Protagoras, or *Republic.* It is hardly surprising, then, that the person being unmasked is often upset and embarrassed at being shown to be a fool, as Socrates often enough points out.[144] Thrasymachus, we are told, even blushes![145] Usually, the "comic fool" who suffers the unmasking is a Sophist, but he need not be. Euthyphro and Meno, in their respective dialogues, are not professional Sophists but pompous know-it-alls, so self-certain in their opinions that their unmasking, too, has a comic dimension. Socrates even portrays himself, occasionally, as suffering at the hands of someone else's elenchus. It is rarely noted, for example, how dramatically amusing is Socrates' characterization of himself as learning about eros at the seat of the priestess, Diotima. Here is a young man (about eighteen?), perplexed (rather than excited!) about the phenomenon of eros which he has witnessed in others but of which he seems to have precious little experience himself. He decides to seek counsel and goes, for advice to a young man in his sexual prime—to a priestess! Diotima herself seems to appreciate the irony here, and is often caustic with her replies to Socrates. When she asks him whether he has noticed how excited humans and animals get when under the influence of eros, Socrates replies, hilariously, that yes, he has noticed it and is quite puzzled about it, thereby revealing that he has no experience of the feeling himself![146]

In a related sense, those dialogues in which a number of definitions are proposed but all are refuted, thus ending in aporia, can be understood as comedies of errors.[147] Socrates, even if ironically, often takes the blame himself for the "failures" at the end of such dialogues, thus claiming that he rather than his

_____

144. E.g., *Charmides,* 162c, 166c, 169c; *Protagoras,* 333b, 333d, 4a, 335a, 348c, 360e.

145. *Republic,* 350d.

146. *Symposium,* 207b–c. For Diotima's caustic treatment of Socrates, see, e.g., 202b, 204b, 206b, 210a. Rosen, *Plato's Symposium,* notices this; see 251.

147. It is important to note that these are not just so-called early dialogues, such as the *Euthyphro, Laches, Charmides,* and *Lysis,* but include, for example, the "later" *Theaetetus* as well.

interlocutors is the unmasked fool.[148] Whoever the specific fool, there is something comical about the endless quest for definitions that never succeed, especially when these dialogues of definition are taken in toto. Socrates can be seen in this sense as almost quixotic, questing after one definition, failing, moving undaunted on to the next dialogue and the next failed definition, then the next, without success and without it apparently dawning on him that perhaps the quest itself is foolish, at least in the form it takes.

In one way or another, then, the central comic dimension of the dialogues revolves either around the claim to *be* wise which gets unmasked, or the foolishly optimistic belief that wisdom can be *attained* (if only we can succeed in properly defining this or that virtue), a pretense, that is, to wisdom either attained or easily attainable. But what is this pretense? It is a claim to a transcendence of our finitude (in this case, the lack of wisdom) more radical or complete than is in fact humanly accomplishable. Aristophanes' account of eros as striving for a completeness we can never attain proves an appropriate account of the erotic source of the comedy of the human situation.

Let us proceed more slowly here. Socrates' undercutting of the Sophists' claims to wisdom, and so to a radical transcendence of a specific form of human finitude, is clearly comical. But insofar as philosophy itself is the striving for wisdom, and so a striving for just the sort of radical transcendence fraudulently claimed by the Sophists, is it not itself comical?

If wisdom were in fact attainable, the answer would clearly be no. There is nothing inherently comical about the aspiration to a project that is attainable, even if such attainment involves a long, arduous path. Only if the end of wisdom is impossible of attainment does its pursuit risk becoming quixotic, and so comic, a comedy based, again, on a claimed achievement (or the claimed achieveability) of a transcendence more complete than is humanly possible.

I have argued throughout this book that the dialogues portray attaining wisdom as an impossible goal: due to the

---

148. E.g., *Laches*, 200e; *Charmides*, 175a–b; *Lysis*, 223b; *Republic*, 354b (the end of book 1).

finitude of human nature itself we could never actually attain a comprehensive knowledge of the whole even if that knowledge were in principle attainable (by a god). Therefore, insofar as philosophy is portrayed in the dialogues as genuinely optimistic about such radical transcendence, it becomes comic. This seems often enough to be true, both in the explicit claims to wisdom on the part of the Sophists and others, as well as in the implicit optimism of Socrates (even if ironic) that success, either at discovering a correct "definition" of a virtue or adequately comprehending the ideas, is possible. In this sense, based on what I have argued in chapters 3 and 4, the *Republic* is one of the most comic of dialogues, even more so than the *Euthydemus*, *Hippias Major*, or *Cratylus*, dialogues often cited as especially comic. The *Republic* is comic insofar as it entertains (on the surface, and ironically, as I have claimed) the prospect of a kind of completeness, the actual establishing of a perfectly just city, complete with philosopher-rulers who have a comprehensive knowledge of the forms and so are truly wise rather than being "lovers" of wisdom. Such an accomplishment, as the *Republic* itself hints clearly, is impossible, and therefore the serious pursuit of it is quixotic and comic. It is indeed "the comedy of the city," as one commentator has noted.[149]

In the previous section, I emphasized that the dialogues have a tragic dimension rather than being simply tragedies. I wish now to make the same qualification regarding their comic dimension. If the dialogues were *simply* comedies, then the "lesson" of these comedies might be something like this: "The fraudulent claim to wisdom of the Sophists and the quixotically optimistic striving after wisdom of Socrates have shown them all to be comic fools. It would be more prudent, therefore, not to strive after such impossible goals. Be content with things as they are and must be. Accept our status as finite, limited beings, particularly as regards wisdom. Resign ourselves to what we

---

149. John Sallis, *Being and Logos: The Way of Platonic Dialogue* (Pittsburgh, Pa.: Duquesne University Press, 1975), 271 ff. See also Bloom, *The Republic of Plato*, who characterizes the *Republic* as a "divine comedy" (381).

have, which is opinion. Custom is the king; follow custom fully and reverently. Accept it and do not question it." I submit that this would be a lesson consistent with that of the conservative comic poet Aristophanes. Strepsiades in the *Clouds*, to take only the most famous example, is made to lament not only his foolish effort to transcend his financial difficulties by going himself and then sending his son to Socrates' "think-tank," but even laments his coming to the city and marrying a city woman in the first place; he should have been content with his quiet, rustic life in the country.[150] "Resign yourself and be content with your situation; you are better off that way" is one lesson of the *Clouds*, even as it would be of the dialogues were they simply comedies in the sense above described, and if Aristophanes' account of eros in the *Symposium* were adequate by itself.

But the dialogues are not comedies simply, though they manifestly have a comic dimension. They avoid the former by characterizing the philosophic stance as a subtle and complex one. On the one hand, philosophy avoids being simply comic by recognizing that the wisdom for which it strives is impossible, by recognizing, that is, that one's transcendence of everyday ignorance will never be complete. That is surely what Socrates's peculiar wisdom, as knowing what he knows and what he does not know, is all about. Yet that stance always risks becoming comic because it always risks falling into the temptation to believe that the wisdom for which we strive is indeed possible, or even occasionally that one has fully achieved it. Philosophy's relation to comedy is thus precarious, as it is in so many other ways; in its proper stance, it avoids being simply comic, but, as it were, only barely.[151]

---

150. Aristophanes, *The Clouds*, lines 40–55. John Anderson argues that an important element in comedy is the recognition that the "reality" against which one fights (or tries to transcend, as I am putting it) is one which we would be better off accepting. See his *The Realm of Art* (University Park: Pennsylvania State University Press, 1967), 109, 110, 131.

151. In an astute set of remarks on this section, Jacob Howland notes that I speak almost interchangeably of *Socrates* or *the philosopher*, but also of *the dialogues* as comic or potentially so. He is right. As I have argued

What, then, is the status of this striving after an impossible wisdom? It is, I suggest again, a kind of *finite transcendence.* It is a transcendence in that it recognizes, against comedy, that our everyday situation is not satisfactory or acceptable, that it should and can be transcended, that, indeed, the best life can be lived in pursuit of this transcendence toward wisdom. On the other hand, it is finite transcendence, in that it recognizes the impossibility of a complete transcendence to achieved wisdom. It thus neither passively accepts our situation as finite, nor does it foolishly claim comprehensively to overcome it. Rather, recognizing both the finitude of our situation and the possibility of a kind of transcendence, it responds openly to that possibility, and in so doing transforms one's life.

Tragedy and comedy in the Platonic dialogues are thus both intimately connected to eros, to our experienced incompleteness and our striving for wholeness. Were that wholeness actually attainable, philosophy, indeed human life, would be neither tragic nor comic. It becomes so because, and only insofar as, that wholeness is impossible, that is, because we are erotic. Insofar as that striving for an impossible goal is accompanied by an ennobling character, philosophy takes on a tragic dimension. Insofar is it falls prey to the temptation to claim wisdom, it becomes comic. Both qualities, as I have tried to show in this chapter, are portrayed in the dialogues, which may therefore aptly be called, borrowing from the *Philebus,* "the whole tragedy and comedy of philosophy."

---

throughout, Socrates is neither "Plato's mouthpiece" nor the unqualifiedly paradigm Platonic philosopher. It is the dialogues as a whole that portray the "philosophic situation." On the other hand, Socrates certainly occupies a special place in that domain. Hence, the complexity of the portrayal of philosophy, and so of its comic dimension.

6

TRUTH AND FINITUDE: ON HEIDEGGER'S READING OF PLATO

In this chapter I want to call attention to one of the most pervasive presences of the theme of finitude and transcendence in the dialogues, the experience of truth as it is portrayed therein. Truth, in Greek, is *aletheia*; the word is not abstract but tells us literally something of the way truth was actually experienced for the Greeks: unhiddenness. Something that has been hidden is brought to unhiddenness; the very experience of truth, then, is an experience of the copresence of hiddenness and unhiddenness. Stated differently, it is the copresence of a distinctive mode of finitude and the finite transcendence thereof. This experience, as the present chapter will show, is everywhere present in the dialogues.

No one in our time has been more sensitive to the significance of *aletheia* for Greek thought than Martin Heidegger. Yet curiously, his interpretation of truth as it occurs in Plato is oblivious to its richness. Indeed, through a misreading of the cave analogy in *Republic* book 7, Heidegger interprets Plato as abandoning the Greek experience of truth as *aletheia* rather than, as I now hope to show, paradigmatically exhibiting it. Through a critical examination of Heidegger's famous reading of Plato, then, I hope at once to call into question a misreading of Plato by no means limited to Heidegger, and to exhibit the power of *aletheia* as it is experienced in the Platonic dialogues.

I begin, for contrast, with Heidegger's well-known and controversial interpretations of the pre-Socratic philosophers. Much as, in the last century, Nietzsche's pathbreaking interpretation of the meaning of Greek tragedy scandalized more-orthodox scholars, so Heidegger's reading of the pre-Socratics, so utterly different from standard readings, has caused similar scholarly shock and initial rejection. If there is a definitive characteristic to Heidegger's readings, I suggest that it is his refusal to interpret the pre-Socratics as if these great thinkers were merely using words in their "ordinary" or everyday senses. Heidegger's strategy tends to be first to give a fairly standard translation of the fragment in question, then ask rhetorically something like the following, in regard to the Greek word *adikia* in Anaximander's fragment: "The literal translation is 'injustice.' But is this literal translation faithful? That is to say: does the word which translates *adikia* heed what comes to language in the saying?"[152] This leads to a radical, often controversial, but always thought-provoking rereading and rethinking of the fragment in the light of Heidegger's famous (or infamous) etymologies.

But whatever one thinks, finally, of the accuracy or acceptability of Heidegger's readings of the pre-Socratics and others, one can surely admire and strive to emulate the enormous care, thoughtfulness, and generosity that he devotes to the utterances of such as Anaximander, Parmenides, and Heraclitus.

In that sense, I submit, there has never been a "Heideggerian" interpretation of Plato, at least not by Heidegger himself. Compared to his exquisitely careful and always generous interpretations of the pre-Socratics, his reading, for example, of the cave analogy in *Plato's Doctrine of Truth* is cursory and orthodox to the point of tediousness. Indeed, the very attribution in the title of that essay of a "doctrine" (*Lehre*) to Plato is already a sign that the sensitivity to the *way* of a thinker, the path of thought, the questioning and questing, has been abandoned in favor of an orthodox reading of Plato's "doctrine."[153] When Heidegger wants

---

152. Heidegger, "The Anaximander Fragment," in *Early Greek Thinking*, trans. David Krell and Frank Capuzzi (New York: Harper & Row, 1975), 41. For other examples of the same strategy within this one book, see 23, 24, 30, 45, 52, 54, 59, 60, 64, 66, 70, 76, 81, 86, 88, 103, 105, 108, 112, 113, 116, 117.

153. This is so even if the "doctrine" is claimed to be what is "unsaid" in a thinker's thought, as Heidegger insists in the opening paragraph of "Plato's Doctrine of Truth." An "unsaid doctrine" remains a "doctrine."

to be sympathetic and generous to a thinker, he says things such as this of Heraclitus: "Heraclitus does not teach this or any doctrine. As a thinker, he only gives us to think."[154] Precisely from a Heideggerian standpoint, I submit, Plato no more has a "doctrine" than does Heraclitus or Parmenides, and possibly even less so, since he never speaks in his own name.

Heidegger's reading of the *Republic*'s cave analogy is defective both in its general standpoint and in its specifics.[155] The defect of the general standpoint can be seen by noticing a similarity between this reading and Heidegger's other interpretations of texts, both philosophic and poetic. I refer to his tendency not to offer "comprehensive" interpretations that go through the work from beginning to end and try to tie all the parts together into a coherent whole, but instead, in a prefiguration of the later deconstructive strategies of Derrida and others, to focus on a few sentences, phrases, or sometimes even a single word, that is, on the "margins," as a way of gaining access to the "unspoken" core of the thinker's thought. It should be obvious that the longer and more complex the work in question, the more problematic the claim to gain access to its essential thought by an analysis of a small segment. Thus, to take one extreme, it is hardly problematic for Heidegger to concentrate his analysis on a single fragment of Anaximander, since that is all we have (although his decision to accept only part of that fragment as genuine enters into controversial territory). But, to turn by

---

154. Ibid., 72.

155. For earlier critiques of Heidegger's Plato interpretation, with somewhat different emphases, see Stanley Rosen, "Heidegger's Interpretation of Plato," in *The Journal of Existentialism* 8, no. 28 (1967): 477–504. More recently, see his comprehensive study of Heidegger's reading of Plato, *The Question of Being: A Reversal of Heidegger* (New Haven, Conn.: Yale University Press, 1993). Also see Robert Dostal, "Beyond Being: Heidegger's Plato," *Journal of the History of Philosophy* 23, no. 1 (1985). Dostal notes that "the critique of Plato remains essentially the same throughout Heidegger's work" (71) and speaks of "Heidegger's lack of recognition of the proximity of his own position to that of Plato" (74). Throughout, he emphasizes the historical background in which Heidegger comes to his Plato interpretation.

contrast to the Plato interpretation in *Plato's Doctrine of Truth*, it is altogether more problematic to claim by an analysis of these few pages to comprehend not just "what Socrates says in the cave analogy" or even "Socrates' view of truth in the *Republic*," but "*Plato's* doctrine of truth." In so doing, Heidegger completely ignores a number of crucial contextual factors about which I shall have more to say later. Here I will simply mention a few of them: First, he ignores the fact that this is Socrates speaking, not Plato. I have already criticized as entirely inadequate the interpretive principle that whatever Socrates says is what Plato believes. As we have seen, one crucial peculiarity and difficulty of the Platonic dialogues is that Plato never speaks in his own name; he is both always present and always absent.[156] We obliterate that subtlety by treating Socrates as merely the mouthpiece for Plato's "doctrines." Second, Heidegger ignores the fact that in every dialogue Socrates or the leading interlocutor always speaks within a certain context, and to certain people.[157] Variations of situation (jail, private parties, the agora) and, crucially, of interlocutors (Sophists, young people, old friends—in the case of the *Republic* primarily Thrasymachus, Glaucon, and Adeimantus), mean that Socrates, much less Plato, is never speaking abstractly, universally, but always *to* given individuals, within a given context. To ignore this fact and simply leap from context-specific discussions to claims about "Plato's doctrine of truth" is surely careless, especially from one who has insisted on other occasions that his own politically loaded words must be understood in their proper context. So the basic procedure employed by Heidegger, to leap into the middle of a dialogue and without reference to context make claims about "Plato's doctrine," is surely problematic.

More specifically, the central point of Heidegger's actual analysis is that Plato brings about a fateful shift in the meaning of truth from *aletheia* as "unhiddenness" to "correctness" of looking.[158] He accomplishes this critique in a relatively small

---

156. Or in the singular case of the *Apology*, present but silent; see *Apology* 34a, 38b.

157. I have developed these considerations at length in chapter 1.

158. "Plato's Doctrine of Truth," in *Philosophy in the Twentieth Century*,

number of steps, all of which are deeply problematic. First, beginning with the important passage in which Socrates (*not* Plato) says of the "idea of the Good" (*Republic*, 517c, 4) that it is "itself master, dispensing both unhiddenness (to what emerges) and the ability to perceive (the unhidden),"[159] Heidegger almost immediately conflates the enormously difficult and mysterious "idea of the Good" with all the other ideas, so that he can say that "*Aletheia* comes under the yoke of the *idea*."[160] But this method overlooks the many decisive differences between the other ideas and the idea of the Good, quite especially and decisively that the Good is not directly knowable (*Republic*, 505a) and "beyond Being" (509a).[161] In this sense, the Good is much more akin to Heidegger's later discussions of the *Es* which "gives" Being and time.[162]

Next, quoting the passage at *Republic*, 515d, where Socrates says of the cave dweller who gets freed from his chains and can turn toward the things that generate the shadows that "turned towards things that are being more, he can have a more correct glance,"[163] Heidegger concludes that "Everything depends on the *orthotes*, the correctness of the glance."[164] Everything? Surely what gets brought to unhiddenness, and what stays hidden, remains decisive. Nevertheless from here, by the end of the same paragraph, Heidegger reaches his crucial conclusion that "Truth

---

vol. 3, ed. William Barrett and Henry Aiken (New York: Random House, 1962), 251–70. See esp. 251, 261 ff, 265 ff. I will occasionally alter the translations.

159. Ibid., 265; I here retain the Heideggerian translation.

160. Ibid., 265; see also 267.

161. David Lachterman is thus correct when he says that "The Good, the visual accents notwithstanding, bears a marked kinship to the Heraclitean *logos* as construed by Heidegger." See "What Is 'The Good' of Plato's *Republic*?," in *Four Essays on Plato's Republic* (Double issue of the *St. John's Review*) 39, nos. 1–2 (1989–1990); 169, n 21.

162. See esp. the essay, "Time and Being," in *On Time and Being*, trans. Joan Stambaugh (New York: Harper and Row, 1972).

163. "Plato's Doctrine of Truth," 265.

164. Ibid.

becomes *orthotes*, correctness of the ability to perceive and to declare something."[165]

But the issue of correct looking is already implicit in the understanding of truth as unhiddenness from the very beginning, certainly including for the pre-Socratics. For something to be brought from hiddenness to unhiddenness someone must be looking. Try to conceive of something hidden being brought to unhiddenness without someone looking. I cannot take a walk in the forest, hide, then come out of hiding, unless I suppose (even if I only imagine it) that someone is seeking me. This ought to appeal to Heidegger; he could tie it in with his claims in *Being and Time* and elsewhere that "Being needs man,"[166] or that man is the "shepherd" of Being. Good shepherds, after all, must watch, and so "look correctly at," their flock. Even in pre-Socratic thought, Heraclitus' well-known aphorisms that "nature loves to hide" and that "a hidden harmony is better than an apparent one" (to take only one thinker as an example) could hardly be comprehended without a reference to "correct looking." So to emphasize the need for "correct looking" in no sense diminishes the significance of what gets brought to unhiddenness and what remains hidden. It is surely not the case, therefore, that by calling attention to the need to look in the right direction, Plato has "changed the essence of truth."

So again, a genuinely "Heideggerian" reading of Plato has yet to be rendered.[167] I certainly do not propose to offer one here.

---

165. Ibid. Heidegger's mild qualification in the next paragraph hardly goes far enough. He goes on to support his claim by citing Aristotle's famous remark that "The false and the true are not in the act (itself)....but in the understanding" (266), as if what Aristotle said was evidence for Plato's view.

166. Heidegger, *Being and Time*, trans. John Macquarrie and Edward Robinson (New York: Harper & Row, 1962), 270, 272.

167. There is evidence that Heidegger himself later realized this. Consider his remark that the interpretation of the change in the essence of truth to *orthotes* is "not tenable." See "The End of Philosophy," in *On Time and Being*, trans. Joan Stambaugh, 70 (Heidegger does not, curiously, refer explicitly to Plato here, but the reference to "Plato's Doctrine of Truth" is surely intended.

But I would like to try the experiment of learning from the care and generosity of Heidegger's interpretations of the pre-Socratics and apply something of those interpretative virtues to a reading of Plato. If we do so, I suggest, we shall find that many of the themes present in the Platonic dialogues (though often not the explicit topic of one of the arguments) are precisely ones that Heidegger claims Plato has forgotten. My suggestion will thus be that these themes are not forgotten by Plato, but presented in the oblique or "nonobjective" way that ought to appeal to Heideggerian sympathies.[168] As we shall see, the theme of the finitude of *aletheia* is especially present in this way. At least as serious as the inaccuracy of Heidegger's explicit interpretation of Plato's supposed "doctrine of truth," then, is his failure to notice the genuine philosophical richness of the "happening" of the Platonic dialogues.

To prepare for such a reading of Plato, I want to engage in a brief recapitulation of a number of important themes in Heidegger's thinking, themes which, for the most part, were sustained throughout his career. I shall be concentrating on issues in his thought that Heidegger understands as, beginning with Plato, having been forgotten or obliterated in the history of the West's "forgetting of Being," issues which, therefore, he would claim to be "remembering" or "recalling" from the "oblivion" of metaphysics.

The first theme to which I want to allude is Heidegger's pathbreaking and sustained reflection on truth as *aletheia*, "unhiddenness." Heidegger's meditation on this word draws out the intimate connection between what is revealed in any happening of truth (what is "unhidden"), and what remains hidden or concealed. The two, he insists, are inseparable. Truth, therefore, is always also "in the untruth," finite, partial, concealing in and by the very manner in which it reveals what it reveals.

---

168. Stanley Rosen puts the point more critically: the late Heidegger is "a defective version of Platonism, namely, the attempt to elicit the senses of Being in myths, poetic dramas, and even in simple accounts of how philosophy emerges from everyday life." See "Is Metaphysics Possible?," *Review of Metaphysics* 45, no.2 (1991): 256–57.

Such a recognition flies in the face of a dominant Western, "metaphysical" conception of truth exhibited, for example, in the Cartesian notion of a "clear and distinct idea," or the Hegelian notion of "absolute knowledge," both of which presume the possibility of an *unqualified* truth, concealing nothing. Such an unadulterated revelation, Heidegger's reflection suggests, is not vouchsafed to finite human being, whose experience of truth, true to it and Dasein's nature, is always finite, partial, revealing, yes, but always also concealing.

Second, and connected to this, so it is with Being, which never brings itself to presence in totality, "infinitely" in the Hegelian sense, but always withdraws even as it comes to presence. Every presencing of Being, then, whether as idea, as God, or as technology, is finite and partial; as Being emerges into presence, again, it always also withdraws, sometimes, in some epochs of Being, more than in others. Any comprehensive analysis of a given revelation of Being, therefore, must also pay heed to the necessary way in which that very revelation is also a withdrawal of Being, in which presencing is also absence.

But, third, the articulation of this element of concealing in the happening of truth or the withdrawal of Being raises an immediate and immensely difficult problem. To articulate, to name, to make the matter for thought the subject of a set of predicates, is to bring it to a kind of presence, namely, a linguistic presence. But if the matter for thought is that which *withholds* presence, which remains concealed or withdrawn, then the very effort to articulate it runs the risk of distorting it, of engaging in the *pretense* of bringing to presence that whose very essence is not to be so. How, then, are we to speak about that which, to use another formulation, is essentially *nonobjective* in a language whose very structure (subject-predicate) invites, perhaps inevitably, the objectification of that of which it speaks?

However complex this issue, it is one that we experience virtually every day, for example, in the phenomenon that in any actual conversation what is explicitly *said* always occurs within a context, an existential or psychological background, which, without ever being brought to explicit presence in speech, is nevertheless so determinative of what is said that what we may call its "unspoken presence" dominates the discussion. A formal or "professional" conversation between two people can be informed by the unstated fact that the two have a personal antipathy for each other. Or a family gathering, superficially jovial, might be profoundly affected by the painful absence of a beloved relative. The question, again, is how we capture this "presence of (or within) absence" adequately in explicit speech without distorting it.

Heidegger struggled with this issue in regard to the question of Being throughout his career. Part of his effort has been critical. Western metaphysics, by and large, has failed utterly at this, or, stated differently, has "forgotten" or even obliterated the non-objective, that which essentially remains concealed or withdrawn, precisely in its interpretation of Being as presence. Given that view, however Being is interpreted, whether as Platonic idea, Aristotelian *energeia*, Christian God, or modern "subject" (such as the Cartesian "Ego"), it will always, in the very project of being named and having predicates ascribed to it, be turned into an object, an objective presence, and therefore, just insofar as it is *not* an object, distorted. The essentially nonobjective has thus been forgotten or obliterated in the metaphysics of presence.

More positively, Heidegger made effort after effort to speak the nonobjective in a nonobjectivizing way. This is a main source, in my judgment, of the notorious Heideggerian obscurity. At least since Descartes and probably before, the ideal of clarity and distinctness has been a virtual demand laid on philosophical speech. To be "unclear" is thus, obviously, a philosophical defect, on the basis of which bad grades are given to students and articles and books are rejected by publishers. But to be "clear and distinct" about something is almost inevitably, again, to objectify it, to make it the subject of a sentence to which "clear and distinct" predicates are ascribed; "clarity and distinctness" is therefore an inseparable accomplice of the metaphysics of presence. By these standards, to attempt to speak in a nondistorting way about that which is precisely *not* an objective presence, about that which is concealed, withdrawn, mysterious, will almost necessarily be to speak "unclearly," at least by the Cartesianesque standards of the metaphysics of presence.

Heidegger's efforts in this regard ranged from the patent and self-defeating to the more complex. Perhaps his most notorious early effort was the printing of *Sein* with an "x" through it, thus, in effect, trying literally to speak of Being *sous rature*, drawing a line through it even as he writes it.[169] More successful was the gradual "poeticizing" of Heidegger's style in his later work. Why the turn to poetry, both explicitly, in his meditations on poets such as Trakl, George, Rilke, and especially Holderlin, and stylistically in his own writing? Because even in the epochs of the greatest dominance of the metaphysics of presence, we have acknowledged in poetry what we have refused to acknowledge and even made unacceptable in philosophic speech: that what can be *bespoken* in language is often more than what is explicitly articulated as the subject of a set of predicates, that the meaning of poetic speech can never be reduced to what has come to be called the "propositional content" of the specific sentences. We thus acknowledge in poetic speech the possibility of *evoking*, literally of calling forth, that which is not and perhaps even cannot be adequately articulated in a proposition. By *not* "bringing to presence" in the mode of propositional content that which is non-objective, withdrawn, or concealed, poets sometimes nevertheless accomplish the paradox of bringing to an oblique or implicit presence that which is itself only obliquely or implicitly present, and so are true to the matter for thought. To be true to that matter for thought in this sense is thus necessarily to speak obliquely, implicitly, evocatively; conversely, to speak "clearly" according to Cartesian or metaphysical standards would be to distort, to engage in the pretense of objectifying the nonobjective. Little wonder, then, that Heidegger, in an effort to bespeak the revealing/concealing of *aletheia*, or the withdrawal of Being, should move increasingly toward poetic modes of speech. It represents, I suggest, a reasonable effort to be true to the matter of his thought.

Even in *Being and Time*, in its style and structure itself still very much part of the tradition of metaphysics, we can locate the

---

169. Heidegger, *The Question of Being* (German and English text) (New Haven, Conn.: Twayne, 1958), 80–81 ff.

beginnings of this recognition and this effort. We see it, for example, in Heidegger's plea for us to hear "the call of conscience," and in his wonderful remark that only those capable of authentic silence truly have something to say.[170] More systematically, we see it in the *Existentiale* of "understanding," one aspect of which is that we always come to any existential situation with a kind of "preunderstanding": we always know more than is explicitly stated.[171]

But it is in his later thought that Heidegger makes a much more sustained effort to find the appropriate language for a matter for thought whose essential character is nonpresence, nonobjective. In this later work, Heidegger can be accused of "talking around" his subject by his critics, but that, I submit, is precisely his intention, the only way he can be true to the matter he wishes to bring to thought and speech. It is, again, a reasonable alternative to the "clarity and distinctness" that has become the dominant paradigm of "technical" philosophic speech.

In this light, Heidegger's own obliviousness to the "dramatic" or "artistic" dimension of the Platonic dialogues is all the more striking and unfortunate. In what follows, I shall draw attention to some of those aspects of the Platonic dialogues that are "forgotten" by Heidegger in his exclusive focusing on Plato's supposed "doctrine," aspects that will show Plato's profound sensitivity precisely to those themes that Heidegger himself characterizes as having been "forgotten" by Western metaphysics, and especially by Plato.

The issue at stake is how we are appropriately to capture that larger and in part unspoken context within which all thought must take place. Plato's response is to write dialogues. But only if we read and interpret the dialogues *as dialogues* will we gain access to what is obliquely present therein. If we pay attention only to what is explicitly said by this or that character—especially by Socrates—if we conclude forthwith that what is explicitly said is "Plato's doctrine" of this or that, then it is we who "forget" the

---

170. Heidegger, *Being and Time*, trans. Macquarrie and Robinson, 316 ff, 208.

171. Ibid., 182 ff.

bestowing power of what is not explicitly present, we who participate in the "oblivion of truth" in the dialogues, not Plato. In what follows, I shall try to call attention to some of those issues and themes presented not explicitly but obliquely by Plato in the dialogues. As I suggested earlier, we shall find that much of what is so presented should be very congenial to a Heideggerian thinking.

Consider first the issue of truth as *aletheia*, the experience of which always includes the recognition of the finitude of truth, that every revealing, in the very manner of its revelation, is also a concealing, hence that there is no "absolute" or unqualified truth, no truth without limit. Heidegger claims that Plato largely abandons this originary meaning of truth in favor of truth as "correctness of vision," but I suggest that truth as *aletheia* is everywhere present in the dialogues, and present just where it should be, not in isolated speeches and doctrines, but in *what happens* in the dialogues, in the *experience* of truth as there portrayed.[172] Let me cite a few of myriad examples.

In the *Republic*, as we have noticed, eros is denigrated from the opening scene to the very end.[173] The aging Cephalos expresses relief to Socrates that he is free of the "monster," sexual appetite; eros is subject to the most rigid strictures and manipulations in the "city in speech"; the legitimacy of sex is virtually mathematicized in the hilarious and obscure "nuptial number" that is to be the measure of who should have sex and when; and in the account of the decline of various cities and individuals, eros is identified with tyranny, indeed is called "eros the tyrant."[174] Yet in the *Symposium* eros is praised throughout as divine (or at least daimonic) and the source of most of the good things in life, including philosophy. Has Plato changed his mind

---

172. In *Radical Hermeneutics* (Bloomington: Indiana University Press, 1987), John Caputo claims that *a-letheia* as Heidegger discusses it moves "over and beyond the Greeks" (183), and is something "which no Greek ever thought or said" (184). In what follows, I try to show that it was thought and said, or better, bespoken by at least one Greek: Plato.

173. The best analysis of this is Stanley Rosen's "The Role of Eros in Plato's *Republic*."

174. *Republic*, 573b, d.

on eros between the two dialogues, as orthodox commentators
have maintained? Or is the difference rather a function of who is
speaking and being spoken to, and what is being talked about? I
suggest that the latter is very much the case. In the *Republic*, the
guiding theme is the question of justice and the possibility of
justice for individuals and, by extension, for cities. The dialogue
quietly asks, what will happen if you make the justice of the city
the overriding concern of your life and of a city? What kind of a
life or city will it be if justice takes precedence over *everything*, if it
becomes the measure of all judgment and all action? *This* is what
will happen, Plato silently suggests; among other things, eros
must be suppressed and poetic inspiration (which in other
dialogues is praised as "divine madness")[175] will be rigidly
controlled and censored, along with all the other draconian
measures presented in the dialogue. The *Republic*, that is, brings
out the recognition, reveals the truth, that, by the measure solely
of justice, eros is dangerous, it can lead to the worst of human
actions, such as tyranny, it can be irrational, it needs to be
controlled. But that is not "the absolute truth," the complete
speech about eros; it is what is revealed about eros if one speaks
from the standpoint of an exclusive concern with public justice,
and in the presence of a young man, Glaucon, given to excess of
that very passion and in need of so controlling it. But it is surely
not "Plato's doctrine of eros" or even Socrates', as a look at the
Symposium, which takes place with different people and different
guiding concerns, attests.

The occasion and the participants at the *Symposium* are
fundamentally different from those of the *Republic*; it is therefore
hardly surprising, or it should be hardly surprising, that what is
said about eros is also fundamentally different. To name only a
few of the most striking features of this drinking party, it is a party
to which Socrates goes willingly in contrast with the coercion of
the *Republic*. Moreover, most of the participants are themselves
involved in erotic relationships with others present. Eryximachus
and Phaedrus are lover and beloved, as are Pausanias and
Agathon. These appear to be relatively standard homosexual

---

175. *Phaedrus*, 244 ff.

relationships. Socrates is involved in much more complicated and ambiguous relationships with Apollodorus, Aristodemus, and especially Alcibiades. Only Aristophanes is involved in no erotic relationship with another participant. Not surprisingly, then, the dominant attitude toward eros is one of praise. The *Symposium* thus presents, as it were, the flip side of the *Republic* on the issue of eros. In the *Republic* the conditions and participants are such that the dangers of eros are highlighted, whereas in the *Symposium* an encomium to eros is presented. Eros is praised throughout as the source of nobility, honor, courage, happiness, political and poetical inspiration, and—in Socrates' speech—as the source of philosophy itself.

Is the *Symposium*, then, "Plato's doctrine of eros"? No more than is the *Republic*. Given the characters and situation of the *Symposium*, the great potential benefits of erotic inspiration are revealed, while its dangers are concealed, even as the converse is true of the *Republic*. The two, not to mention other dialogues, must be read together to appreciate anything of the fuller "Platonic" attitude toward eros.

But to be "concealed" is to have a peculiar, sometimes even an ironic, kind of presence. Midst the predominant criticism of eros in the *Republic*, its positive potential is quietly present in the very possibility of philosophy and philosopher-rulers. Similarly, in the *Symposium*, the enthusiastic praise of eros does not entirely hide the recognition by some of its participants of its potential dangers. Phaedrus subtly quotes part of a line from Hesiod in apparent praise of eros's great age, the unquoted part of which warns us that eros "breaks the limb's strength, in all gods, in all human beings, overpowers the intelligence in their breast, and all their shrewd planning."[176] Pausanias, for all his lavish praise of homosexual love, recognizes nonetheless that there must be some kind of law regarding it, which implies the recognition that its unbridled excess can be dangerous. Eryximachus the doctor proposes the control of the "unhealthy" eros by *techne*, and

---

176. Phaedrus' remark in the *Symposium* is at 178b. The entire sentence from Hesiod's *Theogony* begins at line 115.

Aristophanes warns us that if we do not conduct our love affairs properly we will be punished again by the gods. So the dangers of eros are indeed hidden behind the predominant praise, but they are not entirely absent. In both dialogues, then, we see in play the Platonic recognition of the experience of *aletheia*: that revealing, the explicitly present dimension of truth, is always grounded in what is hidden, in the present-as-hidden. The dialogues, read as dialogues, teach us always of this finite character of truth.

A somewhat more general presentation of the revealing/concealing nature of truth takes place in the well-known phenomenon of Socratic aporia, his peculiar kind of "wisdom." As it is articulated in the *Apology* and exhibited throughout the dialogues, Socrates' wisdom, identical with his self-knowledge, is his recognition that he is *not* wise in the orthodox sense of "knowing the structure of the whole"; more broadly, it is his recognition of what he knows and what he does not know, a recognition that is exhibited not by assertions to that effect but by his questioning: by what he questions, what he does not question, and the manner in which he does so.

This is an enormously important and complex issue, which I have addressed more fully in earlier chapters and elsewhere.[177] Here I wish to concentrate only on what it can teach us about the way truth is at work in the dialogues. In taking his stance of aporia, that is, in preserving almost always his stance of questioning, Socrates again and again brings to presence his own self-knowledge while at once leading others, often kicking and screaming, to their own. But that very self-knowledge is one tinged with negativity. It is in part a recognition, after all, of what he does *not* know. That knowledge which Socrates does *not* have, which he *knows* he does not have, which is missing, exhibits

---

177. For a fuller treatment, see my *The Virtue of Philosophy: An Interpretation of Plato's Charmides*. For contrast, see the active scholarly debate among "analytic" interpreters of Plato about whether Socrates "knows" anything. For a good summary, see "Additional Note 1.1," in Vlastos, *Socrates, Ironist and Moral Philosopher*, 236–42.

thereby the force of its peculiar or ironic presence. What is revealed, again, is modified by what is present-as-concealed. That, and not some impossibly pure contemplation of the ideas in another world, is the way *aletheia* is at play in the Platonic dialogues.

A third way in which the revealing\concealing character of truth is exhibited in the dialogues is contained in the very fact that they are dialogues, between individual people in specific and sometimes defining situations. It is one thing to compose philosophical essays in the first person, written out of no specified situation, to no specific audience, thereby implying that what the writer says is true for anyone, anywhere. Most of the philosophic works in our tradition do something like this, and it is neither surprising nor inappropriate that we speak with such ease of "Kant's doctrine" of this, or "Locke's doctrine" of that. But Plato does no such thing. Every dialogue is between specific people who are never "everyman," although they usually represent certain character types. Each person and each situation is presented so that the thoughtful reader can notice what can be revealed by (and to) that person with that standpoint, and also what is, what perhaps must be, concealed. Let me cite briefly two of a multitude of examples.

Socrates presents the core of his speech in the *Symposium* as having come from his instruction on erotics from his teacher, Diotima. Three things are especially striking about Diotima: she is a woman, introduced by Socrates into this largely homosexual party after the flute-girls had been earlier dismissed; she is a priestess; and she is a stranger, the only non-Athenian in the *Symposium*. Consider here, as I did previously, only the fact that she is a priestess. This means that whatever she says about eros, it is spoken from the standpoint of religious priesthood. It therefore can reveal all that that venerable calling has to offer, but it is also subject to the limitations, the finite constraints, of that standpoint. In a thoughtful reading of that speech, would we not have to "deconstruct" the religious dimension of that revelation (as I began to do in chapter 5), that is, be aware both of the insights of that standpoint but also of its limitations? Yet how often is

Diotima's speech in the dialogue quoted straightforwardly as "Plato's doctrine of eros"?[178]

Consider as a second example that set of dialogues regarded as so decisive especially by philosophers of a technical bent, the *Sophist* and *Statesman*. In those dialogues, Socrates is present but almost entirely silent, a phenomenon on which I shall comment presently. The leader of the discussion is the Eleatic Stranger, a partisan of Parmenides of Elea. Now it is obvious to anyone who studies the Platonic dialogues that Plato has been profoundly influenced by Parmenides. But it should be no less obvious that he is not *simply* a Parmenidean who has taken over the Parmenidean standpoint without qualification or critique. How, then, could we possibly take the words, or the philosophic methods, of the Eleatic Stranger as "Plato's view"? Would it not be more fruitful to read those dialogues as presenting both the insightfulness and the limitations of that Eleatic standpoint, as an exhibition of what it reveals and what it conceals?[179]

These examples could have been replaced by ones from virtually any dialogue. Surely the fact that nearly everyone present at the *Phaedo* is a Pythagorean has something to do with why Socrates presents such straightforwardly Pythagorean arguments for the immortality of the soul in that dialogue. Surely the fact that he is talking to two young friends in the *Lysis*, or to two brothers in the *Republic*, one of whom is a potential tyrant, has something to do with what Socrates speaks about and the way he speaks. Surely in no dialogue, therefore, should we ignore these crucial existential factors and pretend that we are in the presence of an unqualified revelation of "Plato's doctrine." On the contrary, we are always in the presence of *aletheia*, of revealing and concealing, and to allow that to be is Plato's intention in writing dialogues.

---

178. As an example, see my discussion of the Nussbaum/Vlastos debate in the previous chapter.

179. Thankfully, this has been done by some authors, most notably Mitchell Miller in *The Philosopher in Plato's Statesman* (The Hague: Martinus Nijhoff, 1980) and *Plato's Parmenides: The Conversion of the Soul* (Princeton, N.J.: Princeton University Press, 1986), and by Stanley Rosen in *Plato's Sophist: The Drama of Original and Image* (New Haven, Conn.: Yale University Press, 1983).

This much should now be clear; truth as *aletheia*, unhiddenness, is in no sense "abandoned" in the dialogues. To the contrary, they are steeped in precisely that experience. As the examples I have discussed demonstrate, the portrayal of truth in the dialogues at once recognizes the finite origins of the experience, yet recognizes as well the possibility of a transcendence, a transcendence, however, that is also always necessarily finite. Socratic aporia is perhaps the paradigm and most pervasive example of this recognition.

A second important but "forgotten" theme to which Heidegger rightly calls our attention is the power and, again, the peculiar presence, of the unsaid, of silence, of that which is strikingly absent. Like *aletheia* to which they are clearly related, these themes too are present in the dialogues not in specific speeches or arguments which thematize them, but in the exigencies of the dialogue itself. Let me begin with the theme of silence, and first, with the occasional silence of Socrates.

When Socrates is present in the dialogues, he is usually the dominant speaker and questioner. There are, of course, dialogues where he is not even present, such as the *Laws*. But there are several dialogues, such as the *Timaeus, Sophist,* and *Statesman,* where Socrates is present but, for the most part, silent; in the *Timaeus,* Timaeus is the main speaker, and in the *Sophist* and *Statesman* the Eleatic Stranger dominates the discussion. This silence of Socrates is often enough noted but rarely made thematic by commentators on these dialogues. I suggest that a failure to do so, and especially the all-too-easy substitution of the other individual for Socrates as "Plato's spokesman," manifests our own insensitivity to the happening of the dialogue. Perhaps, consistent with the drama of the dialogue, we should attribute as much significance to the silence of Socrates as we would to the striking silence of a well-known and usually forceful person in our own midst. What does it mean? Is it an implied disapproval? A distancing from the physical speculations of the *Timaeus* or the "technical" philosophy espoused by the Eleatic Stranger? We need not definitively answer the question here to recognize that it should be a question raised by a thoughtful attention to the significance of silence.

Second, there is the noteworthy silence of other characters in the dialogues, for example, of Thrasymachus after book 1 of the *Republic*, of Cleitophon in the same dialogue, or of Philebus in the dialogue of that name. Thrasymachus' initial silence at the beginning of book 2 might plausibly be explained by his embarrassment at having just been bested in argument by Socrates, but can we really imagine that such a domineering personality would have nothing further to say about the issues discussed in the ensuing nine books?[180] Should we not wonder what he might have to say, and what validity it might have?

The cases of Cleitophon and Philebus represent a different case, the silence of refusal. Both refuse to participate in the dialogue of philosophy, refuse to risk having their views questioned. But by that refusal they gain something most thought-provoking: they cannot be refuted. The silence of refusal to participate in philosophic dialogue represents a limit to the very possibility of philosophy; philosophy can only penetrate, can only be efficacious, for those who allow themselves to participate. There are people and positions that philosophy thus cannot either refute or incorporate due to the silence of refusal.[181]

Third, there is, occasionally, the silence of the arguments themselves. Perhaps the best example of this is the one I discussed in the first chapter, the strange admission at the end of the *Crito* that not all the arguments for escaping have been considered. But consider also the curious fact in the *Symposium* that Aristodemus, recounting the speeches at the party that he remembers, does not seem to remember his *own* speech, or that after Socrates' speech we are told that Aristophanes was about to

---

180. Diskin Clay shows sensitivity to the various silences in the dialogues in his "Reading the *Republic*," in *Platonic Writings: Platonic Readings*, ed. Charles L. Griswold (New York: Routledge, Chapman, & Hall, 1988), 22–23. Consider also his remark concerning the founding act of injustice which originates Kallipolis: "About this, Socrates, Glaukon, and Adeimantus are silent, precisely where Plato is not" (27).

181. I owe this insight entirely to David Roochnik. See, for example, his fine article, "The Riddle of the *Cleitophon*," in *Ancient Philosophy* 4 (1984): 132–45, and his fuller discussion in *The Tragedy of Reason* (New York: Routledge, 1990).

respond to Socrates but was interrupted by the entrance of Alcibiades,[182] or in the *Republic*, that Socrates never in fact responds to the challenge issued by Glaucon in book 2 to show that the just man, stripped of the rewards of a reputation for justice and saddled with one for injustice, would nevertheless be happier than an unjust man with a reputation for justice. In each case, the manifest silence of the arguments stands as a provocation to the reader. We are invited to wonder what the arguments are that are missing, why they are absent, and how the dialogue would change if they were invoked.

I spoke earlier of the significance of the silence of refusal, as in the case of Cleitophon and Philebus. There is a no less significant silence which we occasionally experience, the phenomenon of silent presence, about which Heidegger is rightly sensitive. This silent presence, I suggest, is everywhere in the dialogues, if only we will be open to it. Consider a particularly striking example, one appropriate in a chapter invoking the thought of Heidegger. If one pays attention to the dramatic time of the dialogues, we notice a remarkable intensity that characterizes the last weeks of Socrates' life. Begin with the *Theaetetus*, which ends with Socrates saying that he must now go to the porch of the king-archon to answer the charges against him, but urging Theodorus that they should meet again tomorrow (when the *Sophist* takes place). If we think through the dramatic time carefully, we see the following sequence of dialogues, all in the last fortnight or so of Socrates' life: *Theaetetus*, *Euthyphro* (apparently on the same day!), followed on the next day by the *Sophist*, on the following day (?) by the *Statesman*, then, presumably, the "lost" *Philosopher*, then, apparently within a day or two, the *Apology*, followed shortly by the *Crito* and *Phaedo*. Should we not wonder at the peculiar intensification of Socrates' philosophic activity as he nears the end of his life? Why might it be? Might the silent presence of his impending death be giving to Socrates' activity a special urgency and stake? Should we not consider the dramatic if silent impact of Socrates' "Being-toward-death"?

---

182. *Symposium*, 212c.

Finally and decisively, there is the silence of Plato himself, concerning which so-called esoteric interpreters of Plato render elaborate interpretations while other scholars completely ignore it. As I suggested earlier, the situation is complex because, given the nature of the dialogue form, Plato is in one sense silent, even absent (his name is mentioned twice in the *Apology*, where he is present but silent and once in the *Phaedo*, where we are told that he is absent), but in another sense, as the author of every dialogue, dominantly present. The question is how to interpret this "Platonic anonymity?"

The easiest response, the one predominant in the Anglo-American scholarly tradition and, unfortunately, adopted by Heidegger, is to virtually ignore it by assuming that whatever the leading character in any dialogue says is, more or less, "Plato's doctrine" concerning whatever is being discussed. This view has been widely and successfully refuted as entirely too simplistic and, in fact, rendering the dialogue form itself a gratuitous literary flourish. At the other extreme is the "esoteric" tradition that suggests that Plato's views are *not present* in the dialogues, that our only clue to them is what we can glean from the doxographic tradition regarding Plato's lectures at the Academy.

My own response to this problem has been developed in detail throughout this book and elsewhere.[183] For the purposes of our contrast with Heidegger's reading, we need only note, critically, that Heidegger has himself failed to "hear" the silence of Plato while being aware only of his presence as author, an ironic defect for this great spokesman for the significance of silence and withdrawal. More positively, however, we can recognize in Plato's ambiguous "place" in the dialogues one more manifestation of his profound sensitivity to the fact that in human things almost never is something completely given or completely absent, that human experience is almost always a complex and profound

---

183. For example, see my "Why Plato Wrote Dialogues," *Philosophy and Rhetoric* 1, no. 1 (1968): 38–50 and *The Virtue of Philosophy: An Interpretation of Plato's Charmides.*

tapestry of presence, absence, and presence-as-absence, of revealing and concealing, of *aletheia*.[184]

So is Plato some sort of proto-Heideggerian? That would be an absurd claim. My point has been, critically, to demonstrate how impoverished Heidegger's reading of Plato has been, and more positively, to demonstrate that there is much in the dialogues that is in fact commensurate with Heidegger's thinking, and so that Plato should present a much more complex and thought-provoking "problem" for Heidegger than Heidegger has allowed. But to do so is not at all to suggest that the two are identical or even "the same." I close this chapter by citing only one decisive difference that remains between the two thinkers, one that bears clearly on our guiding theme of finitude and transcendence. To do so, I shall appeal again, as I did at the beginning of the chapter, to the pre-Socratics.

If we take the general views espoused by Thales, Anaximander, and Xenophanes, we can see that right from the beginning three—perhaps *the three*—decisive philosophic possibilities are established. Thales suggests to us that wisdom, in the sense of knowledge of the structure of the whole, is possible. The *arche* of the whole is intelligible—it is water—and accessible to human thinking (*"Nous* is quickest of all, and runs through

---

184. Why is Heidegger so oblivious to the richness of Plato's writing, and even to its affinity with his own thought? I offer two speculations, one psychological, suggested to me by William Richardson, one more philosophical, suggested to me by Charles Griswold. Psychologically, Heidegger may have been so deeply committed to his account of the "history of Being," which depends so decisively on the critique of Plato as at the roots of the "forgetting of Being," that, even after he recognized its untenability, he could not bring himself to give it up. More philosophically, one dimension of the fact that Plato wrote dialogues is that he always shows philosophy as arising out of a more or less explicitly *political* situation (in the literal sense of the *polis*), in terms of which even abstract philosophic thought must be understood. But Heidegger always claimed in behalf of philosophy, fundamental ontology, or later, "thinking," that it is completely independent of the political. Believing this, perhaps it is less surprising that he ignored the explicitly political dimension of the dialogues.

everything."). He thus presents us with the prototypical version of philosophic optimism that continues through the development of modern science at least to Hegel. The world is "through and through rational," and wisdom is possible.

To this optimism Anaximander articulates the resounding counter. The *arche* is itself inarticulable, inaccessible to human thought, not due to any lack in *our* nature but because of the nature of the *arche* itself; it is *to apeiron*, the indefinite. There is an element of irreducible, primordial mystery in the whole, and its source is, to use a later term, Being.

Xenophanes next articulates a decisive alternative. He agrees with Thales that the whole, including the *arche*, is *in principle* intelligible. Indeed, God knows the whole: "God sees as a whole, thinks as a whole, and hears as a whole" (Fragment 24). "Without toil he sets everything in motion, by the thought of his mind" (Fragment 25). On the other hand, but for a decisively different reason, he agrees with Anaximander that mortals cannot in fact know the whole, not because the *arche* itself is unintelligible, but because we are mortal: "And as for certain truth, no man has seen it, nor will there ever be a man who knows about the gods and about all the things I mention" (Fragment 34). That is, with Anaximander, there is an element of irreducible mystery in the world, or stated differently, the truth vouchsafed to human being is necessarily finite, but the locus of the mystery, of this necessary incompleteness in human knowledge, is not in Being but in us.

These three early but decisive philosophical standpoints having been established, we can now return to the contrast of Plato and Heidegger. Plato is a Xenophanean, Heidegger an Anaximandrean.[185] Both, as I have tried to emphasize, recognize the irreducible mystery, the revealing/concealing character of truth as it is given to humans. For Heidegger, the locus of that mystery is in Being itself, in the way "it gives" itself as always revealing and concealing. But for Plato, the many discussions of

---

185. Both attributions are obviously sweeping generalizations to make my point, and both would need careful nuancing if developed fully.

the ideas suggest that Being is *in principle* intelligible,[186] yet not to finite human being, because of *our* nature as finite, as erotic, as aporetic. Truth remains finite, at once revealing and concealing, but for a decisively different reason.

To put the point perhaps too baldly, for Heidegger, Being is itself the most fundamental source of the *instability* in the human experience of things, whereas for Plato, Being, or the ideas, is the most fundamental source of what *stability* there is in an often unstable, even chaotic, but always finite experience of the world.

Does this mean that Heidegger is finally right about Plato, that the discussions of the ideas suggest a reduction of Being to "presence"? Yes and no. Yes, in that the ideas usually are portrayed as the permanent source of the intellibility and the being of things. No, because given the nature of human being as erotic, therefore as incomplete, finite, aporetic, there will always remain an irreducible element of incompleteness, of aporia, and so of mystery and even absence, in the human experience of things. However, its source, for Plato, is not Being itself but human being.[187]

Plato "gives us to think" in the dialogues, and not just with explicitly articulated "theories" and "doctrines," of forms, immortality, or draconian political systems. He gives us to think as well by presenting us, in an especially dramatic way, with the revealing and concealing, the articulation and the silence, of truth as it might actually happen in a thought-ful human life. In so doing, he invites us to be sensitive to many of the themes so important in Heidegger's thinking, as I have tried to show. But the dialogue form also allows him to present the crucial themes of

---

186. Leaving aside until the next chapter the peculiar status and profound problem of the idea of the Good. Nicholas White alludes to what I here characterize as Plato's "Xenophaneanism" in his "Observations and Questions about Hans-Georg Gadamer's Interpretation of Plato," in *Platonic Writings, Platonic Readings*, ed. Charles Griswold (New York: Routledge, 1988), 249, 256.

187. This claim, again, will need to be qualified by a discussion of the Good as "beyond being"; see *Republic*, 509c. I shall address this issue in the final chapter.

aletheia, withdrawal, and silence in a way true to their own nature, obliquely, implicitly, as instantiations of the finitude of human transcendence.

7

BUT WHAT ABOUT THE IDEAS?

But what about the Ideas? How do Plato's many (but, as we shall note, not ubiquitous) discussions of the ideas or forms[188] fit in with the interpretation of the dialogues I have been rendering? We can begin by noting that the ideas, when considered with regard to our guiding theme of finitude and transcendence, would seem to present an initial problem for my interpretation. Consider first what we can take to be an "orthodox" or standard interpretation of the ideas (to the extent that such a notion is even coherent in Platonic scholarship). The ideas are the principles of intelligibility and of the being of the things of our experience, of phenomena. They are the eternal, changeless intellectual entities that we genuinely know when we say that we "know" something about our world. Therefore, insofar as we "know" an idea (say, "The Equal Itself"), we know what equality is in its various instances, and insofar as we have a comprehensive knowledge of all the ideas (or at least those most important for our lives), we are wise. Moreover, not only do some of us "know" this or that idea, at least a small number of us know the ideas comprehensively, and so are wise. To be sure, different dialogues present different versions of this possibility. Dialogues such as the *Meno*, which introduce the myth (often mistakenly referred to as a "doctrine")

---

188. For the purposes of this chapter, it will not be necessary to honor the subtle distinction between "form" (*eidos*) and "idea" (*idea*). I shall use the terms interchangeably. This is a good time to emphasize, in addition, that the following chapter in no sense claims to be a comprehensive interpretation of the ideas, as if that were possible in a single chapter. The point of my presentation is to show how the ideas fit into and support the general interpretation of Plato I have been presenting.

of recollection, tell us that we all, or at least many of us, had such comprehensive knowledge before we were born, in our previous, disembodied lives. We "forgot" this comprehensive knowledge during the travails of birth, and "learning" during our present, embodied lifetime is a process of "recollecting" our previous knowledge. Compatible with but different from this, dialogues such as the *Phaedo* suggest that, though we cannot know the ideas (and so cannot have true knowledge of what is) during our present lifetime, our disembodied souls can know the ideas after we "die" ("death" here is defined merely as the separation of the soul from the body), when the soul takes flight into the "realm" of ideas. Hence, philosophy, which seeks to know the ideas or be wise, "is a preparation for dying."[189] Perhaps even more optimistically, the *Republic* (if we take its surface meaning as definitive—against the interpretation I have been espousing) argues that at least a certain small group of people, under the right educational conditions, can be brought to a comprehensive knowledge of the ideas in this lifetime—about the age of fifty or so—and can rule in the light of that comprehensive knowledge. If we take only these three dialogues together, then, we get this teaching: one way or another, either in this life, the previous one, or the next one, thorough, comprehensive knowledge of the ideas, or wisdom in the quasi-technical Greek sense of "knowing the structure of the whole,"[190] is possible for human beings. Indeed, the period of time when we do *not* know the ideas, namely, that duration of embodiment which we call our "lifetime" (prior to the age of fifty in the case of correctly educated "philosopher-rulers") is but a brief, if epistemologically painful, interlude.

The above summary, of course, risks parody. Nevertheless, if anything like it is accepted, even if suitably filled out with elaborate "proofs" of a previous life and immortality, of technical accounts of the nature and structure of the ideas, and of step-by-

---

189. *Phaedo*, 64a.
190. This is the sense in which, presumably, the philosopher-rulers will be "wise." Consider also the formulation of Critias's definition—as Socrates elicits it—of *sophrosyne* as "the science of itself and of the other sciences and of the absence of science" (*Charmides*, 166e ff).

step educational plans for preparing us to know them, then all my talk of the necessary finitude of human transcendence, of aporia as definitive of human philosophic living, of eros as the human condition, can be decisively overcome. At least one massively important mode of complete transcendence is possible: wisdom.

In previous chapters I have adumbrated why I do not regard even the gist of the above outline as an adequate characterization of the standpoint of the dialogues. The task of this chapter is to set out with some adequacy how the various discussions of the ideas fit with the interpretation I have been rendering. But before turning to that, it is perhaps worth considering an alternative interpretation of at least some of the dialogues, an interpretation sometimes ascribed to "Socrates" (as opposed to "Plato"). This view takes as a group the so-called aporia dialogues, from "early" dialogues such as the *Lysis*, *Charmides*, or *Laches* to "middle-late" ones such as the *Theaetetus*, and considers them, with this or that qualification, as "genuinely Socratic." In these dialogues, there is no explicit mention of the ideas. Without the ideas, the aporia with which each of these dialogues ends, where the highest human achievement in these matters would seem to be the aporetic one of recognizing that we do not have genuine knowledge, is portrayed as the human condition, at least in this lifetime. Almost as a pole to the optimistic view outlined above as orthodox "Platonism," this view often attributed to Socrates would seem to hold that there is no genuine transcendence at all, or, at most, the rather unsatisfying one of "knowing that my wisdom is worth nothing at all."[191]

It should be clear that the discussions of the ideas function in part to moderate the "pessimism" of this latter, "Socratic" view. One can then even explain the difference between the "aporia" dialogues and those that contain discussions of the ideas as

191. *Apology*, 20e, 21b, 23a. Vlastos, of course, is one of the most famous exponents of this view; see throughout his *Socrates, Ironist and Moral Philosopher*. Vlastos labels the *Lysis*, among others, as "transitional" dialogues (transitional from "the historical Socrates" to "Plato's mouthpiece"), and the *Theaetetus* as a "middle" dialogue. See his chapter 2, "Socrates *Contra* Socrates in Plato."

Plato's movement "beyond" his teacher, Socrates. But if, on the one hand, the optimism of the "Platonic" position outlined above is unfounded, if wisdom in the comprehensive sense is impossible, yet on the other hand, if the sheer epistemological pessimism attributed to the "Socratic" position is excessive, what, then, is the role of the ideas in human life, and what modes of transcendence do they render possible? The task of the present chapter is to begin a response to that massive question.

I want to begin with a set of observations about the way the ideas or forms appear in the dialogues, observations that are independent of each other but that, taken together, will, I hope, furnish the material that will make the interpretation I subsequently develop plausible and persuasive (this, I think, is about as much as one can hope for in regard to the ideas). Before doing so, this is a good place to reiterate my insistence that what follows in no sense claims to develop a comprehensive interpretation of Plato's view of forms or ideas, but only to say enough about it to show how it coheres with the overall interpretation of Plato I have been rendering.

My first observation concerns the way modern scholarship, from the nineteenth century on, tends to discuss the ideas. With few exceptions, modern scholars have referred to and interpreted Plato's discussions as the "theory of ideas" or "theory of forms." Inseparable from the use of that phrase is the concomitant use of what have become technical philosophic terms: "epistemology," "metaphysics," and "ontology." Thus we read regularly of such things as "Plato's earlier metaphysics," "Plato's middle epistemology," or "Plato's late ontology." Now these scholars know well that there is not a single mention in any Platonic dialogue of a "theory" of ideas or forms. Nor does any character in any dialogue use the words "epistemology," "metaphysics," or "ontology." Presumably, therefore, they regard the imposition of these notions on the issues discussed in the dialogues as harmless, perhaps even as helpful. I wish to join with the growing number of commentators who, to the contrary, regard such attributions as inaccurate, misleading, and harmful. My main objection to their use is that each of these terms implicitly invokes nineteenth-century, post-Hegelian notions of a "system," some sort of unified, quasi-scientific "theory," for which there is virtually no evidence in the dialogues themselves. Once such systematic assumptions are imposed on the dialogues, all sorts of interpretive mischief ensues. Since Plato was a sophisticated thinker (at least for "his time"), we must be able to discover, at least germinally, his various "theories," his "epistemology," "metaphysics," and so on. But since, in turn, such a unified system is not there, we are driven to alternative hypotheses such as the "developmental" view (there is no systematic view presented of Plato's theories because he kept changing his mind as to what his theory was; but of course, at any point in his career, he *did* have "theories"), and even the view of the "esotericists" (since no systematic theory is presented in the dialogues, the dialogues must not contain Plato's true philosophy—that is, his systematic theory—which he must have reserved for the members of the academy, or the like.). I shall have more to say about these interpretive standpoints presently. For now, the point is that they all begin with what I believe is an unjustified assumption, the imposition of rather late modern measures of philosophy as necessarily systematic, (therefore containing a set of "theories," technical terminology, and so on), measures that not only are not acknowledged in the dialogues themselves, but are even antithetical to the dialogue form in which Plato has chosen to present his thinking to the public.[192]

But, to return to an objection discussed briefly in my first chapter, surely Aristotle spoke regularly of Plato's "theory of forms," so we can hardly blame this way of reading the dialogues on modern scholarship! If one consults English translations of Aristotle, one surely gets that impression. We read, for example, in the most widely read translation, that of W. D. Ross, in the famous discussion of Plato in *Metaphysics M*, of Plato's "Ideal theory."[193] Vlastos translates the same phrase as "the theory of

---

192. For a compelling suggestion that a similar situation holds with Aristotle's philosophy, see Helen Lang's "The Structure and Subject of *Metaphysics Lamda*," *Phronesis* 38 (1993): 257–80.

193. W. D. Ross, *Aristotle's Metaphysics*, vol. 2 in *The Complete Works of Aristotle*, ed. Jonathan Barnes (Princeton, N.J.: Princeton University Press,

Ideas."[194] But the Greek at 1078b9 is *ten kata ten idean doxan* and at 1078b12 *he peri ton eidon doxa*, which should be translated as "the *opinion* about the ideas" and "the *opinion* concerning the forms."[195] So far as I can determine, this is Aristotle's regular way of referring to Plato's discussion of the ideas. Further, I would argue that Aristotle has it just right, contrary to his English translators; Plato's "opinion" about the ideas or forms strikes me as an entirely felicitous way of speaking of them. So we cannot simply blame Aristotle, if we read him carefully, for the transformation of Plato's writing into a body of "theories."

I therefore agree with those writers who have denied that Plato is even trying to be a "systematic" thinker, and in particular that he has anything like a "theory" of ideas. W. Wieland has developed a sustained and explicit argument for this position.[196] John Sallis has stated the case in the strongest possible terms when he says that "it is highly questionable whether there is any such thing as the philosophy of Plato."[197] Stanley Rosen, in a number of articles and books, has argued for a similar point. As early as his *Plato's Sophist: The Drama of Original and Image*, he argued that "There is no general concept of a form or idea in the Platonic corpus. Each version of the ostensible theory of forms must be studied in its own right, not assimilated into a non-existent comprehensive doctrine."[198] Most recently, he has asserted that "As to the 'theory of Ideas,' it is an invention of

1984), 1078b9, 1078b12. Hippocrates Apostle, in his *Aristotle's Metaphysics* (Bloomington: Indiana University Press, 1973) and Richard Hope, in his *Aristotle—Metaphysics* (Ann Arbor: University of Michigan Press, 1960) translate such passages only slightly less misleadingly as Plato's "doctrine of Ideas."

    194. Vlastos, *Socrates, Ironist and Moral Philosopher*, 91.

    195. My emphasis. Liddell and Scott contain no listing for "theory" or "doctrine" as a translation of *doxa*; see *A Greek-English Lexicon* (Oxford: Clarendon Press, 1985), 444.

    196. W. Wieland, *Platon und die Formen des Wissens* (Gottingen: Vandenhoeck & Ruprecht, 1982), 125–50.

    197. Sallis, John, *Being and Logos: The Way of Platonic Dialogue* (Pittsburgh: Duquesne University Press, 1975), 1.

    198. Rosen, *Plato's Sophist*, 50.

nineteenth-century historical scholarship. Despite much quasi-mathematical rhetoric, Plato presents us with a series of discontinuous poems about the Ideas."[199] As a final example, consider Charles Griswold's remark that "we repeatedly find that in his discussions about knowledge Plato just *assumes* or *asserts* that the Ideas exist, and *then* explains what 'knowledge' is (for example, *Rep.* 476a ff., 507a–b ff., 596a and context; *Pho.* 100b ff.). We do not seem to get an account of how we know these ontological assumptions to be true. Indeed, one is justified in wondering whether Plato has a 'theory' of Ideas at all."[200] I cite these several sources to indicate that there is a growing number of writers (though still a distinct minority) who are calling into question the assumption that Plato can best be understood as presenting a "theory" of ideas or of anything else. That this position is having a difficult time getting a hearing (it has not been refuted, simply ignored by more orthodox scholars) is, I suggest, an indication of how deeply imbued the modern "systematic" assumptions regarding Plato have become.

My second observation concerns the extent of the discussions of ideas within the dialogues themselves. On this point we should note first that many dialogues either do not raise the issue of the ideas at all or do so only implicitly. When they are discussed explicitly, that discussion almost always arises in a context *other* than a thematic discussion of what we would now call the "epistemological" or "ontological" status of the ideas—constructing a just city, defining a Sophist or a statesman, or under-

---

199. Stanley Rosen, "Is Metaphysics Possible?" *Review of Metaphysics* 45, no. 2 (1991): 242. See also his *The Quarrel between Philosophy and Poetry* (New York: Routledge, 1988): "Those who take their bearings by the Ideas, and who elaborate a "theory" (in the modern or constructive sense of the term) of Ideas in direct contradiction to the dialogical procedure of Plato, may very well become Platonists, or at least produce something called Platonism. In no way, however, does it follow from this procedure that Plato was himself a Platonist. The history of Platonism begins with Aristotle, not with Plato" (187).

200. Charles Griswold, "Plato's Metaphilosophy: Why Plato Wrote Dialogues," in *Platonic Writings: Platonic Readings*, ed. Charles Griswold (New York: Routledge, 1988), 148.

standing the relation of pleasure and intelligence. With the possible (though I would argue, doubtful) exception of the *Parmenides*, then, no dialogue is "about" the ideas. It is therefore modern interpreters and not Plato himself who make the ideas the central issue or philosophical core of Plato's work. To judge from these modern interpreters, most of the Platonic dialogues are simply literary devices whose real purpose is to allow Plato to present his latest version of his supposed "theory" of ideas. Or, in some of the best and most imaginative cases, the point of the "earlier" dialogues is to prepare for and lead up to the full, "mature," or most adequate presentation of this "theory."[201] In either case, the assumption is that the real philosophic point of Plato's writing is to present his "theory" of ideas. In support of this, we need only observe the extent to which the scholarly consensus on "Plato's philosophy" is inseparable from, if not identical with, his supposed "theory of ideas." It is hardly an exaggeration to say that "Platonism" *is* the "theory of ideas." I emphasize, again, that nothing in the dialogues themselves tells us this; it is an imposition of modern scholarship.

My third observation is that what we are told about the ideas when they are discussed is in every case generic. The attributes predicated of specific ideas are always ascribable to all the ideas. We are told, for example, that they are "eternal," "changeless," "unities," "paradigms," and principles of intelligibility by which we understand their phenomenal instances.[202] Not once, in all the dialogues, are we ever told what specific knowledge we gain from

---

201. I am thinking of two excellent recent works, Mitchell Miller's *Plato's Parmenides: The Conversion of the Soul* (Princeton, N.J.: Princeton University Press, 1986) and Kenneth Sayre's, *Plato's Late Ontology: A Riddle Solved* (Princeton, N.J.: Princeton University Press, 1983). I should add that Miller contests this characterization of his work, arguing in a personal letter that his work "characterizes Plato's writing as a provocation to the self-selecting reader to *think through for himself* what the Ideas must be and 'do.' What each of those Platonic texts "presents" are *problems and orienting suggestions*, not a 'theory.'" If so, we are in fundamental agreement.

202. E.g., *Symposium*, 211a; *Republic*, 479 ff, 484 ff, 490 ff, 507b ff, 529c ff; *Phaedo*, 74b ff.

a specific idea, what "Beauty Itself" or "Equality Itself" actually is. We must make the stunning admission that this so-called theory of knowledge so closely identified with Plato is not given a single confirming instance in all the dialogues. Despite initial appearances (that "friendship" is the topic of the *Lysis*, "the Equal Itself" is discussed in the *Phaedo*, "what piety is" is the theme of the Euthyphro, and so on), no character in any dialogue ever learns and articulates for us the knowledge actually gained from an insight into a specific idea. All discussions are generic and programmatic.

Fourth, what we are told of the ideas from dialogue to dialogue is radically discontinuous, not to say contradictory. It is these discontinuities that have been in large measure responsible for the monumental quantity of scholarly effort devoted to figuring out just what the ideas are, how they function, what the "argument" for them is, and how to reconcile the conflicting accounts. About what other "theory" in the history of philosophy has there been so much controversy, and has so much been written? To put the point somewhat differently, what other "theory" in the history of philosophy has been presented by its author with so much ambiguity, unclarity, and inconsistency? Was Plato that bad a writer, that muddled a thinker?[203]

This congeries of problems, especially how to make sense of the disparities in presentation of the ideas from dialogue to dialogue, has been primarily responsible for the various "schools" of Platonic interpretation. I mention only three of the most dominant.[204] The "developmentalists" argue that the disparities in presentation from dialogue to dialogue can be explained by reference to Plato's intellectual maturation. He constantly

---

203. I therefore agree with the sentiment expressed by Stanley Rosen: "If Plato possessed a homogeneous doctrine of a fundamentally scientific nature which he wished to communicate in a univocal and explicit manner to all readers, then his choice of the dialogue form betrays a singular incompetence. That is not a charge with which I wish to associate myself"; see *Plato's Sophist*, 14.

204. For a more full account of the history of Platonic interpretation, see E. N. Tigerstedt, *Interpreting Plato* (Uppsala, Sweden: Almquist & Wiksell, 1977).

"corrects" earlier "mistakes" in his "theory" by writing the next dialogue.[205] Obviously, ascertaining the correct date of authorship of each dialogue becomes crucial to this form of interpretation. Depending on where you like to enter your circle, you can argue independently for the dating of the dialogues (for example, on philological or historical grounds), then conclude that whatever is the "last" dialogue is Plato's "final" or "most mature" theory, or you can argue on philosophic grounds for which dialogue has the most adequate statement of the "theory," then conclude that that dialogue must be the latest.[206]

The second main interpretive standpoint, which we may call the "unified theorists," argues that there is in fact a systematic unity to Plato's thought, either that the basic presentation is consistent and unified throughout,[207] or, in the most powerful reading, that apparent inconsistencies can be read as Plato's pedagogically preparing the way in some (usually "earlier") dialogues for the fuller or more adequate statement of the "theory" in the culminating dialogue.[208]

Third, perhaps the most extreme interpretation is that of the "esotericists," most recently of the "Tubingen school." Despairing

---

205. In my judgment, the best example of this standpoint is Kenneth Sayre's *Plato's Late Ontology*. My criticism of the interpretive standpoint guiding his reading in no way denies that his book is full of penetrating insights and imaginative readings. This is, of course, the dominant school of interpretation among "analytic" Platonists.

206. The best refutation of the "date the dialogue" school of interpretation is Jacob Howland's "Re-Reading Plato: The Problem of Platonic Chronology," *Phoenix* 45, no. 3 (1991): 189–214.

207. An early version of this standpoint is Paul Shorey's *The Unity of Plato's Thought* (Chicago: University of Chicago Press, 1903). A more recent (and more adequate) example is the work of Hans-Georg Gadamer; see esp. *The Idea of the Good in Platonic-Aristotelian Philosophy*, trans. Christopher Smith (New Haven, Conn.: Yale University Press, 1986).

208. I am thinking of Mitchell Miller's *Plato's Parmenides*. Again, although I shall later present some objections to the interpretive standpoint of this book, I want to acknowledge its important contribution to our understanding of Plato.

of the possibility of discovering in the dialogues a coherent statement of Plato's systematic "theory," they conclude that it is simply *not there* in the dialogues. Whatever Plato was doing in his written dialogues, he reserved the revelation of his "real theories" for his lectures at the Academy.

I want to emphasize that all three standpoints are assuming something that I believe is not present in the dialogues. They all assume that somehow, Plato must have *had* a "theory," in particular a "theory of ideas," which either was or was not presented in the dialogues. It is that assumption that I wish in what follows to call into question. Obviously some dialogues speak of the ideas. But that the best way to understand those discussions is as a systematic "theory" I wish to contest.

I want to be careful not to overstate my point here. I am not saying that no general statements can be made about the way the ideas are discussed in several dialogues. Nor am I denying that there is a certain coherence in the way they are discussed from one dialogue to another. To the contrary, I shall presently argue for just such a coherence. But to write coherently is not necessarily to have a "system," nor is it necessarily to have a "theory," and it is the imposition of these latter two on the dialogues that has been so misleading in modern interpretations.

First and foremost, to reiterate one of my guiding interpretive principles, what is said about the ideas in a given dialogue must be understood in the light of the specific context in which they are discussed. The discussion of ideas, the choice of which ideas are discussed and what precisely is said about them, is bound to be different when it takes place between Socrates and a group of Pythagoreans, on the day of Socrates' death, when he is trying to convince them that they need not mourn his death, compared to a discussion, say, when Socrates' chief interlocutors are two young men of considerable political ambition, and Socrates is trying to give them an inkling of what would genuinely have to be known in order to form a truly just polity. Contexts as different as these, to take only two well-known examples, demand that different nuances be emphasized, and this has nothing to do with Plato's "changing his mind" from one dialogue to the other.

My first positive point, then, is that one of the things that the dialogue form brings out most clearly about Plato's philosophy is the conviction that philosophical thinking, its "form" as well as its specific "content," cannot be understood as an abstract or universalized "discipline," and certainly not as a set of abstract "theories" comprising a thinker's "system." Philosophy is a human activity occasioned always by specific human predicaments. What is said in any given situation cannot be understood adequately except as a response to those specific predicaments, and will always be tinctured, no matter how "generalizable" the point may be, by the exigencies of that situation and those predicaments. As I have emphasized in previous chapters, this is in no sense to say that Plato is some sort of radical relativist arguing not just for a "situational ethics" but an entire philosophy limited to situationally relative occasions. To arise out of a given context, to be articulated in terms of that context, is not necessarily to be limited to that context. Transcendence is possible, but, as a transcendence *out of* this or that given situation, it will always be tinctured by its context. Transcendence, that is, is always *finite* transcendence. Every Platonic dialogue, I suggest again, teaches us this lesson. On no topic is its message more important than in understanding Plato's various discussions of ideas.

That said, let me begin the task of such finite transcendence by trying to say something of what is true of the forms in their quite varied appearances in the dialogues. Let me return first to the remarks made toward the end of the last chapter concerning the sense in which Plato may be said to be a "Xenophanean." On the one hand, the dialogues seem to be informed by an experience of the world such that the flux of becoming, the phenomena, are somehow grounded in what is not in flux, not becoming. I emphasize that it is an "experience of the world" that guides Plato's thought here, not a Cartesian point of fixed certainty nor a mystical intuition. The dialogues portray an experience of the flux of things such that that experience does not make sense, cannot be understood, in terms no deeper than the flux itself; becoming does not explain itself, is not self-evident. Yet we do, from time to time, come to at least partial understanding of the flux of things; in the midst of constant becoming, we fathom something of the meaning of the flux itself. But to fathom is to go deeper, deeper than the flux. Such understanding as is from time to time ours must then be grounded in an access, however partial and incomplete, to an *arche* of the flux, to Being. The ideas, then, are that *arche* of the flux of becoming. In this sense, the experience of the world portrayed in the dialogues is "foundationalist." The ideas, as the principles of intelligibility of what becomes, *are* Being; this is Plato's "Parmenideanism."[209] Plato rejects Anaximander, in effect, insofar as the *arche* of what becomes is in principle intelligible; the *arche* is not *to apeiron*.

But "in principle intelligible" does not mean "in fact intelligible" and especially not "in fact completely or comprehensively intelligible."[210] For this reason, Plato rejects as well the optimism of a Thales, an Anaximenes, or even a Pythagoras. For two fundamental reasons, the intelligibility of the *arche* will never be entirely accessible to human thinking, and aporia will be an inescapable element of the human situation. The first reason, about which I shall have more to say later in the chapter, is the peculiar status of the idea of the Good. The second reason, which can be briefly addressed here, is human nature itself, and in particular, our nature as erotic. As previous chapters have elucidated, our natures, particularly the erotic dimension of incompleteness, renders us always and necessarily finite, partial. So it is with our insight into the *arche*. We intuit its presence, intuit as well that it is the source or ground of what knowledge we have of the flux; but we do not, in any comprehensive or totalizing sense, "know" the *arche*, "know" the forms. In some dialogues, in the portrayal of some situations and some character types, Plato finds it appropriate to emphasize the intelligibility of the ideas "in

---

209. I am thinking in particular of Parmenides' famous Fragment 3: *to gar auto noein estin te kai einai*; "Thinking and Being are the same," or "For the same thing can be thought as can be." That the ideas are Being indicates my disagreement with Stanley Rosen's claim that "Being is the Good and beings (ta ontos onta) are the Ideas"; see *The Quarrel between Philosophy and Poetry*, 130.

210. An excellent account of how this situation is present in the *Phaedrus* is Charles Griswold's *Self-Knowledge in Plato's Phaedrus* (New Haven, Conn.: Yale University Press, 1986); see esp. 104–5.

themselves." The *Phaedo* or the idyll of the middle books of the *Republic* would be good examples of this emphasis. In other dialogues, such as the so-called "aporia" dialogues or the *Symposium* and *Phaedrus* in particular, he emphasizes the necessary incompleteness of our access to the ideas. Again, these represent different aspects of the human situation, not changes in Plato's "theory" of ideas.

So in different ways in different dialogues, we see the ideas portrayed as the stable ground, the Being, of the unstable flux of becoming, of phenomena; or perhaps better, the ideas are portrayed as the source of what stability there is in an otherwise radically unstable flux of becoming.

But, as I emphasized above, we do not "know" the ideas or even know *that* there are ideas in any strict or comprehensive sense of knowledge. It must be emphasized next, then, that there is no "proof" of the ideas, no "deduction" of them, in any dialogue. It is again a stunning fact that despite the talk, in the *Republic* for example, of a "dialectical" march back to *archai* that are not hypotheses,[211] or of diairetic "deductions" in the *Sophist* or *Statesman*, in no case is anything like a "deduction" of the ideas actually presented. In every case, what actually happens is that we *begin with* the ideas, and from that beginning their great value is developed.[212]

But what, if anything, is the justification of such a beginning? If there is no formal or transcendental "proof" of the ideas, why

---

211. *Republic*, 510b ff.

212. Charles Griswold thus does not exaggerate when he says that "we repeatedly find that in his discussions about knowledge Plato just *assumes* or *asserts* that the Ideas exist, and *then* explains what "knowledge" is (for example, *Rep.* 476a ff., 507a–b ff., 596a and context; *Pho.* 100b ff.). We do not seem to get an account of how we know these ontological assumptions to be true" ("Plato's Metaphilosophy: Why Plato Wrote Dialogues," in Griswold, ed., *Platonic Writings: Platonic Readings*, 148. Stanley Rosen has shown that even in "technical" and "late" dialogues such as the *Sophist*, the forms are assumed rather than diairetically deduced. "The sense of the metaphor (concerning a "gift of the gods") is that we are *given* complex forms as visible. This is our starting point"; *Plato's Sophist*, 76.

should we affirm them? Is such an affirmation some sort of philosophical article of faith, an "unjustified assumption"? It would be ironic indeed if this "doctrine" of ideas, so closely identified with "Platonism" would turn out to have its sole justification in arbitrary assumption. But if not, what is the "justification," short of "proof," that is presented in the dialogues?

We must be careful not to fall into a certain Cartesian trap here. Descartes laid down a demand not only upon himself but, it seems, on modernity, that if a given "knowledge claim" cannot be demonstrated with absolute certainty, such that it is indubitable, then it is not worth believing and should be doubted. Even as we moderns have, with every good reason, fallen back from this demand, it exerts an implicit force on us insofar as we tend, without necessarily *doubting* everything that we cannot prove with certainty, to at least regard those less-than-certain propositions, beliefs, affirmations, and so on, as somehow falling short of genuine knowledge, genuine rationality. If we apply this conviction to the Platonic dialogues we shall again impose a modernist assumption on the dialogues when no such assumption is present therein. On the contrary, as I have argued at length elsewhere, it is taken up and rejected at least as "early" as the *Charmides*.[213]

The Greek word that comes closest to what we moderns would count as "scientific" knowledge is *episteme*, which in fact is usually translated straightforwardly as "science." Although many of the modern connotations of the term make it somewhat misleading, the Greek word does carry with it the sense of "demonstrative knowledge," and so, to an extent, of certainty. As the *Charmides* shows, the word was already in Plato's time being employed as the paradigm of all knowledge. But as that dialogue also shows, Plato calls into question that paradigmatic status, and for good reasons.

In the *Charmides*, at a crucial juncture in the dialogue, Critias replaces Charmides as Socrates' interlocutor and replaces as well

---

213. For a detailed development of what I shall here outline only briefly, see my *The Virtue of Philosophy: An Interpretation of Plato's Charmides*, chaps. 6–7.

the intense introspection that Socrates had demanded of the young man with a sophistic contest to see who can defend the best definition of *sophrosyne*. He does so, ironically enough, with the definition, which he supposes ought to appeal to Socrates, of "self-knowledge."[214] Socrates replies with a question whose answer virtually determines the course of the rest of the dialogue in its ostensibly unsuccessful effort to define *sophrosyne*. Socrates asks, "If *sophrosyne* is indeed knowing something, then it is clear that it must be some sort of science, and a science of something; or no?"[215] Critias answers affirmatively, that it is a science of the self, and the dialogue continues to its unsuccessful conclusion. But it does so, and so is indeed unsuccessful, *only* on the assumption that if self-knowledge is a kind of knowledge, it must be *episteme*. What that assumption leaves out, of course, is that there might be some *other* sort of knowledge that is not *episteme*, and the dialogue quietly gives us the alternative, *to gignoskein*, whose paradigm is precisely Socrates' own self-knowledge as "knowing what he knows and what he does not know."[216] For this latter knowledge is clearly not "epistemic." If it were, it would have to be "demonstrated" with some sort of "proof," presumably a long two-column list articulated by Socrates, labeled respectively "what I know" and "what I do not know." Obviously, nothing of the kind is given. Still, there is a different *sort* of "demonstration" given of Socrates's self-knowledge, through his *questioning*; Socrates exhibits his self-knowledge as what he knows and what he doesn't know through what he questions and what he does not question. Such knowledge is not and cannot be *episteme*. But unless one is locked into a rigid Cartesianism, it is no less clear that it is a *kind* of knowledge, one different, and answerable to different standards, than *episteme*.[217]

---

214. *Charmides*, 164d–5b.

215. *ei gar de gignoskein ge ti estin he sophrosyne, delon hoti episteme tis an eie kai tinos: e ou; Charmides*, 165c4–5.

216. It is instructive (and ironic) in this regard that the Delphic oracle that Critias cites in formulating his definition, *gnothi seautou*, uses the root *gignoskein*, not *episteme*.

217. Vlastos recognizes different senses of "wisdom" in the dialogues; see *Socrates, Ironist and Moral Philosopher*, 3 ff, 239.

The *Charmides* thus establishes a number of crucial points. First, knowledge is heterogeneous. There are different kinds of knowledge appropriate for different issues, and the different kinds are not reducible to a single mode of knowledge or "science." Second, in particular, knowledge of the virtues such as *sophrosyne* is probably not "epistemic." At least, the effort to gain "epistemic" access to what *sophrosyne* is fails (as does the similar effort to "define" other virtues in the other aporetic dialogues). But this in turn means that much of what we regard as philosophical knowledge (knowledge of the virtues, self-knowledge, and the like) will not be *episteme* and therefore will not be susceptible to the kind of demonstration, not to mention rigorous certainty, that we associate with *episteme*. Why not, and what sort of alternative "knowledges" might there be? The answer to these questions, I think, centers on the crucial distinction between *noesis* and *dianoia*.

Dianoia as it is used in the dialogues is something like "discursive reasoning." For our purposes and for the contrast with *noesis*, its crucial characteristic is that it is *articulated* thinking or reasoning, expressed, in principle with complete adequacy, in discursive speech. *Noesis*, by contrast, is typically translated as "intuition" or "insight." Its crucial characteristic differentiating it from *dianoia* is that it is nondiscursive. As does Plato, we usually speak of our "intuitions" metaphorically; we speak of "seeing" something, of a "moment of insight," *in the light of which* we speak about this or that, but which cannot be reduced to the speech that occurs in its light.[218]

For *episteme* to be comprehensive and complete, it would have to be pure *dianoia*, in which any initiating *noesis* would be fully articulated, and therefore replaced by, discursive speech. The desire to accomplish this is the clear source of the Hegelian, and modern, effort to develop a "presuppositionless" science, to replace what we tend to call our "vague intuitions" with demon-

---

218. As with most of the key notions in the dialogues, these are not terms whose distinctions are maintained throughout Plato's writings with rigid consistency or without regard to context. I am articulating here what I take to be a *pervasive* sense of the distinction.

strable science. The question is, is the achievement of a comprehensive philosophical *episteme*, which means the reduction of all *noesis* to *dianoia*, possible?

I suggest that the lesson of dialogue after dialogue is that Plato's answer is no. As I have again argued in detail elsewhere, every philosophic speech is bounded at its beginning and its end by a noetic vision. What we may call its "archaic" *noesis* is the insight into what the matter for thought is, into how to begin our speaking. Something "strikes us" as at stake, as a matter for thought that needs reflective clarification, or that we do not know and needs to be known. That originating insight is the *ground* of the speaking; it is not spoken itself. We rather speak *in the light of* that insight. Similarly, the "telic" *noesis* is the final or culminating insight *toward* which the speech hopefully leads us, but which again is not reducible to the speech itself. Our speech, we hope, leads us to "see" something that we did not "see" before, and that seeing is the *result* of the speaking, not the speech itself. Philosophic speech, we may say after the manner of the discussion of eros in the *Symposium*, attempts to bridge the gap between the originating and the culminating noetic insights.[219] But to bridge the gap between them is not to replace them. Neither the originating nor the culminating *noesis* is reducible to dianoetic speech itself.

As one instructive example of this, we may again turn to the *Charmides*. The dialogue begins with a dramatic portrayal of the presence of an initiating *noesis*. Socrates somehow "sees" that the young Charmides is lacking in, and in need of, *sophrosyne*, and so by the ruse of Socrates' being the doctor who can cure Charmides' morning headaches, he turns the topic of the conversation to that virtue.[220] When he begins his questioning of Charmides, he formulates his question in a curiously complex way which I quote at length:

"It seems to me, I said, that it would be best to approach the examination in this way. It is clear that if *sophrosyne* is present in you (*parestin*), then you must have an opinion

---

219. *Symposium*, 202e.
220. For extended consideration of this point, see my *The Virtue of Philosophy*, chap. 2.

about it. If indeed it is in you, it necessarily will grant to you the means of perception (*aisthesin*) out of which you will be able to offer an opinion of what *sophrosyne* is and of what quality it is. Or do you think not?

I think so, he said.

Since you know how to speak Greek, I said, you must be able to express your opinion.

Perhaps, he said.

In order that we may divine (*topasomen*) whether it is in you or not, tell me, I said, what, in your opinion, do you say *sophrosyne* is?"[221]

There is obviously much to be said about this rich and complex formulation of what one would expect to be the straightforward question, "What is *sophrosyne*?"[222] For our purposes, we need note only the crucial presence of the term *aisthesin*. If *sophrosyne* is in Charmides, we are told, it will offer him the "means of perception" or "sense of its presence," out of which he will be able to offer an opinion. Socrates' complex question, as against a simple "What is *sophrosyne*?" shows that he does not expect or even hope for some sort of direct access to or unmediated articulation of "*sophrosyne* itself." What Charmides will thus attempt to articulate is not "*sophrosyne* itself" but its "means of perception," in the light of which Charmides will express his opinion. Socrates is not even asking Charmides to articulate "*sophrosyne* itself;" he knows, I suggest, that that would be impossible, for it would imply a direct *dianoetic* access, without the mediation of *noesis*, to *sophrosyne* itself.[223] Instead, Socrates asks Charmides to articulate

---

221. Charmides, 159a; my translation. Rosamond Kent Sprague translates *aisthesin* appropriately as "a sense of its presence"; see her *Plato's Laches and Charmides* (New York: Bobbs-Merrill, 1973), 65.

222. For my more extended analysis, see *The Virtue of Philosophy*, chap. 3.

223. Kenneth Sayre makes a somewhat similar point, arguing that the various "definitions" fail because "philosophic understanding is a kind of intellectual discernment that cannot be adequately expressed in language"; see his "Plato's Dialogues in the Light of the Seventh Letter," in Griswold, ed., *Platonic Writings: Platonic Readings*, 103.

the "means of perception" which *sophrosyne* will grant if it is indeed "in" Charmides. Whatever else this complex formulation signifies, it surely means that a beginning *noesis* will be necessary in the light of which Charmides might speak intelligently. It is instructive, therefore, that Socrates' closing formulation of the question expresses the hope that he may "divine" (*topasomen*) whether *sophrosyne* is in Charmides. We are not in the presence of deductive certainty or the possibility of *episteme*.[224]

If Plato were a very different philosopher, he might have had Socrates say something like "In order that we may deduce whether *sophrosyne* is in you..." or "In order that we may prove whether...." But as Socrates' reference to the hope of "divining" whether *sophrosyne* is in Charmides suggests, there is something epistemologically unstable, uncertain, about the presence of a virtue in us and about our access to knowledge of it. I have tried to suggest why there is good reason for Socrates' caution. Our necessary reliance on *noesis* both at the beginning and at the culmination of our cognitive efforts, the irreducibility of those noetic insights to *dianoia* and so to the potential demonstrative rigor of *episteme*, means that our self-knowledge, and the knowledge of virtues and implicitly of forms that such self-knowledge entails,[225] is not the sort of rigorous demonstrative knowledge that

---

224. For excellent discussions of the necessity of *noesis* and its irreducibility to *dianoia*, see Rosen's important study of the *Sophist*, *Plato's Sophist*. For a formulation of a similar argument in a contemporary context, see his *The Limits of Analysis* (New York: Basic Books, 1980). In his insightful study of the *Phaedrus*, Charles Griswold argues that "Men are endowed with a partial and possibly blurred noetic vision of Truth that has been digested and reshaped by dianoia into linguistic form"; see his *Self-Knowledge in Plato's Phaedrus* (New Haven, Conn.: Yale University Press, 1986), 108. In his analysis of the "divine banquet" of that dialogue, Griswold suggests, in the case of the gods, a close affinity if not identity between *episteme* and *nous*. *Divine episteme* would seem to be noetic, not discursive—a decisive difference between the divine and we mortals (106–7, and note no. 48).

225. Even, I suggest, in "early" dialogues such as the *Charmides*, where the ideas are not mentioned explicitly. But the sense of passages such as the one I am presently discussing could hardly be rendered coherent without thinking of the implicit presence of the ideas.

we associate with *episteme*. But since, fortunately, Plato is a pre-Cartesian, he does not infer from the impossibility of *episteme* in this realm that *knowledge altogether* is impossible. To the contrary, we are in the realm of a different sort of knowledge, one which, difficult as this is for modern minds to appreciate, is a knowledge that does not entail certainty. We must now ask, if the process of knowing ourselves, of knowing the virtues, and so of knowing the ideas has about it a necessary instability owing to the dependence on *noesis* and its irreducibility to *dianoia*, what then is the "cognitive state," other than certainty, that characterizes such knowledge?

I want to suggest that if there is a generalized answer that shows up in the action of the dialogues, it is a kind of trust. Let us begin by discussing what the word implies, then move on to a consideration of its relation to our access to the ideas. On the one hand, trust needs to be differentiated from "faith." As Kierkegaard understood so well, there is in faith a much larger "leap" beyond what experience warrants than occurs in trust. Trust, as we often say, is earned; someone may or may not be trust-*worthy*. We trust someone or something, therefore, when our experience tells us that the person or thing can be depended upon. Trust, unlike faith, is not blind. We say that we *know* that we can trust someone; that does not mean that we have some sort of deductive proof, but that the person's dependability has been sufficiently established through experience that we are willing to count on it, to act, and live, in the light of our assumption of that dependability, our trust. On the other hand, trust is not certainty, it is not a question of proof. If, in a certain context, someone says to another, "Prove that you love me," we know not that trust is being established but that it has broken down. Trust does not demand "proof" or certainty; perhaps better, trust has transcended the need for such certainty. It is especially instructive in this context to note the etymological connection between the English word *trust* and "truth." The "truth," at least etymologically, would seem to be what is trustworthy, as when we say that someone is a "true friend." We do not mean by that that we can deduce a large number of propositions about that person with certainty. We mean that he or she can be trusted. Trust, we might then say, is the affirmation of an experienced dependability, a willingness to count on that dependability in an always uncertain future.

Something like that, I want now to suggest, is what we have, or rather, is the most we can hope for, vis-à-vis our noetic insights. They are almost never certain, never "scientific," never provable with apodictic certainty. But we come to learn through experience that they are more or less dependable, that some are more dependable than others, that some are sufficiently dependable that we can live our lives by them. Crucial, surely, to our efforts to come to these decisions is our speech about and in the light of our noetic insights, our "intuitions about the world." *Dianoia* thus always occurs in the light of our *noesis*, and at the same time is one source of the always incomplete confirmation of those insights. We therefore do *not* usually trust someone who asks us to accept their intuitions without supporting speech. The philosophic life, as always part *noesis*, part *dianoia*, will always also be informed in part by trust. Because the philosophic life originates and is lived out in the phenomenal world of becoming, it is therefore altogether appropriate that Socrates, in the famous "Divided Line" analogy of the *Republic*, names the cognitive state that characterizes our experienced world *"pistis,"* trust.[226]

The philosophic life will consequently always be one of aporia, and not just in one's "early" writings. Socrates' interrogative stance, and Plato's commitment to the writing of dialogue, are perfectly compatible with the position I am here outlining. One might say that the stance of trust generated by the disjunction between our noetic insights and our dianoetic efforts to speak in their light puts us in the middle between a stance of doubt or skepticism, in which we begin, as it were, by *presuming the dubiousness* of our necessarily unstable insights, and the apodictic certainty that we associate with *episteme* or scientific deduction. This is the crucial difference between anything like Cartesian "doubt" and Socratic questioning. Whereas Descartes recommends that we doubt, and so distrust and reject in advance, that which is not apodictically certain, Socrates again and again

---

226. *Republic*, 511e.

begins with the opinions of the day, and so reveals that he trusts them to be worthy of question, even if the result of our questioning is to transform radically the original opinion. The trust we have in our guiding intuitions is compatible with our holding them as question-worthy. And the question-worthiness of our deepest convictions is precisely the stance with which the dialogues again and again begin.

I suggest that something like this is the cognitive stance called for in the dialogues by Plato's account of the human condition, the disjunction of our *noesis* and *dianoia*. This is why, as writers such as Rosen and Griswold have pointed out, there is never a "proof" or diaresis, no "transcendental deduction" of the forms. We simply do not have that sort of access to them. Nor, we must add, are they simply *assumed* as some sort of Platonic article of faith. Plato, it seems, has had a noetic experience of the formal structure of the intelligibility of things. He has learned that that experience can be trusted, while at once holding it open to question. In his dialogues, he portrays to us both the kinds of experience that led him to those insights and the kinds of experience that confirm their trustworthiness. By these "phenomenologies," he can hope to lead us to experience the trustworthiness of affirming that formal structure of intelligibility. He cannot prove it and does not try.

I want to emphasize again that what I am here saying is necessarily very general because the details of any specific development of the insight into what I am calling the formal structure of intelligibility, the ideas, or Being, will always vary with the specific context. That is why Plato's "phenomenologies" give us very different contexts, and thus why the details are very different one dialogue from another. The dialogues, I suggest, are written to show us some of the different possible paths, perhaps appropriate for different kinds of souls, to an insight into Being.[227]

227. As Mitchell Miller has suggested to me, it is also possible, and compatible, that certain *collections* of dialogues have a similar pedagogical function for certain types of readers, in such a way that certain dialogues "play off each other."

This, and not Plato's development or changes of mind, is the most basic reason for the differences of one dialogue from another.[228]

But if what is said about the ideas in the dialogues is unsystematic and even sparse, the same is even more true of that idea of all ideas, which seems to be the absolute foundation of what some regard as Plato's "system" or "theory," the idea of the Good, to which we can now turn.

We should begin by emphasizing this most striking fact about the idea of the Good (or "the Good" as it is more usually called), that so very little is said about it in the dialogues. About the Good we have a few pages in the *Republic*, most of it highly metaphorical, an even shorter discussion in the *Philebus*,[229] and vague hints in a few other dialogues. Perhaps Plato means to suggest something quite serious through this striking paucity of discussion. Perhaps we are meant to recognize that however foundational this idea may be—not to Plato's "system" but to the intelligibility and being of life—not much can be said about it. Perhaps, then, part of what we should try to understand about the Good is why it is at once the foundational theme of life itself, yet we understand and can say so little about it.

I begin with an important insight of David Lachterman concerning the positions of scholars on the Good.[230] He observes that

---

228. This is the source of the one basic disagreement I have with Mitchell Miller's fine book on the *Parmenides*, *Plato's Parmenides: The Conversion of the Soul* (Princeton, N.J.: Princeton University Press, 1986). Miller gives the presentation in the *Parmenides* a privileged status as being the most "non-imagistic" of the presentations of the forms. His interpretation is thus that the more imagistic presentations (such as the *Republic*) are, though pedagogically important to some readers, intellectually inferior to the non-imagistic (and therefore presumably purer) presentation of the *Parmenides*. But I fail to see why a non-imagistic account is superior to an imagistic one; in fact, it strikes me as at least as likely that the *Parmenides* is written to show the limits of a purely non-imagistic discussion of the forms, in a world necessarily involved with images. I believe I can accept most of Miller's detailed analysis of the dialogue within this general interpretation.

229. It is not even uncontroversial that the discussion of the good in the *Philebus* refers to the "idea of the Good" in the *Republic*.

230. Lachterman, "What is 'The Good' of Plato's Republic?, 139–71. This short work is of the greatest help in understanding how the Good

they tend to divide into two camps, the one emphasizing almost exclusively the ethical or moral dimension of the Good, the other emphasizing with similar exclusiveness the metaphysical or ontological function that the Good plays.[231] He emphasizes that the disjunction is artificial and destroys the integrity of the dialogue and the Good itself; the *Republic* "invites us to hear the baffling connectedness or kinship within living speech of those preoccupations artificially set apart as 'ethical' and 'onto-logical.'"[232] Lachterman's point is well taken; Plato never separates these "functions" of the Good, so perhaps we should not either. We should seek, as does Lachterman, to understand how the Good serves both functions at once, as one.

I want to refer again back to my closing remarks of the previous chapter regarding the extent to which Plato is a Xeno-phanean. I there suggested that the presence of the ideas as eternal, stable principles of intelligibility, and as Being, meant that Being was *in principle* intelligible for Plato. But that intelligibility in principle is not fully attainable in fact because of the human condition of finitude and partiality, encapsulated for Plato in his discussions of eros. At that time I noted in several places that a complicated qualification would have to be made regarding the Good. Let me now turn to that qualification.

The first thing we are told about the idea of the Good when it is introduced in the *Republic* is that it is "the greatest study, (*megiston mathema*) and that it's by availing oneself of it along with just things and the rest that they become useful and beneficial."[233] The Good is "the greatest study [or learning]" because through it other things become not only intelligible but "useful and bene-ficial." Here is a first instance of the inseparability of the meta-physical and ethical powers of the Good, which gets emphasized

---

"works" in the *Republic*. Two other enormously helpful works are Mitchell Miller's "Platonic Provocations: Reflections on the Soul and the Good in the *Republic*," in *Platonic Investigations* (Washington, D.C.: Catholic University Press of America, 1985), 163–93; and Stanley Rosen's penetrating discussion in his *Nihilism: A Philosophical Essay* (New Haven, Conn.: Yale University Press, 1969), esp. chap. 5: "The Good."

231. Ibid., 139–41.
232. Ibid., 140.
233. *Republic*, 505a; Bloom translation.

even more in the subsequent pages when Socrates shows Adeimantus that the nature of the Good is of the greatest dispute among humans, yet that we are most unwilling of all to be content with the *seeming* good. We desire not the seeming but the real good, a distinction that is literally incoherent without invoking the issue of intelligibility.[234] The pervasiveness of this concern is summed up well by Socrates when he says that "Now this is what every soul pursues and for the sake of which it does everything."[235] The generality of the claim here is striking and important. We are not just talking about epistemology or our "ontological commitments." We are talking about the whole of human life. "Everything" that we do is founded in, has its telos in, the Good.

But no sooner does Socrates make this crucial claim regarding the foundational status of the Good than he states for the first time what is perhaps the most oft-reiterated point in the whole discussion, that we do not know the Good adequately. The next sentence after his opening claim that the idea of the Good is the source by which everything becomes useful and beneficial (505a) states, "And now you know pretty certainly that I'm going to say this and, besides this, that we don't have sufficient knowledge of it."[236] In the next few pages, this denial of knowledge regarding the Good is reiterated no less than four times (505e, 506e, 509b, 509c).[237] Plato thus sees us as in the following predica-

---

234. *Republic*, 505a–d. Stanley Rosen states the connection nicely: "The good as the source of intelligibility is necessarily the source of the good as the useful or valuable, because the satisfaction of desire in both the vulgar and the philosophic sense always depends upon knowledge, and so upon the knowability of the kinds, shapes, or Ideas of things"; see his *Nihilism*, 167.

235. Ibid., 505e.

236. Ibid., 505a.

237. *Republic* 506e might seem to qualify this denial, since Socrates says there of the Good only that "it looks to me as though it's out of the range of our present thrust to attain the opinions I now hold about it." This at least suggests that Socrates, in some different context, would have more to say about it. But it is crucial that what he might then add but cannot now do so is not his *knowledge* of the Good but his "opinions" concerning it. And in any case, Socrates never explicitly fulfills this tantalizing expectation.

ment. That which is the source of our knowledge of things, of the being of things, of their usefulness and benefit, the Good, is itself not directly knowable. *Being* (the forms) may indeed be in principle intelligible. But Being itself has a source or foundation, and that source or foundation, though it "gives" being and intelligibility, is itself "beyond being" and intelligibility—as we will learn at 509c.[238]

We cannot know the Good in any straightforward sense of the term. Is there a way by which we can at least gain a sense of how something could function as the source of what is and of our knowledge of what is, yet itself be beyond being and knowledge? Yes, by an analogy, the famous analogy of the sun, presented at 508a ff. It is presented as an analogy the closeness and appropriateness of which is signaled by Socrates calling the sun "the offspring" of the Good (508c). The general point of the analogy is well known. The sun is the source both of the visibility and the being of the visible things, yet is not itself an *object* of visibility (at least not focally or adequately). It is rather the medium of visibility and visible being, that power which enables visibility and visible being to happen. It is literally *in the light* of the sun that things become visible; but the sun itself cannot (without blindness) become an object of visibility itself.

So it is, by analogy, with the Good. The Good is the source of the intelligibility and the being of what is intelligible, while not itself one of the intelligible objects. Like any analogy, this can only *suggest* how the Good functions, how it "works." The account itself implies that that is the best we can have. We do not have knowledge but we do have *intimations* of the Good.[239] In perhaps

---

238. That the Good is beyond intelligibility would follow from its being "beyond being," though Socrates does not at this moment make that Parmenidean point. The parallels—but also the crucial differences—with Heidegger's late discussions of *Ereignis* are obvious and striking; see especially the essays in *On Time and Being*.

239. Perhaps the very best icon of which, as Stanley Rosen has so well pointed out, is "the good man": "A good man, as we observe him within our daily lives, is not 'useful for...' in the same sense that tools, food, acts, even just and beautiful things exhibit utility. Entirely apart from the happiness which may justly accrue to the good man because of his

the most striking set of remarks in the entire discussion of the Good, toward its close, Socrates tells Glaucon that knowledge and truth are *like* the Good but not the Good itself (509a) and that "not only being known is present in the things known[240] as a consequence of the good, but also existence and being (*to einai te kai ten ousian*) are in them as a result of it, although the good *is not being but is still beyond being*, exceeding it in dignity and power."[241]

We can now see why so little is said directly about the Good. We do not, cannot, know it directly, but can only *intimate its presence and power*, and talk, not of it itself but of its effects, in the light of our intimations. That is not "knowledge of the Good" or wisdom, but it is not ignorance either. What, then, can we say about our intimations of the Good?

If I understand Plato correctly, the world exhibits, or is itself an exhibition of, a structure of intelligibility, which is *there* (as opposed to "constructed" by human consciousness). He called that permanent structure of the intelligibility of things the forms, ideas, or sometimes, Being. Because of the structure of things that I set out above, in which the *dianoia* of human discourse is bounded at its beginning and its end by *noesis*, and because both the originating *noesis* and the culminating *noesis* are partial, and in addition, because the *dianoia* that attempts to join them is, as linguistic and therefore participant in becoming, itself partial, wisdom, in the sense of comprehensive knowledge of the structure of the whole, is impossible on the Platonic view of things. But we *do* have noetic insights, however precarious, and we *do* speak in the light of those experiences, however partially. Although we can neither intuit the whole (which would make us gods) nor articulate the whole (which would make us Hegel), we nonetheless, from time to time, *intuit the presence* of that formal structure of intelligibility which Plato called ideas. In the light of

---

consciousness that he is good, there is a certain fulfillment, completeness, or perfection which shines forth from such a man, and which we too admire, even perhaps without envy or desire, because of its splendor"; see his *Nihilism*, 172.

240. It is noteworthy that the words for "known" here are both forms of *gignoskein*, not *episteme*. *Kai tois gignoskomenois toinun me monon to gignoskesthai phanai....*

241. 509c; my emphasis.

these intuitions, we "know" not the ideas, but the world; we save the phenomena, not the ideas.

So for Plato, the phenomena, the things of our experience, are grounded in the ideas. But Plato also suggests that the ideas are themselves grounded in what we might call the ground of all grounds, the idea of the Good. As the analogy of the sun suggests, the Good functions as the "light" of intelligibility by which we see something of what phenomena are by seeing their relations to ideas. But a "third man" argument or infinite regress is avoided because the Good is *different* from the other ideas, indeed in a way, as others have observed, it is really not an idea at all.[242] For the ideas are, as principles of intelligibility, themselves intelligible beings. But the Good, which is the ultimate source of the intelligibility of what is most intelligible, is not itself an intelligible being. It is rather "beyond being" and intelligibility. One consequence of this Platonic view is that there is at once a truly wonderful amount of intelligibility available in the world and to human being; we can know myriad things. But there is also, if I may cautiously use this word, ultimate and irreducible mystery.

But this idea of all ideas, this ultimate if mysterious source of the intelligibility and being of things, is not called the idea of Intelligibility, of Knowledge, of Being, nor of Mystery. It is called the idea of the Good. Why? It suggests nothing less than that the irreducible ground of the whole is inseparable from the question, the issue (but not necessarily the answer) of goodness. The issue of the Good literally in-forms all things. Things are what they are only within the context or realm of a certain good. Again, about any thing, about any act, the question of whether or not it is good (or in some contexts, what it is good for) is an integral part of what it means to understand things.[243] It is in a sense the most pervasive of all issues, in the light of which we understand

---

242. E.g., Hans-Georg Gadamer, *The Idea of the Good in Platonic-Aristotelian Philosophy*, trans. Christopher Smith (New Haven, Conn.: Yale University Press, 1986), 124: "The good is the being of the ideas generally and not an idea itself."

243. Mitchell Miller argues cogently that the good really functions as "the perfect," the standard toward which all aspiration, whether intellectual or ethical, moves, however imperfectly; see his "Platonic

everything, to the extent that we understand anything. And, the dialogues suggest, that issue is *there*, that is to say, it is not created by us, or "constituted" by human consciousness. To be sure, the actual response that we make to the issue in any given situation always risks being "perspectival," a function, that is, of the exigencies of the specific situation. The *response* we give may indeed be perspectival; but the *issue* of the Good is not. It pervades all situations and is thus the source of the integrity, the coherence (in both the intellectual and ethical senses) of life; hence its fundamentality.[244]

But this is to say that the Good is less a pervasive "answer" to things or a pervasive item of knowledge than a pervasive question or issue. The good of an act, situation, or thing is less an item of knowledge about it, part of its formal structure, than it is an irrevocable concern. The good of acts, situations, or things is always more precarious, more open to question, than is its formal structure. Perhaps that is why the ontological status of the Good is so different for Plato. Forms, as principles of intelligibility, are each a kind of entity, or to use Hegelian language, they are *determinate*. As such, for Plato, they are Being. But the Good is not so determinate, not an answer, again, but an issue. For this reason, the source of the pervasive presence of the Good is "beyond being" and intelligibility. It is a mystery, to be sure, but a mystery that is always with us. Plato sheds light on that mystery, not, to be sure, by "explaining" it, getting rid of it, but by bringing it and keeping it before us with clarity and power, by showing us how it might be. We know, and more fundamentally, we live, in the light of our intimations of the Good; our actions, our aspirations, our convictions, are always informed by our best sense of what is good. We do not and never will "know" the Good in the sense of *episteme*. But neither are we condemned to utter ignorance. Our noetic visions or intimations of the Good, always precarious and worthy of question, allow us nevertheless the kind

---

Provocations: Reflections on the Soul and the Good in the Republic," in *Platonic Investigations*, ed. Dominic J. O'Meara (Washington, D.C.: The Catholic University Press of America, 1985), 163–94.

244. This is the guiding point of David Lachterman's insightful article, "What Is 'The Good' of Plato's *Republic*?"

of knowledge perhaps adumbrated in the Delphic oracle's command and encapsulated in Socrates' own sense of self-knowledge. That knowledge is exhibited in part by our speech about things, but more fundamentally by the conduct of our lives. It amounts to something like the "wisdom" of Heraclitus: "speaking and acting the truth, according to the nature of things."[245]

It should now be obvious how the ideas, at least as I think they should be understood, fit in with the overall theme I have been developing concerning finitude and transcendence. The ideas, the whole question of knowledge, present us with one more framework within which we come to understand the human situation as one informed at once by finitude and the possibility of a transcendence, not to "absolute knowledge" or "wisdom" in a comprehensive sense, not to "solutions" to our problems, political, aesthetic, or metaphysical, but a movement nevertheless out of the limitations with which we begin, toward a more (but never total) comprehensive understanding. There is therefore no conflict between the "Socratic" stance of aporia and the "Platonic" teaching regarding the ideas, and certainly no need to invent a theory of Plato's "development" beyond his teacher. The ideas are the source of the possibility that in knowledge, too, a transcendence of our situation, in this case of ignorance, is available; the stance of aporia is the consequence of the recognition that such transcendence is always finite. When we articulate our sense of the world in the light of our best intuitions into the way things are, we come to a better understanding of our world. When, in addition, we from time to time succeed in thinking and acting in the light of the Good, we move as well toward a better, more worthy life, a life *kalos k'agathos*, "noble and good."

---

245. Heraclitus, Fragment 112.

BIBLIOGRAPHY

Greek Texts:

Aristotle. *Metaphysica.* Edited by W. Jaeger. Oxford: Clarendon Press, 1957.

———. *De Re Publica.* Edited by Immanuel Bekker. Berolini: George Reimeri, 1855.

Plato. *Platonis Opera.* 5 vols. Edited by J. Burnet. Oxford: Clarendon Press, 1958.

———. *The Republic.* 2 vols. Edited with translation by Paul Shorey. Cambridge, Mass.: Harvard University Press, 1953.

———. *The Symposium of Plato.* Edited by R.G. Bury. Cambridge: W. Heffer & Sons Ltd., 1932.

Other Works Cited:

Adams, James. *The Nuptial Number of Plato: Its Solution and Significance.* London: C.J. Clay & Sons, 1891.

Allen, Reginald. "The Speech of Glaucon in Plato's *Republic.*" *Journal of the History of Philosophy* 25, no. 1 (1987): 3–11.

Anderson, John. *The Realm of Art.* University Park: Pennsylvania State University Press, 1967.

Aristophanes. *The Eleven Comedies.* Anonymous translator. New York: Tudor Publishing Co., 1912.

Aristotle. *The Complete Works of Aristotle.* 2 vols. Edited by Jonathan Barnes. Princeton, N.J.: Princeton University Press, 1984.

———. *Aristotle's "Metaphysics."* Translated by H. G. Apostle. Bloomington: Indiana University Press, 1984.

———. *Aristotle—"Metaphysics."* Translated by Richard Hope. Ann Arbor: University of Michigan Press, 1973.

Bloom, Allan. "Reply to Hall," Political Theory 5, no. 3, (1977): 315–30.

——, ed. and trans. *The Republic" of Plato*. New York: Basic Books, 1968.

Bluestone, Natalie Harris. *Women and the Ideal Society: Plato's "Republic" and Modern Myths of Gender*. Amherst: University of Massachusetts Press, 1987.

Bowen, Alan C. "On Interpreting Plato." In *Platonic Writings, Platonic Readings*, edited by Charles Griswold (New York: Routledge, 1988), 49–65.

Buber, Martin. *I And Thou*. Translated by R. G. Smith. New York: Charles Scribner's Sons, 1958.

Caputo, John. *Radical Hermeneutics: Repetition, Deconstruction, and the Hermeneutic Project*. Bloomington: Indiana University Press, 1987.

Clay, Diskin. "Gaps in the 'Universe' of the Platonic Dialogues." In *Proceedings of the Boston Area Colloquium in Ancient Philosophy*, vol. 3, edited by John J. Cleary. (New York: University Press of America, 1988), 131–57.

——. "Reading the *Republic*." In *Platonic Writings, Platonic Readings*, edited by Charles Griswold (New York: Routledge, 1988), 19–33.

Cornford, F. M. *The Origins of Greek Comedy*. London: Edward Arnold, 1914.

——, trans. *Plato: "The Republic."* (New York: Oxford University Press, 1956).

Dostal, Robert. "Beyond Being: Heidegger's Plato." *Journal of the History of Philosophy* 23, no.1 (1985): 71–98.

Friedlander, Paul. *Plato: An Introduction*. Vol. 1. New York: Pantheon Books, 1958.

Gadamer, Hans-Georg. *The Idea of the Good in Platonic-Aristotelian Philosophy*. Translated by Christopher Smith. New Haven, Conn.: Yale University Press, 1986.

Griswold, Charles. "The Ideas and the Criticism of Poetry in Plato's *Republic*, Book 10." *Journal of the History of Philosophy* 19, no. 2 (1981): 135–50.

——. "Irony and Aesthetic Language in Plato's Dialogues." In *Literature As Art: Essays in Honor of Murray Krieger*, edited by Douglas Bolling (New York: Haven Press, 1986), 71–102.

——, ed. *Platonic Writings, Platonic Readings.* New York: Routledge, 1988.

——. "Plato's Metaphilosophy: Why Plato Wrote Dialogues." In *Platonic Writings, Platonic Readings,* edited by Charles Griswold (New York: Routledge, 1988), 143–67.

——. *Self-Knowledge in Plato's "Phaedrus."* New Haven, Conn.: Yale University Press, 1986.

Hall, Dale. "The *Republic* and the Limits of Politics." *Political Theory* 5, no. 3 (1977): 293–313.

Harman, John. "The Unhappy Philosopher: Plato's *Republic* as Tragedy." *Polity* 18, no. 4 (1986): 577–94.

Heidegger, Martin. *Being and Time.* Translated by John Macquarrie and Edward Robinson. New York: Harper & Row, 1962.

——. *Early Greek Philosophy.* Translated by David Krell and Frank Capuzzi. New York: Harper & Row, 1975.

——. *Platons Lehre von der Wahrheit: Mit einem Brief uber den <<Humanismus>>.* Bern, Switzerland: Franke Verlag, 1947.

——. "Plato's Doctrine of Truth." Translated by John Barlow. In *Philosophy in the Twentieth Century,* vol. 3, edited by William Barrett and Henry Aiken (New York: Random House, 1962), 251–70.

——. *The Question of Being* (German and English text). New Haven, Conn: Twayne, 1958.

——. "Time and Being." In *On Time and Being,* translated by Joan Stambaugh (New York: Harper & Row, 1972). 1–24.

Howland, Jacob. "Re-Reading Plato: The Problem of Platonic Chronology." *Phoenix* 45, no.3 (1991): 189–214.

Hyland, Drew A. "Philosophy and Tragedy in the Platonic Dialogues." In *Tragedy and Philosophy,* edited by N. Georgopoulos (London: Macmillan Press, 1993), 123–138.

——. "Plato's Three Waves and the Question of Utopia." *Interpretation* 18, no. 1 (1990): 91–109.

——. "Potentiality and Presence: The Significance of Place in the Platonic Dialogues." *Journal of Speculative Philosophy* 8, no. 1 (1994): 28–43.

———. *The Question of Play.* Lanham, Md.: University Press of America, 1984.

———. *"Republic* Book II and the Origins of Political Philosophy." *Interpretation* 16, no. 2 (1989): 247–61.

———. "Taking the Longer Road: The Irony of Plato's *Republic." Revue de Metaphysique et de Morale,* no. 3 (1988): 317–33.

———. *The Virtue of Philosophy: An Interpretation of Plato's "Charmides."* Athens: Ohio University Press, 1981.

———. "Why Plato Wrote Dialogues." *Philosophy and Rhetoric* 1, no. 1 (1968): 38–50.

Kiekegaard, S. *The Concept of Irony: With Constant Reference to Socrates.* Translated by Lee Capel. London: Collins, 1966.

Kraut, Richard. *Socrates and the State.* Princeton, N.J.: Princeton University Press, 1984.

Lachterman, David. "What Is "the Good" of Plato's *Republic?"* In *Four Essays on Plato's Republic* (Double issue of *St. John's Review* 39, nos. 1–2 [1989–1990]: 139–71.).

Lang, Berel. *Philosophy and the Art of Writing: Studies in Philosophical and Literary Style.* Lewisburg, Pa.: Bucknell University Press, 1983.

Lang, Helen. "The Structure and Subject of Metaphysics Lamda." *Phronesis* 38 (1993): 257–280.

Lattimore, Richmond, trans. *Hesiod.* Ann Arbor: University of Michigan Press, 1959.

Marx, Karl. *Karl Marx: Early Writings.* Edited by T. D. Bottomore. New York: McGraw Hill, 1963.

Mattei, Jean-François. "The Theater of Myth in Plato." In *Platonic Writings, Platonic Readings,* edited by Charles Griswold (New York: Routledge, 1988), 66–83.

Miller, Mitchell. "Commentary on Clay." In *Proceedings of the Boston Area Colloquium in Ancient Philosophy,* vol. 3, edited by John J. Cleary (New York: University Press of America, 19880), 158–64.

———. *The Philosopher in Plato's "Statesman."* The Hague: Martinus Nijhoff, 1980.

——. "Platonic Provocations: Reflections on the Soul and the Good in the *Republic.*" In *Platonic Investigations,* edited by Dominic J. O'Meara (Washington, D.C.: Catholic University of America Press, 1985), 163–93.

——. *Plato's "Parmenides": The Conversion of the Soul.* Princeton, N.J.: Princeton University Press, 1986.

Nails, Debra. "Problems With Vlastos' Platonic Developmentalism." *Ancient Philosophy* 13, no. 2 (1993): 273–92.

Nietzsche, Friedrich. *Thus Spoke Zarathustra.* In *The Portable Nietzsche,* edited by Walter Kaufmann (New York: Penguin Books, 1982), 103–439.

Nussbaum, Martha. *The Fragility of Goodness: Luck and Ethics in Greek Tragedy and Philosophy.* Cambridge: Cambridge University Press, 1986.

Orwin, Clifford. "Liberalizing the *Crito*: Richard Kraut on Socrates and the State." In *Platonic Writings, Platonic Readings,* edited by Charles Griswold (New York: Routledge, 1988), 171–75.

Plato. *The Collected Dialogues of Plato.* Edited by Edith Hamilton and Huntington Cairns. New York: Pantheon Books, 1961.

——. *Plato's "Laches" and "Charmides."* Translated by R. K. Sprague. New York: Bobbs-Merrill, 1973.

——. *The Symposium.* Translated by Suzy Groden. Amherst: University of Massachussetts Press, 1970.

Riginos, Alice Swift. *Platonica: The Anecdotes Concerning the Life and Writings of Plato.* London: E.J. Brill, 1976.

Roochnik, David. "The Riddle of the Cleitophon." *Ancient Philosophy* 4 (1984): 132–45.

——. *The Tragedy of Reason.* New York: Routledge, 1991.

——. "The Tragic Philosopher: A Critique of Martha Nussbaum." *Ancient Philosophy* 8, no. 2 (1988): 285–95.

Rosen, Stanley. "Heidegger's Interpretation of Plato." *Journal of Existentialism* 7, no. 28 (1967): 477–504.

——. "Is Metaphysics Possible?" *Review of Metaphysics* 45, no. 2 (1991): 235–57.

——. *The Limits of Analysis*. New York: Basic Books, 1980.

——. *Nihilism: A Philosophical Essay*. New Haven, Conn.: Yale University Press, 1969.

——. *Plato's "Sophist": The Drama of Original and Image*. New Haven: Yale University Press, 1983.

——. *Plato's "Symposium."* New Haven, Conn.: Yale University Press, 1968.

——. *The Quarrel between Philosophy and Poetry*. New York: Routledge, 1988.

——. *The Question of Being: A Reversal of Heidegger*. New Haven, Conn.: Yale University Press, 1993.

——. "The Role of Eros in Plato's *Republic*." *Review of Metaphysics* 18, no. 3 (1965): 452–75.

Rousseau, Jean-Jacques. *"The First and Second Discourses": Jean-Jacques Rousseau*. New York: St. Martin's Press, 1964.

——. *Of The Social Contract*. Translated by Charles Sherover. New York: Harper & Row, 1984.

Sachs, David. "A Fallacy in Plato's *Republic*." In *Plato's "Republic": Interpretation and Criticism*, edited by Alexander Sesonske (Belmont, Calif.: Wadsworth , 1966): 66–81.

Sallis, John. *Being and Logos: The Way of Platonic Dialogue*. Pittsburgh, Pa: Duquesne University Press, 1975.

Saxonhouse, Arlene. "The Net of Hephaestus: Aristophanes' Speech in Plato's Symposium." *Interpretation* 13, no. 1 (1985), 15–32.

Sayre, Kenneth. "Plato's Dialogues in the Light of the Seventh Letter." In *Platonic Writings, Platonic Readings*, edited by Charles Griswold (New York: Routledge, 1988): 93–109.

——. *Plato's Late Ontology: A Riddle Solved*. Princeton, N.J.: Princeton University Press, 1983.

Schaerer, René. "Le Mecanisme de l'ironie dans ses rapports avec le dialectique." *Revue de Metaphysique et de Morale* 48 (1941): 181–209.

——. *La Question Platonicienne: Etudes sur les rapports de la pensee et de l'expression dans les dialogues*. Neuchatel: Memoires de l'Universite de Neuchatel, 1969.

Shorey, Paul. *The Unity of Plato's Thought*. Chicago: University of Chicago Press, 1903.

Strauss, Leo. *The City and Man*. Chicago: Rand McNally & Co., 1964.

———. *Persecution and the Art of Writing*. Glencoe, Ill.: The Free Press, 1952.

Taylor, A. E. *Plato: The Man and His Works*. New York: Meridian Books, 1959.

Thorson, T. L., ed. *Plato: Totalitarian or Democrat?*. Englewood Cliffs, N.J.: Prentice Hall, 1963.

Tigerstedt, E. N. *Interpreting Plato*. Uppsala, Sweden: Almquist & Wicksell, 1977.

Vlastos, Gregory. *Platonic Studies*. 2d ed. Princeton, N.J.: Princeton University Press, 1981.

———. *Socrates: Ironist and Moral Philosopher*. Ithica, N.Y.: Cornell University Press, 1991.

———. "The Third Man Argument in the *Parmenides*." *Philosophical Review* 63 (1954): 319–49.

White, Nicholas. "Observations and Questions About Hans-Georg Gadamer's Interpretation of Plato." In *Platonic Writings, Platonic Readings*, edited by Charles Griswold (New York: Routledge, 1988), 247–259.

Wieland, W. *Platon und die Formen des Wissens*. Gottingen, Germany: Vanderhoeck & Ruprecht, 1982.

INDEX OF NAMES

INDEX OF SUBJECTS

Noble lie p. 51
Fatted beast p. 52